SOME HABITS AND CUSTOMS
OF THE
WORKING CLASSES

[THOMAS WRIGHT]

SOME HABITS AND CUSTOMS

OF THE

WORKING CLASSES

BY

A JOURNEYMAN ENGINEER

[1867]

REPRINTS OF ECONOMIC CLASSICS

AUGUSTUS M. KELLEY · PUBLISHERS
NEW YORK · 1967

First Edition 1867
(London: Tinsley Brothers, *Catherine Street,
Strand*, 1867)

Reprinted 1967 by
AUGUSTUS M. KELLEY PUBLISHERS

Library of Congress Catalogue Card Number

67 - 19960

PRINTED IN THE UNITED STATES OF AMERICA
by SENTRY PRESS, NEW YORK, N. Y. 10019

SOME HABITS AND CUSTOMS

OF THE

WORKING CLASSES.

SOME HABITS AND CUSTOMS

OF THE

WORKING CLASSES.

BY

A JOURNEYMAN ENGINEER.

LONDON:

TINSLEY BROTHERS, CATHERINE STREET, STRAND.

1867.

PREFACE.

THROUGHOUT the papers that form this volume it is clearly implied, and in several places distinctly stated, that the writer is a working man; but since an implied identity of the author with the person supposed to be writing is a legitimate and frequently-adopted means of giving a realistic air to fancy sketches, and as any merit the present volume may have comes of the fact that the sketches that compose it are not fancy ones, I wish my readers to understand that in the present instance there is no assumption of character for the sake of literary effect. I am really a working man—a unit of the great unwashed—and having nothing but personal experience and observation to go upon, use them alone. So that however deficient the papers may be as pieces of literary workmanship, they are, as regards their substance, entitled to such a degree of consideration as may be fairly awarded to actual experience.

While the broad generality, that the working classes of this country form one of the most important sections of its social system, is admitted by all who have a knowledge of the constitution and aims of that system, great and extreme differences of opinion exist among men in every rank of life as to the exact relative position and power which those classes should hold, or

are entitled or fitted to hold, in the State, and most
important questions of home policy hinge more or less
on these debatable points. And as, to all who regard
the social progress and well being of the country the
solution of these vexed questions is a consummation
devoutly to be wished, and the first and an absolutely
essential step towards the desired solution is a thorough
understanding of the character, education, habits, and
modes of thought of the working classes, as embodied in their personification "The Working Man,"
the result has been that this typical individual has
been done times innumerable by more or less eminent
hands, and from very various points of view. Many
of these word-pictures of the working man are, as
word-pictures, masterpieces, and are, considering that
they are written by men outside of the classes of
which they treat, surprisingly accurate; but still, to a
working man even the best of them plainly show a
want of that knowledge of the minutiæ of the inner
life of the working classes which can only be thoroughly known to members of those classes. And it
is in the hope of, and with a view to throwing some
light upon this inner life—which in the aggregate has a
most important bearing upon the general character of
the working classes, and *must* be taken into consideration by all who wish to form an approximately correct
estimate of that character—that the following papers
have been written. While some of the pictures of the
working man that have been given to the world have
been as impartial and accurate as it was possible for
them to be made from an outside point of view, others
have, as was naturally to be expected, gone to either
extreme; some representing him as something very like

A monster of such hideous mien,
As to be hated needs but to be seen;

while others picture him as an all-perfect being, a living incarnation of "all the talents" and the whole of the cardinal and moral virtues. In this case, however, as in most others in which extreme views are taken, the truth lies near "the happy mean." The working man of actual life is, like most other human beings, a compound of good and evil; he has virtues, but he has also his faults and weaknesses. He will maintain a battle for what he conceives to be his rights, "and never count the cost;" he will stand by his friend in cloud as well as sunshine; and he will often endure the woes of want, and the still more terrible grief of seeing his wife and children suffering those woes while he is powerless to relieve them, with a degree of fortitude which, were it displayed in a more startling situation, would be deemed heroic. And take him for all in all, and his comparatively limited opportunities considered, he is not a bad fellow; and is in any relation of life—according to my full belief —an infinitely better man, and a more useful and creditable member of society, than the snobby-genteel kind of person who, with the manners and education of an underbred counter-skipper, and an income less than that of a good mechanic, sacrifices comfort and honesty to keep up appearances. Nevertheless, in him human nature has not attained the maximum of perfectibility just yet; his character has its seamy as well as bright side. He is often drunken, and not always ashamed thereof; and sometimes his love of drink leads to his being guilty of conduct which—to put it mildly—is not all that may become a man; moreover, he frequently, in a too literal sense, takes no heed for the morrow. And though he is undoubtedly endowed with a considerable amount of natural shrewdness, he is constantly allowing himself to be cajoled out of money and used as a tool by gangs of idle, ignorant, blatant harpies, who are his own inferiors in everything except one questionable gift, " the gift of the gab." He is not, generally speaking, so well educated and well informed as he might be; his language is scarcely " pure English undefiled," and is too often and too habitually " full of strange oaths;" while his ideas upon history, political economy, and the constitution of society, are noticeable rather for their confusion and their exceedingly " pronounced" tone, than for their extent or accuracy—in short, they are derived for the most part from the " Sunday Smasher," whose terrific correspondent, " Wat Tyler," he will tell you, is the boy for them—them being a vague and generic synonym for that bloated and bloodthirsty aristocracy, on which the redoubtable " own correspondent" in question is constantly, but as it would seem unavailingly, pouring the vials of his wrath.

But his faults and shortcomings all admitted, the average working man of every-day life, when not misled by the mis-statements or puffed up by the flatteries of self-seeking adventurers or ill-informed, injudicious friends, is, upon the whole, a pretty good fellow; and if in trying to show him in his habit as he lives, I have not hesitated to speak of or attempted to conceal his faults when they have come in course, I have not, I trust, on the other hand, failed to do justice to his good qualities. At any rate, I can conscientiously aver that if I have extenuated nothing, neither have I put down aught in malice; I have, according to my lights, told the *whole* truth, but *nothing but the truth*.

To speak of the working man as having faults at all, will be regarded as a libel upon him by those who take the view that he is the perfection of humanity. But so far as I am able to judge, the working man of these observers exists only in imagination; and it is of the original, and not an idealized copy, that I speak. By remembering this, by remembering that it is not of their working man I speak, gentlemen of an idealizing turn will be saved from any useless waste of indignation, or from undertaking a Quixotic defence of an individual that is not attacked. As there is no rule without an exception, I cannot say with absolute certainty that no such working man ever existed as the all-perfect and grievously sinned against being which sundry writers and speakers delight to picture as the representative working man; but I do say, that in the course of an unusually extensive and diversified experience I never met with such a one; and I beg also to say that were such a paragon to turn up in a workshop, he would stand a remarkably good chance of being chaffed out of it, unless he speedily toned himself down to something approaching the natural standard. But should some such bright particular workman actually exist at the present moment, he must be regarded as so thoroughly exceptional a being, that he cannot justly be taken into account in any general consideration of the working classes; and it is with a view to aid in the important work of arriving at *a correct general estimate* of the working classes that I write.

The various papers forming the volume have not been written with any view to continuous connexion, nor do they profess to embody the history of " The Working Man " from the cradle to the grave; they simply treat, as the title of the volume expresses, of some of his habits and customs, and are occasionally written in a somewhat discursive style, in order that episodical features of working-class life or manners which, though interesting in themselves, would not afford materials for separate papers, may be touched upon. As I am not in any severe sense of the term an educated man, my book, considered from a purely literary point of view, will doubtless present numerous and serious defects to learned critics, but while asking that such defects when found may be made a note of, I trust that the "extenuating circumstances" of my education having been of an elementary character, and my pleading guilty on that point, will be taken into consideration in passing sentence on such shortcomings. But should the book, or any part of it, be considered deserving of condemnation apart from such errors or defects as are fairly attributable to a want of education, I have no wish to shelter myself under the plea of being "only a working man." A working man should, in my opinion, be held as fully responsible as other men for every statement or expression of opinion that he may put forth ; and, personally, if I am to be damned, I would much rather be damned outright than damned with a qualification.

CONTENTS.

PART I.
WORKING MEN IN THEIR PUBLIC RELATIONS.

PART II.
WORK AND PLAY.

PART III.
SOCIAL AND DOMESTIC LIFE.

PART I.

WORKING MEN IN THEIR PUBLIC RELATIONS.

THE WORKING MAN'S EDUCATION.

OF the many means that have been tried or suggested
with a view to aid in effecting that very desirable
thing, the social and moral elevation of the working-
classes, education is admittedly the most important,
and has been the most productive of beneficial results.
In all civilized communities a wholly uneducated man
is an imperfect member of society, however great may
be his natural abilities ; and the self-evident corollary
is, that to give " the masses" such degree of education
as the circumstances of their position will admit of
their receiving, and as is best adapted to their mode
of life, is a first and important step towards not only
their intellectual, but also their social elevation. To
cultivate the mind of a man, who with his family is
condemned to live in some den inferior in every essential of health and comfort to the sty of a prize hog,
and compared with which a prison cell would be a desirable residence, and who would regard prison fare as
riotous living, may seem to be beginning the task of
elevating him at the wrong place, or even to be doing

him a positive injury. But practically such is not the
case, for though the cultivation of the mental faculties
gives rise to a keener and more painful consciousness
of physical degradation, that consciousness is essentially of the nature of an ardent desire for better
things, and the creation of such a desire is an important step towards its own fulfilment. For while outside help, the help of those above the masses, the help
of wise legislation and private benevolence, must aid
in any elevation of " the lower orders," it is to their
having a thorough and comprehensive sense of their
own position in society, abstractly and relatively, to
their having an earnest desire for a better state of
things, and being capable of self-help, that these orders
must chiefly look for any general or permanent ame-
lioration of their condition. And taking it for granted
that education is to be the chief instrument in quali-
fying the working classes to achieve their own social
elevation, the questions naturally arise,—Are the working-classes, as a body, as well educated as they might
be, and as their circumstances would fairly admit of
their being? and has the enormous expenditure of
money and labour, which for years past has been bestowed upon the education of these classes, been productive of proportionately great results? And to these
questions the reply of any person having a practical
knowledge of the working-classes, and of the state of
education among them, would be in the negative.   It
is true that a large proportion of the working-classes can
now read and write, and, thanks to cheap educational
literature, there are not a few men among them who
are, even in a scholarly sense, well educated; but the
ignorance, and the want of anything like real or beneficial education, that still prevails among them as a
class, and which is seen most markedly in those who

have received all the benefits of the educational machinery at present applied to their benefit, is unpleasantly astonishing, and would, I fear, scarcely be
credited by the admirers of " the intelligent artisan."

As this last-named individual is supposed to be the
best representative of the education and general intelligence of the working-classes, it would be doing both
the working-classes and those who take an interest in
their welfare a service if some admirer would favour
the world with a plain definition of what an intelligent artisan really is.   The phrase " intelligent artisan," like many other well-sounding stock phrases, is
somewhat vague, and may mean a variety of things,
and have different meanings to different people.   The
mere fact of being an artisan of course implies a certain degree of natural intelligence, and, in many instances, a certain degree of education also ; and used
in this broad sense, " intelligent artisan" and " artisan"
are of course synonymous terms.   Again, if by an intelligent artisan is meant a working mechanic having
considerable natural shrewdness of character, and
capable of holding his own in the battle of life, the
class will still be found pretty numerous, as it will
also should an intelligent artisan be taken to mean a
working man who, without having any definite idea of
their meaning, can talk about " the rights" or " dignity" " of labour," " the tyranny of capital," electoral
rights, universal suffrage, and other kindred topics.
But if by an intelligent artisan is meant a working
mechanic who has acquired a tolerably sound education, who is moderately well read in the popular and
standard literature of the age, capable of forming opinions for himself upon those topics of the day that
more particularly affect the well-being of his own
order, and of expressing those opinions in plain and

proper language—if you mean a man whose reason must be convinced, or at any rate appealed to, as well as his passions roused, before he will consent to any plan of action pointed out to him by others—if by an intelligent artisan is meant (as many people suppose) a man having such qualifications as these, then intelligent artisans are much scarcer than many persons seem to suppose them to be. They do exist. I have the pleasure of being acquainted with many of them; and, indeed, they may be said to be a numerous body, but, considered in relation to that vast aggregation known as the working classes, they must be regarded as exceptional beings: the exceptions that prove the rule, that the working-classes, as a body, are not as well educated as they might and (taking into account the vastness of the resources that have been brought to bear upon the task of promoting education among them) ought to be, or as, from the manner in which they have been belauded by admirers more ardent than judicious or well-informed, large numbers of those belonging to other sections of society believe them to be. They must be regarded as so exceptional as to make the somewhat prevalent idea, that intelligent artisans are a large and well-defined section of the working-classes, an utterly erroneous and misleading one.

I have no wish to speak disparagingly or unkindly of the working classes. Very far from it. I am myself a working man, " native and to the manner born." All my relations, friends, and companions belong to the working classes; my life has been spent among them; my best sympathies are with them; and if I appear to speak to their disadvantage in trying to show them as they are rather than as I would wish them to be, or as many of their well-wishers in the higher ranks of society suppose them

to be, it is in no unbrotherly or recreant spirit that I
do so; but rather in the belief that I shall be doing
them a greater service by showing to those who are
willing to befriend or anxious to understand them, or
even to some of themselves who may not have given
the subject any serious consideration, where they are
weak, and in what matters and in what manner assistance would be valuable to them, than by adding another
layer of tinsel to any of the philanthropically or oratori-
cally highly-gilt and embellished pictures of "the
working man," which represent him as having virtues
and advantages which he really does not possess; and
which pictures too often cause those who believe in
their truthfulness to feel disappointed or disgusted
with him for not coming up to the pictorial standard.
Working men as a body have many virtues : they are
honest, industrious, and provident, and none but
themselves can know with what fortitude they face
the hardships incidental to their sphere of life, or how
kind they are to each other in the hour of need : and
they have a fair share of natural intelligence.   But in
the sense in which intelligence implies a certain degree
of general knowledge and refinement of manners, the
working-classes generally are *not* intelligent.   As this
want of educational intelligence cannot be attributed
to any lack of easily-accessible educational appliances,
the promoters or advocates of the systems on which
these appliances are based, or by which they are regulated, are naturally prepared with statistics and state-
ments showing to their own satisfaction that the working-classes, the classes for whose special benefit most
of the pet educational schemes and institutions of the
day have been founded, *are*, in an educational as well
as a natural sense, intelligent.   But while believing in
the general utility of statistics, I think they should be

received with reservation when they are brought forward by the supporters of a theory or system, to demonstrate the success of their system ; and at any rate it is admissible in such cases to put the facts sought to be proved to the test, on the principle involved in the text—" By their fruits ye shall know them."

I suppose that it will not be disputed that the workshops of the manufacturing districts, the districts in which artisans are most largely employed, are the best places in which to look for the ripest and best developed specimens of educational fruit among the working-classes; and if such is the case, then the small quantity and unsatisfactory quality of that kind of fruit to be found in workshops, must inevitably convince the inquirer that the system of which they are the best productions must be an unsound one. If the working-classes were, in the educational sense of the term, intelligent, would eight men out of ten in a large workshop habitually use blackguard and blasphemous language in their ordinary conversation, and a still larger percentage of them be unable to express themselves emphatically upon any subject without resorting to the same kind of language, as is the case at present ? Would the majority of the jokes and jests current in the workshop, and in many of which there is real wit, be so inextricably mingled with, and dependent for their point upon, indecencies and blasphemies, as to be unfit for repetition ? Or would there still be in the workshop an almost entire absence—not of substantial kindness, for that is a marked and general characteristic of working communities—but of those little courtesies and civilities which, while costing nothing, enhance the value even of kindness, and are, in fact, in themselves a sort of kindness, softening the dis-

agreeableness of disagreeable things, and making pleasant things still more pleasant ; and the non-practising
of which upon the part of the working-classes, offers a
prominent and ready means of unfavourably contrast-
ing their character with that of other classes of society ?
If the working-classes had in their degree benefited as
much as under a wiser dispensation they might have
done, in those boasts of our age, "the march of
intellect," and "the spread of education," would there
still be large bodies of highly-paid artisans notorious
for their addiction to drunkenness and to brutal and
brutalizing sports, and for an ignorance—except in
what pertains to their trade—probably as dense as that
which characterized their ancestors in the days when
"wild in woods the noble savage ran." And, above
all, were they as well educated as the circumstances of
their position would admit of their being, would the
great bulk of the working-classes still be "led by the
nose as asses are," by a number of writers and spouters,
who trade upon their weaknesses and passions, and live
and thrive by the misery which it is their selfish
business to create among the classes whose greatest
benefactors they claim to be ? Would *educated* working men be blindly led to their own destruction by
frothy professional agitators, whose only qualifications
for the office which they assume of "guide, philo-
sopher, and friend" of the working-classes, are a knowledge of the weaknesses and a belief in the gullibility
of those classes, a fixed resolution never to do any
hard work, an utter want of principle, an unbounded
stock of impudence and power of coarse flattery, and
the capability of talking an infinite deal of rubbish
about the "bloated aristocracy," the "tyranny of
capital," and so forth ?

What arrant nonsense in the present day is this—

among the working-classes—yet unexploded bloated-
aristocrat doctrine.   What do the present generation
of working men, or the individuals whom to their
sorrow they allow to be their counsellors, know about
aristocracy, bloated or otherwise, that justifies them in
regarding the aristocracy and aristocratic institutions
as being necessarily and specially antagonistic to their
interests ?   Taking that disgrace to humanity, George
IV., as the great original bloated aristocrat, the man
who in theatrical parlance created the character, there
will still probably be found aristocrats as bloated as
the spirit of the age will permit them to be.
There are doubtless silly and vicious aristocrats, dukes
who are duffers, scamping marquises, knavish earls,
blackleg baronets, dishonest right honourables, officers
who have far greater claims to be considered rogues or
blackguards than gentlemen, and younger sons as
shameless and impudent spungers as any of the land-
less, moneyless, long-titled German serenities, who are
supposed to fatten upon the loaves and fishes of English " place" or pension. But if among the aristocracy
there are, as in other grades of society, bad and worthless members of the body, there are also good and
useful ones.   In no great national or philanthropical
movement for the benefit of the people have some
greater or lesser portion of the aristocracy failed to
take a worthy part.   In the last memorable instance,
in which a large section of working men, from no
fault of their own, stood in need of the substantial
sympathies of all other classes—the cotton famine—
did the aristocracy as a body show a less kindly or
liberal feeling than others ?   The subscription lists to
the Lancashire distress fund show that they did not.
In those lists many of the noblest names in the land
will be found credited with amounts as noble as the

names of their donors ; and far larger—making every allowance for their relative wealth—than the subscriptions of the wealthy traders and manufacturers whose colossal fortunes had been made directly out of the labours of the men who stood in need of assistance. And the newspapers of the time prove that their sympathy was not limited to giving individual subscriptions, for they were among the warmest advocates of the cause of the distressed operatives, and materially assisted in securing for them the practical aid which their case required. So far as the working-classes have any real knowledge of the aristocracy, they have no cause to regard them with hatred ; and I believe that, as a rule, working men would be treated with more courtesy, consideration, and equality by the aristocracy than by the moneyocracy, the holders of the bulk of the trading and manufacturing capital of the country,—the capital that is, as the professional agitators put it, " wrung out of the sweat and blood" of the " ground-down" labouring-classes. And though, as an abstract principle, any system which supports a large number of unproductive consumers must necessarily be an unsound one, yet, practically speaking, it is one which, it must be evident to all, save visionaries who believe in the possibility of a system of universal brotherhood, must exist *in some shape* in all civilized communities ; and the English aristocracy, as it at present exists, is perhaps the least offensive form of it. An English nobleman is usually wealthy enough to support his nobility without *directly* preying upon " the people," and gentlemanly enough to be civil to all men ; and he is amenable to the law, and to that perhaps still more dreaded power, public opinion. And if there are noblemen deriving large incomes from landed property who house the labourers on their

estates in hovels less wholesome and comfortable than
piggeries, are there not manufacturers employing large
numbers of " hands" in unhealthy and laborious occupations, and paying them wages that forces them to
live in those filthy overcrowded dens that abound in
the poor neighbourhoods of large towns, and in which
the poorer orders of the working-classes linger out
their miserable and unhealthy existence?—men who
neither know how or where their hands live, nor care
whether they live at all. In short, as I said before,
the working-classes have no *special* grievance against
the aristocracy, yet such is the state of intelligence
among them (the working men), that a majority of
them give credence to the clap-trap talk of agitators,
who represent the aristocracy as though they were still
" ruthless barons," robbing and killing the people at
their own sweet will, and roasting Jews or drawing
their teeth whenever they could lay hands on them.

Again, what is the meaning of " the tyranny of
capital" of which the professional agitator talks so
much? To ninety working men out of a hundred the
phrase conveys no definite meaning, while the remaining ten would probably give as many different definitions of it. If it means anything it is, that whatever
philanthropic theorists may say about the true interests
of capital and labour being identical, those interests
are really antagonistic, and that whenever the capitalists are masters of the situation, they make the
most of their opportunities for putting the screw on
labour. And upon this principle the capitalists might
as well talk of a tyranny of labour, as labour is not
slow to return the compliment by putting the screw
on capital when it has a chance; the great difference
in the respective positions of capital and labour in
this respect being, that capital being a thing that

enables a man to bide his time, and capitalists understanding the relations between capital and labour
better than the working-classes, capital is much oftener
master of the situation than labour. Though were
working men sufficiently well-informed and intelligent
to rid themselves of the spouting knaves who prey
upon and bring disgrace upon them by using their
name, and to trust to their own sense and powers
of observation for understanding the true relations between capital and labour, those relations would soon
be better equalized, and more satisfactory than they
are at present.

The whole tone of workshop life is a practical pro-
test against the belief that working men of the present
day are in point of educational intelligence equal to
the age they live in. There are still large numbers of
them unable to read or write, while many of those
who can read and write only do so in a merely mechanical sense : it would be putting it mildly to say
that fifty per cent. of them are unable to write a
decently readable letter, and that eighty per cent. of
them have no knowledge at all of the literature of the
country. Many of them who can read, but whose
reading is confined to the police intelligence of their
weekly newspapers or the leading tales of their halfpenny or penny serials, are ignorant of the meaning
of many of the common words in the language, and of
the point or source of the most hackneyed of the
quotations that are daily coming under the notice of
" the general reader." They have no knowledge beyond the vaguest hearsay of the history of their
country or its great men, or of those topics of the day
a proper understanding of which would conduce to the
welfare of themselves and the class to which they
belong. A working man who is moderately well read,

who is capable of expressing himself in proper and appropriate language, of writing a well-phrased letter, or drawing up an address or the heading of a sub-scription-list in suitable terms, is a rarity in a work-shop, and is regarded and honoured as such by his fellow-workmen, who speak of him as a great "scholard," refer to him to decide disputes upon general matters, ask him to write for them, or tell them how to write their most particular letters, put their grievances into addresses or petitions, act as secretary to their meetings and associations, and be their spokesman when occasion shall require. Yet such a working man as this ought not to be the comparative rarity that he is, and is only an average specimen of what the bulk of working men might be.

Unsatisfactory, however, as is the state of education among artisans, it is still more deplorable among the lower-paid orders of the working-classes, many of whom are totally uneducated—never having as children enjoyed those opportunities of gaining that little education of which artisans have generally had the advantage, or else they were sent to work at such an early age as to make them speedily forget any little rudimentary education they may have previously received. Artisans are sometimes the sons of men slightly higher in the social scale than themselves, and as a rule they are the sons of artisans or the better kinds of unskilled workmen—of men who have a far-off sense of education, and who, setting a high value on it, determine to give them the best instruction in their power, and—the smallness of their incomes considered—spend large sums of money in carrying out their determination. They send their boys to school at an early age, keep them at it till they are fourteen—when of course they must leave to be " bound 'pren-

tice"—and then send them into the workshop fine
scholars, according to workshop ideas of fine scholar-
ship. That is to say, the boys will be able to read
and write, work the great horseshoe-and-nails sum,
repeat whole chapters of the Bible "off book," and
tell the names of the great personages and places of
scripture-history; will be able to give a list of the
sovereigns of England from the time of the Conquest,
with the names and dates of the principal battles that
took place during their reigns; give the names of the
highest mountain and longest river in the world;
tell the distance of the sun from the earth; and even
speak a little of what they are pleased to call Latin
and French. But boys on leaving school soon forget
the fine things that they "knew by heart," or could
"say off book," and on becoming men the majority of
these fine scholars will be found to be ill-informed
members of society, with little legitimate claim to be
considered intelligent in any save the primary and
natural sense of the term.

It will naturally be asked, How comes it, then, that
educational and general literature being so cheap and
abundant, educational facilities so wide-spread and easy
of access, and artisans endowed with a considerable
share of natural intelligence, they should, as a class,
be ignorant and ill-informed? The answer to this
question is, in my opinion, that the system of education applied to the working-classes is a thoroughly
unsound one. The great fault of it is that it attempts
too much—attempts to make *scholars* of children, instead of merely trying to pave the way to their becoming intelligent men,—that it is a sort of Jack-of-all-
trades-and-master-of-none system, touching in a dry
and elementary manner upon a great many branches
of education, without going far enough into any one of

them to make it sufficiently interesting to the pupils to make them pursue it for the sake of the pleasure it gives after they have left school; and one that sacrifices the cultivation of the higher faculties to the development of a mechanical and comparatively useless power of memory.

Take the case of a well-to-do mechanic's son. Having been taught to read in a woman's school, or a national infant school, he is at seven or eight years of age removed probably to one of those schools known as British schools; in which the general body of pupils pay from fourpence to sixpence a week each, and an " upper class " a shilling a week each in consideration of learning " extras." On the day on which he is to enter his new school, the hope of the Joneses, attired in the cloth suit which up to the previous day has done duty as his " Sunday clothes," and with hands and face as clean as water and soap can make them, and hair carefully oiled and brushed, is taken to the school by his mother, it being necessary that one of his parents should have an interview with the master. On coming into the master's presence, Mrs. J. makes her best curtsey, and explains that she wishes her boy to be enrolled as a pupil in that school; whereupon the schoolmaster having taken a look at Master Jones, and blandly asked him whether he is a good boy, proceeds to take down his name and age and the address of his parents. He next asks whether he has been to school before, and if so, where; and then tests his powers by putting him to read a few sentences aloud; after which he assigns him a class. The boy being thus disposed of, the master addresses himself to the mother, telling her in the first place that they are very strict as to the personal cleanliness and regular attendance of their pupils, and she having expressed

her approval in these matters, he goes on to inform
her that "our course" consists of reading, writing,
arithmetic, grammar, geography, including the use of
the globes, the Scriptures, astronomy, composition,
history, elocution, singing, and elementary science; in
addition to which, French, Latin, and geometry are
taught in the upper class, for admission into which,
however, Master Jones will not be qualified for some
time to come. Mrs. Jones listens to the recital of
this numerous and high-sounding list of studies respectfully but appalled—wondering why the master
should enter into all these details with her; but she
is speedily enlightened upon this point by his going on
to say that they find some of the books, but that her
son will also require a number of books which they do
not find, but with which he will be happy to supply her
at the same price as the booksellers. Mrs. J. of
course takes and pays for the books, which are duly
handed over to her son, who may then be considered
fairly established in his new school. And now let us
look at the plan of education followed in the school.
The hours of attendance are from nine in the morning
till four in the afternoon, with an hour and a half for
dinner, and half an hour—a quarter of an hour morning and afternoon—for play; besides which each pupil
has "night lessons," the preparation of which will take
from one to two hours, according to the length of the
lessons and powers of memory of the learner. The
pupils are divided into from seven to ten classes, irrespective of the upper class; and taking it that our
illustrative school has ten classes, we will suppose that
our new pupil is placed in the fifth. This class will
be "taken" by pupils from the first class, or the
younger "pupil-teachers," boys destined for the teaching profession, but who as yet are mere schoolboys,

whose inaccessibility to the corrupting influence of marbles cannot be relied upon, and many of whom, it is well known in schoolboy circles, are given to secretly eating the toffee that has been taken from pupils who have been detected devoting greater attention to it than their lessons ; and who openly make favourites of some pupils, and take " picks" at others.   One of these boys will in the morning " take" the night lessons and sums, this operation consisting in examining the sums, and seeing that a certain percentage of them have the right answers, and listening to the repetition of the lessons, passing those who are tolerably perfect in them, and making those who are very imperfect or totally ignorant " stand on the line," in order that the master may deal with them.   After the taking of the night lessons, come (say) the scripture lesson, which consists in the reading—each boy in the class taking a verse in his turn—of one or more chapters in the Bible, and the asking of a number of questions by the teacher to test the *memory* of the boys concerning what they have been reading.   When this has been gone through, it will be time to go into the playground.   On assembling in school again, the whole of the pupils are formed into one large class for a singing lesson, at the end of which they break up into their ordinary classes for their writing lessons, which last till dinner-time.

After dinner, the time up to the hour for going into the playground will be occupied by grammar and geography lessons, which in the fifth class will be taught, the former by the pupils' repeating in a monotonous sing-song tone after the teacher, " There are nine parts of speech—article, noun, adjective, pronoun," &c. ; and the latter, by their repeating in the same tone and manner, that the Earth is divided into

two hemispheres and four continents ; that an island
is a piece of land entirely surrounded by water, and a
peninsula a piece of land almost surrounded by water.
On returning from the playground, the remainder of
the afternoon will be taken up by the reading lessons,
consisting, in the fifth class, of "moral lessons in
words of two syllables," and the setting of the night lessons, which last will, in the case of our young friend,
be confined at this time to the working of half-a-dozen
sums, and the learning by heart of a table of weights
and measures, and a column of "spellings." But
even with this limitation in the matter of the night lessons, Master Jones's scholastic task will be a tolerably
heavy one for an eight-year-old boy, fond of play, and
having to go to bed at eight o'clock in the evening.
This, however, is only the beginning of his educational
sorrows.   We will suppose that he is a moderately
good and intelligent boy, that he does not get "put
on the line" with unusual frequency, that he never
gets sent home for having dirty shoes or face, that he
does not occasionally spend his school wages, play
truant for a week, and bring a forged note of excuse
for his absence ; that when he gets a caning he grins,
or howls, and bears it, and does not go home crying,
and bring his mother with him on the following morning to indignantly state in the face of the assembled
pupils, "which her boy is as good a boy as ever
breathed, and she ain't a-going to have him beat black
and blue to please any nasty puppy of a teacher ;"—
we will suppose all this, and that he gradually rises
from class to class, and takes prizes at the half-yearly
examinations, until, at twelve years of age, he reaches
the first class, and the full force of the cramming
system is brought to bear upon his devoted head.
His night sums will now be in the higher rules of

arithmetic, which he finds exceedingly difficult, from
his having been forced through the earlier rules without being taught the principles of their application;
and the lessons will embrace half-a-dozen different
subjects besides. These and his day lessons tax his
powers of memory to an unnatural extent, while
leaving his other faculties dormant. But still the
system enables him to shine at the heavily-crammed
and oft-rehearsed half-yearly examinations, to take
prizes at them, and to cover himself and his master
with glory in the presence of the parents of the pupils
and others who attend such examinations. Having so
distinguished himself, it is considered advisable by his
proud and gratified parents either to remove him to a
"finishing school" (generally a "genteel academy" at
from one to two guineas per quarter), or place him in
the upper class of the school he is already attending;
this latter being the plan most usually adopted. In
consequence of this proceeding, lessons in mathematics
and a couple of languages are added to the boy's
already cruel mode of educational misery. He will
now have little or no time for play; his memory will
be strained to a stupefying degree; he will begin to
sincerely hate school and all pertaining thereto, and
urge his parents to send him to work; and when he
is sent to work his sense of relief at being freed from
the thraldom of lessons will give an additional zest to
the general feeling of joy and importance which all
boys feel on first going to work.

Nor is it at all surprising that such a system as I have
attempted briefly to describe should produce a hatred
rather than a desire for education in the minds of
those who suffer under it. In the first place it attempts too much. A moment's consideration must
make it evident that boys of from twelve to fourteen

years of age, and of only ordinary strength of mind, cannot simultaneously study ten or twelve subjects— several of which really are, and all of which as they are taught to them appear to be, wholly distinct— with any reasonable probability of attaining a useful proficiency in them all ; while the distraction of mind consequent upon this multiplicity of studies makes it very improbable that they will learn any of them well. The mode of teaching practised under this system, and indeed necessitated in order to secure its *apparent* success, is also utterly objectionable. Its chief aim is to produce prize pupils and organize showy public examinations, rather than to lay the foundations of a good education. By this mode only the barest and driest outlines of each subject are taught : no attempt is made to interest the pupil in his studies by teaching him the broad principles or general applications of the various branches of knowledge which those studies embrace, or to amalgamate or generalize such of the studies as admit of it. Under this system of teaching, proficiency is sought to be attained by cramming the pupils to bursting-point with definitions, dates, and figures, all of which, though of the utmost importance as parts of the subjects to which they pertain, and essential to the thorough understanding of them, are wholly uninteresting and practically useless to students having no further knowledge of those subjects. Let any person look, for instance, at the class-books from which history and geography—the two most interesting branches of an ordinary English education—are taught in those schools more particularly devoted to the education of the children of working men, and they will find that the best of them are little better than chronological tables recording the dates of the births and deaths of sovereigns, and the names and dates of famous battles and sieges, and catalogues of the principal countries, rivers, and mountains of the earth. These books are a good illustration of the striving-to-do-too-much feature which disfigures the system to which they belong, for they profess to give a *detailed* history, or geographical description of the world, in a small volume of about a hundred and twenty pages. That a knowledge of the physical sciences and the ancient and modern languages is a highly desirable thing there can be no doubt, but the circumstances of working men do not admit of their boys being taught these branches of education, and the attempt to teach them during the last year or two at school is a mere waste of time. The smattering he gets (and that is the utmost he can hope to gain) is not sufficient to induce him to continue the study after he has left school, and the smattering itself is speedily forgotten.

Speaking from experience, I have no hesitation in saying that considering that the children of the working-classes must under the most favourable circumstances leave school at fourteen years of age, and many of them much earlier ; it is a mistake to attempt to extend their school studies beyond the plain foundations of reading, writing, and arithmetic. But these, and more especially the first of them, might be taught in so comprehensive a manner as to embrace a useful general knowledge of a variety of subjects. Working men cannot be made *scholars*, but by reading they may gain knowledge, and to create and direct a taste for reading should be the chief aim of their education. Under a system having this object in view, the education of the working-classes would be continued after they left school; for literature of all kinds is so abundant and easy of access that no youth or man who has a taste for reading experiences much difficulty in gratifying it.

The merely mechanical power of reading must be taught in some more or less mechanical manner; but as soon as the pupil is able to read sentences intelligibly the work of interesting him in his studies might be commenced. Let there be a " first reader" consisting of short fables and tales selected—and if necessary altered—from Æsop and the fairy histories. Let the next " reader" consist of stories of travels and voyages, in connexion with which the study of geography might be incorporated, by the teacher pointing out on the globe and map the various places referred to in the readings, showing in what position a ship would be whose latitude and longitude are given, and explaining other geographical points that would necessarily arise. Indeed, in the hands of a judicious and well-informed teacher such a series of readings would supply texts not only for the teaching of geography, but also of some of the most interesting features in astronomy and navigation. These might be followed by an " historical reader" and " scientific reader" for the higher classes; the former consisting of selections—with short explanatory head notes—from the works of Gibbon, Robertson, Macaulay, Froude, Strickland, and other celebrated historians, and the latter of dialogues, in the style of Joyce's " Scientific Dialogues," and allegories illustrating in an interesting manner the principles of science.* And these might be supple-

* Of the thousands of reading lessons which I had during a five years' pupilage in a large school which is still famous as a working-class school, only two left anything like a lasting impression upon my mind, or were regarded with feelings of real interest, and not as mere task-work. The first was a tale called " The Three Giants," in which, under the guise of a pleasant story, the powers of air, water, and steam were explained and exemplified; though it was only in after years, when I had acquired a practical knowledge of the nature and operation of these natural forces, that I discovered

mented by a "general reader" made up of selections
from the works of the most eminent British poets,
essayists, and novelists.   I leave it to be taken for
granted that a knowledge of the Scriptures would form
part of this or any other system of English education,
but a much higher knowledge of them would be conveyed to the pupil if, instead of setting him to learn
chapters of the Bible by way of punishment, or cramming him with the genealogies of the Patriarchs and
Apostles just previous to examinations, he was shown
what a really valuable lesson in physical science "The Three
Giants" contained.   But had the teacher under whom I read the
tale pointed the moral of it—as under a more rational system of
education he would have done—he might have taught me more
science in a few hours than I learned in the course of two years in
the "finishing school" to which I was sent to complete my education, and in which "the sciences" were among the too-numerous-
to-be-mentioned subjects taught—or rather supposed to be taught.
The second of these long-remembered reading lessons was a story
of Irish peasant life, called, if I remember rightly, "The Foster
Parents," in which one Mickey Flood was a prominent and favourite
character.   Both stories were contained in a "class-book" issued
by an Irish educational society ; and I can still remember the thrill
of joy which ran through the class, and the smile which lit up the
countenance of every pupil, whenever it was announced that either
of these had been selected in preference to the "moral" and other
dry lessons which usually formed our reading exercises.
    A copy of Joyce's "Scientific Dialogues" was the prize that fell to
my lot at one of the half-yearly examinations at the working-class
school of which I am speaking, and I remember that I read it
during the holidays that followed the examination with as much
pleasure as I did "Nick of the Woods," which I read during the same
holidays ; and I established quite an enviable reputation as a con-
juror, by performing some of the simple experiments explained in
the book before a number of my schoolmates whom my parents had
invited to take tea at our house.   The book made an equally
favourable impression upon several of my school friends to whom I
lent it—and one of whom, of course, failed to return it ; and there
can be no doubt that such a book would be a valuable class-book,
and, aided by such experiments as might be easily and inexpensively
conducted in a school-room, would do much to popularize science.

the geographical positions of the various countries mentioned in Holy Writ, and told the changes they have undergone, and their present social position among the nations of the earth; and had pointed out to him the glorious poetry and wisdom of such parts as the Psalms, the Proverbs, and Christ's Parables and Sermon on the Mount, and the applicability of many of the lessons contained in them to the affairs of every-day life at the present time.

That some such educational system as this, administered by competent teachers—teachers qualified to do something more than stolidly listen to their pupils repeating the lessons they have "learned off book," and count the number of mistakes they make—would be more beneficial to, and better suited to the circumstances of the working-classes than the high-pressure system at present applied to them, no person having a real knowledge of those classes can for a moment doubt. It is true that *scholars* would not be produced under it, nor would the pupils be *perfected* in any single branch of education, but they would gain a considerable amount of general knowledge, and gain it in a manner that would create a desire for further knowledge, in the shape of a taste for reading; and thus induce them to continue what would be practically their education, after they had left school, instead of regarding it as completed when they walk out of the school-house for the last time. Such a system as this might be still further developed, by having attached to each national or other large school attended by the children of the working-classes, a library, consisting of such works as "The Pilgrim's Progress," "Robinson Crusoe," a selection of Scott's, Cooper's, and Marryat's novels, books of voyages and travels, works upon natural history, interesting biographies, historical works,

popular books of science, and any works of general interest that might be considered likely to attract and
instruct youthful readers. The privilege of borrowing
these books could be granted as a reward for diligence
in their studies to the boys of the first and second
classes, and the condition of each borrower writing out
some sort of an epitome or criticism of each work lent
to him might be attached to the privilege; and thus,
by making it an incentive to application and a means
of exercising pupils in composition, the library would
be fairly converted into an educational engine, and be
quite consonant with the system of which it would
form a valuable part. The cause of education among
the working classes might also be materially assisted,
if in large towns a number of memberships, varying in
length from one to five years, of local mechanics' institutions or literary institutions were given as prizes
at school examinations. This form of prize need only
be given to boys in their last year at school; and,
under a rational system of competitive examinations,
they would fall to the cleverest boys, who would thus
be in a position to immediately follow up the work of
education commenced at school.

It may be urged against any system of this kind
that it would produce a desire for light reading rather
than solid education; but then, what is generally understood by a solid education cannot, under any system, be completed between seven and fourteen years
of age; and among the working-classes it is only those
who have a strong natural liking for some particular
branch of learning, or men of more than ordinary
strength of mind who have resolved to rise in the world,
and are determined to educate themselves as an essential means to that end, who will devote their leisure
time to direct study, or who could do so profitably.

And as it seems to be a law of nature that boys who do read *will* read fiction, it would be much better to turn them out of school eager to run riot among the Waverleys, and ready to smuggle candles to bed in order to finish the enthralling adventures of Hawkeye or Mr. Midshipman Easy, than to send them forth hating all books together, and with minds so uncultivated in all save the rudimentary technicalities of a cut-and-dried education that when a reaction sets in— if it ever does set in—they first become readers of that pernicious thieves' literature which the legislature, in its wisdom, still allows to be sown broadcast throughout the land; and finally settle down as " constant readers" of *The Weekly Denouncer* agitation newspaper, and *The Three Farthings Miscellany* sensation serial. Besides, this universal inclination of boys for works of fiction, which such a system of education as I have been speaking of would merely guide, becomes, like the juvenile taste for tarts and toffee, moderated as the boys advance in life, and in the meantime it paves the way to more general or solid reading.　Whatever disciples of the Gradgrind school may think or say, there can be little doubt that one of the working-classes who has gone through the Waverleys and the Cooper, Marryat, and Mayne Reid series of novels during the first two or three years after leaving school, read the works of Dickens and Bulwer at a later period,and learnt to appreciate Thackeray by the time he reaches manhood, has had a good preparation for profitably reading and reflecting upon those graver subjects which affect the constitution and well-being of society.　The reading of good fiction almost necessarily gives rise to a large amount of incidental reading.　Few persons can read Scott's novels without being led to read historical works relating to the same periods as the novels; and the allusions to, and quotations from, standard works, contained in modern novels, often lead to the reading of those works; while the delineation of character, powers of description and satire, and other valuable literary qualities that characterize the higher works of fiction, enable the reader of such works to appreciate those qualities when he meets with them in the current literature of the day. And it should be borne in mind that as a working man's actual experience of society is almost exclusively confined to his own class, it is principally to reading that he must trust for gaining a knowledge of other classes of society and the relative position of his own class : and were it for this reason alone, the importance of developing a sound taste for reading among the working classes must be apparent.

These remarks upon the state of education and intelligence among the working-classes apply chiefly to the artisan section of them, the section of them on whom the highest efforts of the system under which the working-classes are at present educated are expended, and the want of general intelligence among whom is one of the most conclusive proofs that the system is an unsound one. But while its defects must be held to account for a great deal of the want of general intelligence amongst working-men, there are other causes that materially contribute towards it. Many of the children of the working-classes, children of very poor, very ignorant, or drunken parents, are never sent to any kind of school; while others who are sent to school have to leave it at such an early age to go to work, that any little glimmer of education they may have received during their brief period of schooling is almost entirely forgotten long before they attain manhood; and of course among the working-classes, as

in other ranks in life, there are some men so stupid
or debased that no kind or amount of instruction
would ever make them intelligent. That there is an
abundance of natural shrewdness, and what is generally called rough common sense, among the working-
classes, there can be no doubt; and all who have any
considerable personal acquaintance with them are
aware that there are numbers of well-informed, really
intelligent men among them; but these are so few in
number compared with the general body, that they are
totally inadequate to the leavening of the mass, and
in any question affecting the relations between their
own and other classes of society, their influence is
utterly swamped by that of the many-headed multitude who acknowledge the sway of the professional agitators. No system of education could produce a state of society in which all men would be intelligent; but, under a system specially designed to
suit the circumstances of their position and develope
the natural powers of mind which they undoubtedly
possess, a large majority of them might be made really
intelligent members of society, and a decided tone of
educated intelligence given to the whole body. That
a system capable of producing such highly desirable
results could be constructed and successfully carried
out by educated, liberal-minded men having a practical
knowledge of the working-classes, there can be no reasonable doubt. And though the working details of
any such system could only be decided upon by actual
practice, and would have to be varied with varying
circumstances, I think the general principles of it
should be such as I have indicated.

The vast national and private means furnished for
promoting education amongst us have undoubtedly
been productive of good. But it is certain that they

have not effected anything like the amount of good that they might have done. The general result of the present state of things is to place a large number of working men in a position to affirm—as I heard a mechanic doing the other day when asking a shop-mate to write a letter—that they were very good scholars once, only they have forgot all their education; and to send forth a number of boys capable of performing a number of surprising but for practical purposes useless feats in educational gymnastics. There are means in plenty; what is wanted is that those who are interested in promoting the welfare of the working-classes should try to bring about the substitution of another and a better plan of using them.

WORKING MEN'S FRIENDS.

THE working man is certainly a man of many friends and protectors—that is, if he believes the self-glorifying and interested assertions of a number of individuals who dub themselves " friends of the people," " the working man's friend," and so forth. But if the working man does not choose to take these assertions for granted, but, on the contrary, prefers to inquire how far they are true, and what are the motives for making them, it is much to be feared that he will often have occasion to exclaim, " Save me from my friends !"

A friend of the working classes being now a character that is deservedly appreciated and respected, and one that brings more or less of a coveted publicity to those sustaining it, is evidently also a character that offers attractions to all manner of men ; and troops of friends, true and false, wise and unwise, candid and sugar-candid, and all other kinds of friends or professing friends, " the working man" must look to have. To mere popularity hunters, to stump-oratorically inclined individuals who are from time to time seized with a feeling under which they must speak or " bust," to social theorists, to budding

or would-be politicians, and to matured but ma-
nœuvring politicians, to all these does the character
of a friend of the working-classes present irresistible
attractions ; and men of each and all these classes are inflicting themselves upon the working man. A number
of really well-meaning and benevolent persons—whose
benevolence, however, is greater than their knowledge
of the subject they deal with—have also of late years
indulged largely in the friend of the working-man style
of philanthropy ; and the result of their proceedings
has been, that the unfortunate working man has, in
a most objectionable and unfortunate Exeter Hall
fashion, been made an " object of interest." He has
been dinnered and tea-partied, and had the inestimable honour of shaking hands with the squire,
and of being waited upon at tea by the squire's wife
and daughters, and exhibited to the neighbouring
gentry at "feeding time." He has had prizes presented to him for growing the largest cabbage, and
bringing up the largest family in the parish, or on the
estate, " without troubling the union ;" and he has
even had an opportunity of cutting a dash, by the
winning and wearing of prize breeches. And, while
agricultural Giles has been lionized in this style,
his brother Jack of the manufacturing districts has
been made the subject of May meetings ; has been
lectured to, and upon, and been publicly assured by
men of wealth and position that they, too, are working
men, and work as hard as he does for their living, and
that consequently his cause is their own : a kind of
statement which though perhaps substantially true,
is, under the circumstances, a piece of vain bombast
which the more sensible of the Jacks set down at its
true value.

From this class of friends, however, the working
man has little to fear, as what they do is generally
done with a good intention and from disinterested
motives; and though their plans may not be very
wise ones, or likely to effect the end they have in
view; and though their exceedingly patronizing manner
may possibly demoralize some of the patronized, by
causing them to regard themselves as an inferior race
of beings, still, upon the whole, little harm can, and
some good may, result from the proceedings of these
well-meaning if not very wise people.

There is, however, one class of self-constituted friend
to whom the working man should ever say, " avoid
thee ;" a class whose chief object it is to " put money
in their purse," and who adopt the character of the
working man's friend as the readiest means of accom-
plishing that object. It is this class of friend who
tells the working man that he is an outraged and
oppressed individual, against whom all classes of society are leagued; and that it is to them—the said
friends—and to no one else, that he must trust for
guidance and protection. At the head of this peculiar class of friends stands the great C. G. B., or
" Alphabet" Crusher, proprietor of Crusher's newspaper. Crusher's newspaper is the oldest of its class;
but age has only increased its influence as the leading
and most pronounced organ of the labouring classes,
the most energetic discoverer and denouncer of the
abuses to which those classes are subject at the hands
of every other. Since the abolition of the paper
duty, Crusher has had many rivals for the proud
and profitable position of journalistic agitator and
toady-in-chief to " the working man;" but he has
always acquitted himself in a manner that proves

him paramount, and his paper can still boast of
having the largest circulation in the small but not
altogether unimportant world in which papers of its
class are read. And the continuous success of the
veteran Crusher in his own line of business is by no
means surprising to those having a knowledge of the
subject. " Crusher's newspaper " for many years
reigned alone in its glory, and its name became a
household word among a large section of the working-
classes, while its teachings, as propounded by the great
" C. G. B. C." himself in weekly articles of the most
terrifically " scathing" character, formed the political
ideas of more than one generation of the men of that
section. Of late years the proprietor seems to have
deputed the scathing business to his leading contri-
butors ; the fact that his name forms part of the title
of the paper, and the remembrance of his former deeds,
still keeps his memory green ; and in the estimation
of the bulk of the agitator-ruled portion of the working-classes, Crusher, or as his admirers delight to
call him, "The Old 'un," is more emphatically "the
boy" than any of his younger rivals. And it is
only due to Crusher's newspaper to say that it has
gone with the age ; for however sycophantic to the
working-classes, or senselessly abusive of all other
sections of society might be the tone of its rivals, it
has always managed to advance a little beyond them
in either direction.

A working man may be in constant employment,
earning good wages, and enjoying good health ; he
may have a comfortable home, and be a depositor in
the savings bank, and with all these advantages he
may consider that he is a comparatively happy man.
But let him become a reader of Crusher's newspaper,

and he will soon find that, so far from having any claim to consider himself in any sense happy, he is one of the most oppressed and miserable of human beings. He will learn that he is the prey and victim of a " bloated, vicious, blood-sucking aristocracy," unjust taxation, unfair and unequal laws, and a host of other national and personal wrongs. He will be persuaded that the chief aim of capitalists and the employers of labour is to crush and " grind him down," and to annihilate " the rights of labour." In this conscientious and comforting publication he will find the government of his country described as an organized swindle, the principal design of which is to oppress and rob him, and to prevent him from ever attaining any elevation in the social scale. To corroborate this description the actions and conduct of the Government are distorted and commented upon in a style of unquestionable vigour, but of very questionable fairness. The members of the legislative and executive bodies, and all who are in any way actively concerned in carrying on the work of government, he will find described either as arrant fools or self-interested knaves, who, however they may differ about other matters, are unanimous upon the two points of enriching themselves, and of deliberately oppressing the working-classes. And, finally, he will be led to infer that all the friendship for, and interest in, the welfare of the working man, and all the administrative talent in the country, is centred in the We's of Crusher's newspaper.

" We are a nation that must be cracked up," observed one of our most remarkable men to Mark Tapley, during the period of that jolly gentleman's residence in the American " Eden ;" and though there are few persons who would like to speak as plainly as the Yankee colonel, there are, I fancy, still fewer who object to being cracked up occasionally. And so it is with the working-classes. They do not say that they *must* be cracked up, and they would scorn the idea of asking any one to crack them up; but still when they *are* cracked up they are pleased, and are disposed to view the motives of the flatterer in a favourable light. It is to this feeling that Crusher's newspaper, and others of the same class, are indebted for the influence they undoubtedly exert over a considerable portion of the working-classes. In these journals the working man finds himself cracked up to an almost unlimited extent. He is described in their pages as an injured innocent, against whom every man's hand is raised; he is told that it is he who is the only real producer of the national wealth, and that it is he who, as the chief producer, should have the lion's share of the produce, out of which he is unjustly kept by a "bloated aristocracy," and a "servile middle class." In these papers he finds himself habitually alluded to in favourable terms as "a bold bread winner," or "a brawny son of toil," is applauded to the very echo for his "sturdy independence," "rough common sense," and a host of other good and great attributes of which he may or may not be possessed. And in addition to reading all these fine things about himself, the working man, in this kind of papers, has the satisfaction of seeing his enemies (that is, according to these said journals, all who are in a higher rank of society than himself) denounced in the most emphatic language.

The working man who reads and believes in newspapers of the "Crusher" class soon becomes a discontented and unhappy person, and learns to regard himself as an oppressed member of society, on whom all other ranks of society constantly wage warfare. He

becomes a person of intensely class feeling, and believes in the sentiment that whatever is beneficial to
or approved by people above him, must necessarily be
antagonistic to his interest, as in a foregone conclusion; and, while he constantly rails against the
aristocracy, thus speaking of them as the natural and
avowed enemies of the working classes, he is himself
generally the most aristocratic—in his own offensive
sense of the word—of working men. Whenever a
man of this kind is by any chance " clothed in a
little brief authority" he exerts that authority to its
utmost limits and exacts the honour due to it with
the greatest rigour. If a foreman, he scorns the idea
of associating in any but a business way with the
men under his command; if a mechanic, he would
indignantly repudiate any proposition to associate him
with a labourer; and even when a labourer he will
usually find some set of persons with whom he will
refuse to associate—upon some such plea as maintaining
the dignity or the rights of labour, or of upholding
the respectability of the order to which he belongs.
And men of this kind, narrow-minded, ignorant, ill-
informed men, whose ideas upon the constitution of
society and the relative position and value of its various
sections have been derived from the toadying
of papers whose circulation depends upon their persistent writing up of " The working man " are among
the greatest obstacles to the social progress of the
working classes. They are men of little strength of
mind, and, being fooled to the top of their bent, are
firmly impressed with the belief that themselves, and
their class, *are* perfect; and that consequently there
remains nothing more for them to do in the way
of self-improvement, with any view to aiding in the
work of their own advancement. All such disadvan-

tages as they labour under, they assume are entirely attributable to the general wrong-doings and special machinations against them of the rich and powerful, and they lay the flattering unction to their souls that their friends of the agitator persuasion will yet find find them a royal road to wealth and social elevation. Hugging themselves in this belief, they remain stationary, grumbling at their position, but refusing to " move on," and are as a mill-stone about the neck of the more liberal, intelligent, and energetic section of the working classes, who have learned and are striving to carry out the principle that working men themselves must be the chief workers in achieving their own elevation, and that self-denial and self-improvement are primary means to the desired end.

Another and if possible more dangerous " friend " against whom the working man should be on his guard, is the one who comes forward in the character of a delegate. This kind of working man's friend, though not a very numerous, is an exceedingly mischievous one. The members of it generally commence life as journeymen, and during that portion of their career (though still plain Bill or Jack) have probably been noted for their aversion to hard work, and what among their fellow workmen is called the " gift of the gab." And it is to this gift, added to effrontery and idleness, that they owe their elevation to the position of delegates. Should any meeting of the workmen employed in the establishment in which they are engaged be convened for the purpose of consulting upon any subject in which they have a common interest, Bill Spouter or Jack Gabbler will at once seize the opportunity to " hold forth." And as men of this kind have a great flow of language, and a ready command of long, hard, and high-sounding words, they

soon succeed in attaining great ascendancy over their
less fluent fellow-workmen, for there are few things
that exert a stronger influence over uneducated men
than this same "gift of the gab," more especially when
that gift is in the possession of one of their own class,
and is exercised in favour of what they consider to
be their cause. By means of displaying his frothy
eloquence upon every available occasion, the delegate
that is to be acquires the reputation among his shopmates of being able to " speak like a book." In these
days of frequent change and rapid locomotion their
reputation for eloquence soon becomes known throughout " the trade," and then when any occasion arises
for choosing a trade delegate, Spouter or Gabbler is
probably the man selected. It is then that the working
man's friend of the delegate species comes out in all
his glory. It is then that he ceases to be Bill or Jack
and becomes the great Mr. Spouter, who addresses
crowded meetings of his " dear brethren," to whom
he professes that he is quite overcome by the sense
of their wrongs, on which wrongs, if *real* he enlarges
in the most exaggerated language : though the wrongs
have often no existence at all, being in fact simply the
result of imaginations heated by the clap-trap rhapso-
dies of the Crushers and Spouters. It is when he has
become a trade delegate that Spouter discovers that
masters and all others connected with the labour of
production, except the manual workers, are hard and
designing tyrants, whose sole objects in life are to
grind down the working man, and to amass wealth
by " wringing it out of his sweat and blood ;" and it is
when he has made this discovery that he urges his
" down-trodden brethren" to submit no longer to such
a state of things, but to resist the tyranny of masters
and capitalists : urges them, in a word, to take one

of the most disastrous steps that any body of working men can take,—namely, to strike. It is still Spouter who, when the men have struck, and they and their families are reduced to distress and starvation as a natural consequence (though Spouter as a trade delegate is meanwhile drawing a salary, the payment of which will cease with the termination of the strike), urges them—despite their own inclination to accede to the terms offered by the employers—to "hold out" to the last; and tells them that they will be guilty of selfishness and desertion of their cause and their fellow-workmen if they "go in," thus engaging one of their best feelings—their sense of honour—to aid in their own destruction. It is also Spouter who writes furious letters to Crusher's or any other paper that will publish them, denouncing, as an ignorant officious meddler, or a base sycophant, any person who has ventured through the press or otherwise to offer a suggestion for the purpose of bringing about an amicable arrangement between masters and men.

That men of the Crusher and Spouter school should be esteemed as friends, and that "organs" of the Crusher's newspaper stamp should be admired and believed in by working men, may appear strange, but it is nevertheless true ; for, as I have already stated, these men and their journals undoubtedly exercise a great influence over a certain portion of the working classes. But that portion, though a very considerable one, is by no means—and I say it with no feeling of disrespect towards them—the most intelligent or proportionately influential portion of the ranks to which they belong.

There are now, fortunately for the working classes, many men among them who by the aid of cheap education and educational literature, an ably and independently conducted newspaper and periodical press, and the formation and extension of mechanics' institutions, working men's clubs and other kindred institutions, have been enabled to keep pace with the intellectual advance of this rapidly progressive age. And to these men the worthless and even dangerous character of their Crusher and Spouter friends are painfully apparent through all the frothy sentimentality with which they surround themselves. It is to these men —the better educated and deeper thinking portion of their body—assisted by *practical, appreciative, disinterested friends from other sections of society,* that the working classes will be ultimately indebted for freedom from the injurious thraldom at present exercised over a large portion of them by men who, in the guise of friends, are their greatest enemies; since they are constantly striving, and with too much success, to create and sustain a feeling of hatred and antagonism against everybody above them in the social scale. And so long as this feeling of enmity exists, it will be impossible for working men to attain any decided or permanent social elevation; for, next to co-operation among themselves, a feeling of friendly unity for the other portions of society is the thing most requisite for the promotion of their own interest and welfare.

To represent working men as a class who ought to be perfectly happy and contented with their position in life would be doing them a great and manifest injustice. That they are sometimes wronged, that there are employers of labour who in the pursuit of gain look upon and treat them as so much live stock or machinery, and that their position when considered in relation to their important place in the community is often a hard and sometimes even an unjust one, are facts altogether indisputable. But when they reflect upon their position, working men should consider that some of the wrongs of which they reasonably complain are incidental to other sections of the community besides their own, while many of the restrictions peculiar to their class are in a great measure attributable to some injudicious proceedings upon the part of some greater or lesser portion of that class, or are the result of that class antagonism which the Crushers and Spouters of society do their best to create and foster.

Apart, however, from wrongs which they suffer in common with others, or restrictions which may have been caused by their own imprudence, working men are well aware, and all other persons who have given any attention to their condition must admit, that there are points in connexion with the social position of those classes on which amendment and redress are very greatly needed. But while the necessity for such amendments is obvious to all who have seriously considered the subject, I think it must be equally obvious that it will never be by means of men of the Spouter or newspapers of the Crusher school, that they will be brought about. On the contrary, there can be very little doubt that they have a most prejudicial effect upon the interests of those whose cause they profess to advocate; for with the exception of strong drink there is nothing so dangerous and injurious to working men (as a body) as the flattering, bombastic, inflammatory speeches and writings of the kind of men and papers I have spoken of. And though the exaggerated tone which these men and journals always assume when treating of any real or supposed wrong often aggravates the sense of injury, yet both men and papers seem to be utterly powerless for the purpose of obtaining redress for the

wrongs complained of or even of directing public
attention to them. Common sense and experience alike
demonstrate that a solemn *Times* leader, round-about
Telegraph article, or a sarcastic or smashing paper
in the *Saturday Review* or the *Pall Mall Gazette*, will
do more towards remedying the matter complained of
(by directing upon it the current of that impalpable,
but in this country generally irresistible, power,
public opinion) than all the senseless bombast and
vulgar invective with which the columns of Crusher
newspapers teem " all the year round." And I think
that even the warmest partisans of the Spouters
would be compelled to admit that in any case of
dispute between masters and workmen, the former
would be much more likely to come to a satisfactory arrangement through the intervention of some
disinterested person who understood the relations
between men and masters, than by means of men
who are constantly denouncing them (the masters) in
the strongest possible language as selfish tyrants.

When it is suggested to that misanthropic show-
man, Mr. Codlin, that little Nell is probably the child
of wealthy parents, and that those who are kind to her
during her wanderings will doubtless be rewarded, he
becomes very anxious to impress upon her that it is he
and not his kind-hearted fellow-showman who is her
friend. Codlin's the friend, not Short, he constantly
reiterates to Nell when Short is out of hearing. It
mayn't appear like it, he is constrained to confess; but
appearances notwithstanding, he assures her it *is*
he and *not* Short who is the friend; and he impresses
upon her mind that she is to be sure to remember that
important fact. So warm does Mr. Codlin's feeling of
friendship for little Nell become with the prospect of
reward, that it induces him virtually to make prisoners

of her and her grandfather, in order that he may make sure of appearing in the character of her friend and protector before the relatives whom he supposes must be in anxious pursuit of her; and he is very much disappointed when Nell and her grandfather effect their escape from his *friendly* watchfulness.

Now there is a great spice of Codlinism in the friendship of the Crushers and Spouters for the working classes. They are constantly calling upon the working man to observe that it is they who are his friends. " Crusher and Spouter are the friends," they say to their hearers and readers, not Short, the good man and liberal statesman who devotes his time, knowledge, and power to the promotion of the spread of education, the extension of the principles of free trade, and the unity of society. Not Short, the thoughtful learned writer who devotes his talents, or Short, the publisher who devotes his time and risks his capital to produce valuable educational works at a price that places the means of a good education within the reach of every working man. None of these nor any of the other Shorts who assist him in his endeavours to attain social and intellectual elevation in the same kindly spirit with which the veritable Short assisted little Nell when on her painful journey, none of these, they repeat, are your friends; but we, the Crushers and Spouters. Like Codlin, they are compelled to acknowledge that " it mayn't appear like it." Friends of the Short type who kindly and unobtrusively strive to help the artisan by placing him in a position to help himself, may impress an unprejudiced mind with the idea that it is *they* who are the friends. But the giant intellect of Crusher is not to be imposed upon. For friendly services to " the working man " coming from persons in the higher ranks of

life are, Crusher warns the working classes, " analo-
gous to the saliva with which the boa-constrictor
slavers his victim, being intended to aid the descent of
the victim into the stomach of the noble reptile."
On the other hand the fact that the Crushers and
Spouters never give the working man anything but
words, and are constantly urging upon him the
necessity for presenting one or other of their brotherhood with a testimonial or dunning him for subscriptions to leagues and associations of which they are the
organizers and self-constituted and irresponsible managers, would make it appear to most people that they
were *not* altogether the friends of the working man.
But then Crusher and Spouter remind " the brawny
sons of toil " that appearances are deceitful, and fer-
vently assure them that, though it mayn't appear so, it is
Codlin and not Short who is their friend, and the
brawny sons of toil believe them and suffer accordingly.

That a true friend is indeed a treasure, feeling, experience, and Shakspeare alike assure us, and the latter
makes Polonius say, when giving counsel to his son :—

" The friends thou hast, and their adoption tried,
Grapple them to thy soul with hooks of steel ;"

And working men would do well to ponder upon this
advice and mark the qualification which it contains,
for if they would act upon that advice and only
" Grapple to their souls " friends whose " adoption "
they have tried, they would soon find themselves freed
from the dangerous wiles of the Crushers and Spouters.
For to test the " adoption " of those characters would
inevitably lead to the discovery that while professing
to be the friends of the working man they are in reality
the most dangerous enemies to his social progress.
The working classes require friends to assist and cheer
them in the work of improving their condition and

prospects, and fortunately they do not lack real friends who have done and are still able and willing to do them good service.   But the real friends of the working classes are very few in number compared with the host of pretenders to that character, and many working men have yet to learn to distinguish the true from the false friend, and to realize the fact that flatterers and parasites are the most pernicious foes.

A PROSPEROUS TRADE-UNION.*

Much has been done of late years to improve the condition of the working classes, and the working man of the present generation enjoys many advantages that were beyond the reach of his less fortunate brethren of former times. The tommy-shop system of robbery has been abolished, and the payment of workmen's wages in public-houses made illegal. Government enactments and inspections have compelled those who employ men in dangerous occupations to take proper precautions for insuring the safety of those employed; and the law now provides against the overworking of children of tender years. Mechanics' and other institutions of a similar character have been established; beautiful parks have been thrown open to city-pent communities, and a variety of other means taken with a view of elevating the intellectual faculties and social position of the working man.

But though a wise legislature has suppressed many of the abuses to which the working classes were formerly subjected, and though private philanthropy and public benevolence have striven, and with a considerable amount of success, to improve both their mental and physical condition, yet they (the working classes) are fully and wisely convinced that it is principally to themselves they must trust if they wish to permanently rise in the social scale, or to be prepared, as far as their circumstances make it possible, to meet those

* The substance of this paper originally appeared in Chambers's Journal.

fluctuations in trade by which they are so often severe sufferers. This feeling led many thoughtful working men to consider how they might best help themselves and the class to which they belonged, and gave rise to the movement which has culminated in the present gigantic system of trade-unions.

Trade-unions, like other institutions, have their opponents, and some of these assert that " trade societies" are unjust monopolies ; that they encourage strikes, and foster a spirit of insubordination among workmen. But such assertions as these are extreme, and are generally made by interested parties, or those who know very little about the subject. Cases can, of course, be brought forward in which men who belonged to trade-unions have attempted to destroy establishments into which some " new-fangled" machinery, which for a time had thrown some of them out of work, had been introduced, and others in which they have ill-treated persons who were obnoxious to " the trade ;" and no doubt instances could be pointed out in which a few lazy, brawling pot-house orators have induced the members of a trade-union to strike for some very slight, if not altogether imaginary cause, and to hold out, despite the remonstrances of their real friends, after they have struck. Such cases as these always occur among men with whom the true principle of trade-union has been but very imperfectly developed ; and no one deplores and condemns them more sincerely than do the thinking and educated members of the trade-unions. That trade-unions, if upon a comprehensive scale, and conducted in a business-like manner, are extremely beneficial to their members, and favourable to the interests of the employers of those members, will be amply demonstrated by an account of the formation, objects, progress, and present condition of one of the strongest, best conducted, and most successful of these unions—" The Amalgamated Society of Engineers, Machinists, Millwrights, Smiths, and Pattern-makers." The trades incorporated in this society bear about the same relation to each other as do those of the bricklayer, carpenter, and stone-mason in the building-trade ; and members of each branch are generally employed in every workshop, where locomotive, marine, or stationary engines, or any of the numerous machines at present in use, are manufactured or repaired.

Previous to the year 1851, each of these trades had a society of its own, into which only members of that particular trade were admitted : but as the advantages of the union principle became more fully apparent, the members of these societies, finding that their interests were substantially identical, resolved to further develop the system of trade-unions by uniting their respective bodies, and forming one large one. On January 1, 1851, this union accordingly took place, and they then assumed their present title of the " Amalgamated Society." Their objects are thus set forth in the preamble which precedes their rules. " The object of this society is to raise from time to time, by contributions among the members thereof, funds for the purpose of mutual support in case of sickness, accident, superannuation, emigration, for the burial of members and their wives, and also for assistance to members out of work." Concerning the management of the society, the preamble says : " For the benefit of its members, it shall be divided into branches, which shall be appointed in such numbers and districts as may be deemed necessary, in conformity with the rules provided for that purpose. Every branch of this society shall appoint its own officers, and conduct its own business in the manner set forth in the following rules." The rules are thirty-five in number, are all drawn up in plain language, and provide for every conceivable contingency. From these rules we learn the system by which the society is managed, the qualifications necessary for membership, the benefits to be derived from it, and the sum each member has to pay to participate in those benefits. The branches of the society are conducted by presidents, secretaries, stewards, and treasurers; and in branches where the number of members make it necessary, vice-presidents and assistant-secretaries are added. The presidents, vice-presidents, and treasurers fulfil the usual duties of such officers; and the steward takes charge of the book which is used as a check upon the secretary. The principal duties of the secretary are to receive, enter, and sign for the contributions of the members; to see to the payment of members who are entitled to any of the benefits of the society; and to conduct the correspondence incidental to his office. He must write to the general secretary of the society at least once a month, and within the first six days of each month, " reporting the state of trade in his district, the number and profession of the members out of employment, and the probability of men being wanted."

From these reports, the general secretary compiles a monthly report of the state of trade throughout the country, and a copy of this report is furnished to the secretary of each branch. Secretaries are thus often in a position to materially assist members who may be out of employment, as from the monthly report they can at once inform them where trade is good or bad, and where men of any particular trade are wanted. The books of each branch are audited every quarter by members who are elected (as are all the officers of

the society) by the remaining members of the branch ;
and each secretary has to forward the quarterly ac-
counts of his branch, duly signed by the auditors, to
the office of the general secretary.   There is an executive council, consisting of twenty-five members, who
are appointed from as many different branches, and
are elected by the members of those branches.   This
council acts for the society in cases of emergency,
fulfils the functions of a court of appeal, and appoints
auditors to examine the books, receipts, &c., of the
general secretary, and report upon the state of the
same to the council.   The central office of the society
is in London, and its business is conducted by the
general secretary, whose time is exclusively devoted to
the affairs of the society.   Such is an outline of the
general system upon which this society is conducted—
a system that, after fifteen years' experience, has been
found eminently satisfactory and successful, and which
has been productive of the most beneficial results.
In a society like this, " union is strength," the greater
the number of members, the greater will be its stability and importance, and it is to the interest of all
members to enrol as many as possible in their society.
But still it is necessary to the continuance and well-
being of the union that each person admitted should
be a " fit and proper" one ; and to insure this, each
candidate for admission must be possessed of certain
qualifications, which are set forth in the rules of the
society.

No person is admitted who is under twenty, or
above forty years of age, except in the case of candidates who have formerly been members of the society,
and who wish to rejoin it, in which case they are admitted up to the age of forty-five years.   No person
is eligible for admission unless he has worked five

years successively at the trade which he professes, or
has served five years to it before the age of twenty-
one. Each candidate for admission must be proposed,
seconded, and recommended by two members of the
branch which he wishes to join; the proposer and
seconder must be prepared to state (and if necessary,
prove by evidence) that the party whose election they
are proposing is possessed of good abilities as a workman, is of steady habits, and good moral character;
and every one who is elected must be a member twelve
months before he is entitled to the benefits of the
society. The avowed objects of this society are to
render support to its members in cases of sickness,
accident, &c., and likewise to give them assistance
when out of work; and I will now proceed to show
how these objects are carried out.

First, with regard to members who are out of work,
the rules of the society provide that, " should any free
member be thrown out of employment under circumstances satisfactory to the branch to which he belongs
. . . . ; he shall be entitled to the sum of 10s. per
week for fourteen weeks, 7s. per week for thirty, and
6s. per week so long as he remains out of employment
—making a total of 19l. 18s. in one year." And these
donations are so calculated that no member can receive more than that sum in any one year; though it
seldom occurs that members are out of employment
for so great a length of time as a year, when trade is
in anything like an average state of briskness. If a
member who is out of work wishes to travel in search
of employment, he receives from the secretary of the
branch to which he belongs a travelling card, which is
filled up in accordance with rules existing for that
purpose. This card establishes the identity of the
travelling member, and enables him to draw the dona-

tion which is due to him in any town in which there is a branch of the society ; and the secretary of each branch which he may visit directs him to where he (the secretary) thinks he is most likely to find employment. The rules of the society provide for the distribution of its other benefits in an equally just and comprehensive manner. Any member who, in consequence of sickness or lameness, is unable to follow his ordinary employment, must send a written notice to that effect to the secretary of his branch within three days of his indisposition ; and he is then entitled to a sum of 10s. per week for twenty-six weeks, and 5s. per week for as much longer as he may continue ill. Provision is likewise made for members who may fall sick while travelling in search of employment ; and should the exigencies of the case require it, the officers of the branch in which any travelling member falls sick, apprise the friends of the sick member of his condition, and send the member to those friends at the expense of the society. Any member who, through accident, blindness, imperfect vision, apoplexy, epilepsy, or paralysis, is rendered incapable of following any of the branches of trade connected with the society, receives the sum of 100l.* Members who are fifty years of age or upwards, and who have been eighteen successive years in the society (the time to count from the date of their entrance into the society of which they were members previous to the amalgamation), and who are not in regular employment, can, if they choose to apply for it, have a retiring allowance of 7s. per week for life. At the death of a

* It is, of course, provided that no member shall receive this or the sick benefit if the accident has been caused through, or the disease brought on by, intemperance, or other improper conduct of the member.

member, his widow or next of kin receives the sum of
12*l.* to defray his funeral expenses ; or, at the death of
his wife, any member, by applying for it, may receive
the sum of 5*l.*, leaving 7*l.* to be paid to his representatives at his own decease. In addition to these specified benefits, there is a benevolent fund (taken out of
the general funds of the society), and from this fund
any particular or unusual case of distress is relieved,
upon the recommendation of the branch to which the
distressed member belongs.

The revenue of the society is derived from the
entrance-fees and contributions of its members, each
member upon his admission into the society having to
pay an entrance-fee varying from 15*s.* to 3*l.* 10*s.*,
according to his age at the time of entrance ; and all
members, when in employment, pay a fixed contribution of *one shilling* per week. Thus, for a weekly payment of one shilling, the working mechanic can assure
himself of assistance when out of employment, or in
case of sickness or accident ; he entitles himself to a
pension, should he be unable to work in his old age ;
and he has the pleasing assurance that at his death
the last rites of humanity will be decently carried out.
Small as this contribution of one shilling per week
may appear for carrying out so many benevolent purposes, it is, nevertheless, amply sufficient when a feeling of co-operation animates the directors and members of such institutions. The society of which I have
been speaking annually issues a blue-book, which, for
accuracy and completeness, is equal to anything of the
kind that leaves the press. The one for 1866 (the
latest issued at the time of writing) is now before me,
and from this may be gathered some interesting facts
concerning the operations and extent of the society
which have an interest for all classes, as they serve to

show what may be effected by association. At the
close of the first year of the amalgamation of the
several societies which now form the present one, the
total number of members was 11,829, and in December,
1865, they had increased to 30,978. The society, at
the date of the report from which I am quoting (which
gives the transactions of the society from December,
1864, to December, 1865), consisted of 295 branches,
230 of which were in England and Wales, 31 in
Scotland, 11 in Ireland, 8 in the United States of
America, 6 in Australia, 5 in Canada, 2 in New
Zealand, 1 in France, and 1 in Malta. The income of
the society for the year was 77,373*l*. 5*s*. 6½*d*., the
expenditure, 49,172*l*. 6*s*. 2*d*., and the total balance
in hand at the end of December, 1865, was
115,357*l*. 13*s*. 10½*d*., exclusive of arrears. In years of
anything like an average state of good trade the
society, after paying all claims upon it, is enabled to
add in a greater or lesser degree to its reserve fund;
but its stability and beneficial character will perhaps
be more satisfactorily demonstrated by showing its
working under extraordinary pressure.

Owing to the " cotton famine " and other causes,
the year 1862 was one of the most disastrous in the
annals of trade, and the calls upon the funds of the
society (which then numbered 24,234 members) were
consequently much larger than the average of former
years, the total expenditure of the society for that year
amounting to 63,565*l*. 18*s*. 5½*d*., being 2*l*. 12*s*. 5½*d*.
per member; since 1853, the greatest expenditure ever
reached in one year previous to 1862, only came to
1*l*. 13*s*. 10½*d*. per member; while some years it did
not amount to even half of that sum per member.
But, notwithstanding the great demand upon the
resources of the society in 1862, they had at the end

of that year a fund of 67,615*l.* 16*s.* 6*d.* in hand. The principal items of expenditure for the year were: Donations to members out of work, 38,881*l.* 16*s.* 4½*d.* Sick benefit, 10,430*l.* 2*s.* 7*d.* Funeral benefit, 3,031*l.* Superannuation benefit, 2,654*l.* 5*s.* Grants to members who, through accident, blindness, or any of the diseases previously mentioned, had been rendered incapable of following their employment, 1,200*l.*, being twelve grants of 100*l.* each. Grants from the benevolent fund, 1,086*l.*, being 241 grants, varying in amount from 8*l.* to 2*l.* Working expenses, 3,219*l.* 10*s.* 3½*d.* This item includes the salaries of all branch officers, secretaries, auditors, trustees, and the members of the executive council, besides the expenses of all committees and delegations; and when we consider the magnitude and extent of the society, and the variety of purposes which it fulfils, it is a surprisingly small one. Printing, stationery, postage, and parcels, 1,149*l.* 12*s.* 4½*d.* Rents, rates, gas, and coal, 700*l.* 2*s.* 2*d.* In looking at this item it must be borne in mind that, in addition to central offices in London and Manchester, each branch of the society has to rent a room in which to transact its business, and as many of the branches number upwards of 300 members, some of these rooms have to be of tolerably large dimensions. Loans to other trades, 240*l.*; and gifts to other trades, 154*l.* 11*s.*

The income of the society in 1862 was 57,783*l.* 13*s.* 11*d.*; their balance in hand, in December 1861, was 73,398*l.* 1*s.* 0½*d.*—making a total of 131,181*l.* 14*s.* 11½*d.*—which the society had in hand to meet the demands upon them in 1862; so that, after paying away in that year the sum of 63,565*l.* 18*s.* 5½*d.* —and by far the largest sum ever paid by this or any similar society in one year—they had a balance in hand of 67,615*l.* 16*s.* 6*d.* The rapid growth and success of this society, and the important position to which it has attained, are sufficient proofs, if proofs were required, that trade-societies, if conceived in a just and liberal spirit, and carried out with no other object than the protection of the lawful interests, and alleviation of the unavoidable distresses of their members, are the most beneficial to which a working mechanic can belong.

TRADE-SOCIETIES AND STRIKES.

I HAVE said that trade-unions such as I have described are favourable to the interests of the employers of their members; and I think that if any unprejudiced person will look at the facts of the case, they will arrive at the same conclusion. In the first place, none are admitted into a trade-union unless they are known to possess good abilities as workmen, and are of steady habits and good moral character; so that, by employing a member of a trade-society, an employer secures a workman possessing those qualifications; and again, any member of a trade-union who is discharged from his employment for misconduct, is debarred from the benefits of the society till he again finds employment; so that the members of a trade-union have an additional inducement to conduct themselves properly while at work.

It is often asserted by the opponents of trade-unions, that one of the objects of these societies is to have all workmen, whether good or bad, paid alike; but this is a mistaken notion. All that the rules of such societies insist upon is, that as they admit no one to be a member unless he is possessed of good abilities as a workman, no member must work for *less than the average rate of wages paid to members of the same branch of trade in the district in which he is employed.** But

---

* This same regulation is practically observed among all bar-risters and physicians of repute.

they by no means seek to place the *superior* and the only average workman upon an equal footing, as there are superior workmen in all trades who are paid at a considerably higher rate than ordinary workmen. And though the rules upon this point savour of trade dictation, they are found in practice to be as much in favour of masters as workmen; for though they forbid a man to work for less than the average wages of the district in which he is employed, they compel him, should he be out of employment, to take work in any district in which it is offered to him, at the rate of wages current in that district, however much higher a rate he may have been previously earning. We will suppose, for instance—and it is a very common case—that there is a " slap" of dull trade in the London district, and that in consequence a number of the London workmen—who are, as a rule, the pick of the trade—are on the funds of the society. Matters being in this state, the secretary of a London branch of the club hears, through the secretary of a provincial branch, that men are wanted in his (the provincial secretary's) district. The London secretary then instructs some of those who are out of employment to go and apply for work in the district in which men are wanted, and if work is offered them in reply to their application, they must take it or forfeit the out-of-work pay of the society, though the wages of that district may be ten shillings a-week less than they have been in the habit of getting in London. And as there is not one working man in a thousand who would refuse work offered under such circumstances, even if he were in such a pecuniary position as would justify him in running the risk, the result is, that masters, through the influence of the club, frequently get first-rate workmen at a third-rate price.

Whether or not the protectionist principle that enters more or less into every trade combination, under whatever name or form such combination may exist, is in the abstract justifiable, is a question that admits of much debate, and which need not be discussed here. But so long as that principle is permitted to be put into practice, I think that the mechanic who has paid a premium and worked for five or seven years at a merely nominal rate of wages, to acquire the knowledge of his art, has quite as much right as doctors, lawyers, or members of the stock exchange, to protect the interests and exclusiveness of his trade. When a case occurs in which a number of working men threaten to "turn out" against an unqualified man who is working for under wages—" here, my masters," exclaim the opponents of trades-unions, " is a case of tyranny and monopoly for you !" and perhaps it is ; but would a persevering solicitor's clerk, or a clever apothecary, who tried to force themselves into the legal or medical professions have fared any better at the hands of the " qualified practitioners"?   Doctors and lawyers could not well, even if they were willing, resort to so vulgar a proceeding as a turn out, but legal and medical " etiquette," or the legal enactments which guard the trade combinations of the " learned professions," would soon, I ween, "do for" the unqualified aspirants to professional honours and profits.   To object to a person's employing the services of whomsoever he may choose, or to a man's selling his services at his own price, is, as a first principle, utterly and self-evidently unjust. But it is as self-evident that it is acting upon the equally unjust first principle that that's in the captain but a choleric word which in the soldier is rank blasphemy, to condemn such proceedings on the part of comparatively ignorant and uneducated mechanics, while approving of their practice by those who should set the example of sacrificing self-interest to abstract justice, and who are more capable of understanding the poetic beauty of appeals founded upon first principles.

It will probably be said that the society of which I wrote in a previous chapter is an exceptional one, and to a very considerable extent this may be said with truth. The trades which form that society are not confined to any particular district, and owing to the great competition and frequent fluctuations in trade, and the abundant facilities for travelling, the bulk of the men following the trades have to knock about the country a great deal. And this same knocking about, although frequently involving considerable suffering and regarded as somewhat in the light of a grievance, has a wonderful tendency to eradicate from the working-class mind that bigoted, narrow-minded tone of feeling which gave rise to the old aggressive style of trade-union, and which, in districts almost exclusively devoted to one particular branch of trade, and where the great majority of the workmen are natives of, and never remove from, the district, still retards the development of the true principles of trade-unions. In their knockings about these men have learned that whatever may be the much-talked-of rights of labour, capital has also its rights, and that a mutual respect and toleration of rights is likely to be most beneficial to all parties concerned. They have also learned that masters as well as workmen require to be allowed some little freedom of action, and that it is a waste of time, money, and energy to assume a position of antagonism towards employers upon merely technical grounds which do not materially affect vital principles, or the ever-to-be-remembered, but apparently never-to-be-defined rights of labour; and they have further learned to abolish all

secret proceedings in connexion with their union, and
to work with union and non-union men in equal good
fellowship.* But to those who know the working
classes, and the mode of thought and action prevailing in
some trades-unions, the mere fact of the various trades
that form " the amalgamated society " having combined, will furnish the strongest proof of the advanced
intelligence and liberality of the general body of the
members of the society. For though, broadly speaking,
the interests of the trades are identical, there is such
divergency of interests among them on minor points
as would in such districts as Sheffield and some of the
iron and mining districts have kept them apart, if not
in direct antagonism for ever and a day. The members of this society have learned, in short, that a trade-
union, to be really beneficial to a trade generally,
and the members of it individually, should have nothing
in its constitution antagonistic to the just rights and
interest of the possessors of capital or employers of
labour ; or of a dictatorial or aggressive character
either as regards employers or workmen ; but should
be conducted solely with a view of assisting—by an
organized system of mutual insurance—its members
when suffering under any of the adverse circumstances
incidental to the condition of the working man ; and
of so associating the artisans engaged in the trade as

* On this last point, however, no particular credit is due to
them. The benefits of the society in question are so manifest, that
the difficulty is not to get members to join it, but to keep out applicants for admission who, as workmen, do not come up to the society
standard, and every year numerous candidates for admission are
rejected, and numbers who have obtained admission under false
pretences are excluded. But though not qualified for admission
into the society, many of these men are able to earn a living at the
trade ; and for society men to refuse to work with them, or object to their working for whatever rate of wages they can get,
would be simply dastardly.

to enable them to act together and spontaneously in promoting their common interests, or resisting any manifestly unjust or unnecessary attempt to depreciate the fair market value of their labour. And the general result of the liberal policy which these lessons have induced them to adopt in the management of their society, is that since the great lock-out of 1852 (which was the second year of the existence of the society), there has been no general dispute between masters and workmen in the engineering trade, and the few partial misunderstandings affecting single workshops, or localities, that have arisen since then have generally been speedily and amicably arranged, while the work-men in the trade are amongst the highest paid class of mechanics, and the capital invested in it yields large profits. The great majority of the masters, and more especially those of them who are practical men as well as capitalists, or who have risen from being working men, give a decided preference to society men, knowing that in them they are sure to secure skilful workmen, while masters and workmen have a mutual and salutary respect for each other's power of making a determined stand should any misunderstanding upon really vital points be allowed to go to extremes; and the tone and self-respect of the trade are materially improved by the members of it—the great bulk of whom are also members of the trade-union—being by their title to the various benefits of the union placed in a comparatively independent position when out of employment, or when permanently or for a time inca-pacitated by accident, disease, or old age from following their ordinary occupation.

That the *principle* of trades-unions is sound, and that when well conducted such unions are useful and beneficial institutions, there can, I think, be no doubt.

But unfortunately there can be equàlly little doubt that this principle is in some instances grossly perverted, and that in these instances the conductors of such societies, instead of aiming at making them mutual assurance societies, with benefits regulated to meet the ordinary drawbacks to which all working men are liable, and such others as may more particularly affect the particular trades with which they are connected, try to make them into weapons of offence against capital and freedom of action either in masters or workmen who do not belong to the societies, and to secure for their members a monopolizing and dictatorial power. And it is the tone of feeling prevailing in trades-unions of this kind, that gives rise to those most diabolical and cowardly of all modern crimes—trade outrages. The unions connected with the trades that have become notorious for these outrages may not be legally responsible for such crimes, no member of the union may know by whom the outrages have been perpetrated, and many of the more manly and better educated of the unionists may regard them with all the abhorrence they deserve ; but still, speaking broadly, the unions of this class, by their generally aggressive policy, their unwritten but perfectly understood laws, their blatant inflammatory spouters, and their lukewarm, half-hearted condemnation of the outrages and the unscrupulous ruffians by whom they are committed, are morally responsible as instigators of, and accessories to, the crimes. And so long as a monopolizing and aggressive spirit is permitted to enter into the composition of trade-unions, so long will trade outrages continue to be perpetrated, so long will the unions of the trades in connexion with which these outrages take place be held morally responsible for them, and condemned by

the public voice, and so long will those whose political
or pecuniary interest it is to do so continue to use the
dastardly proceedings of isolated trades as arguments
for the condemnation of *all* trade-unions, and so
injure such unions in the estimation of those who have
but a superficial knowledge of the constitution and
aims of, and benefits derived from the better class of
them, by the most pernicious, and hardest to refute
of all misrepresentation—generalization founded upon
distorted and insufficient, though not absolutely false,
premises and deductions. And for these reasons it
becomes the duty of the members of the more liberal
and advanced trade-unions, to do all in their power to
raise the moral tone and alter and improve the constitution of those unions in which the true principles
of trade union are as yet but little understood, and in
which the opinions, traditions, and practices that have
come down from a ruder and less civilized period still
prevail.

As trade-unions are intimately connected with the
question of strikes, a few observations upon strikes will
not, perhaps, be considered out of place in concluding
this paper. That strikes are serious evils, and are
ultimately detrimental to the commercial and manufacturing interests of the country in which they take
place, and should, consequently, be avoided whenever
it is possible, are, I believe, regarded as understood
truisms by all who have either a practical or theoretical
knowledge of political economy. Still, circumstances
may arise under which a strike would be the lesser of
two evils between which a body of workmen were
driven to choose ; and in that case a strike would be
justifiable, however much the necessity for adopting
such a mode of settling or attempting to settle a vexed
question between employers and employed might be

deplored.　But the evil that is greater than a strike
must be great indeed, so great that the probability
of it arising in the present age of competition
is very small; and the frequency with which strikes
occur is, in my opinion, in a great measure attributable to the fact, that the general run of working
men do not fully comprehend the nature and magnitude of the evils involved in a strike, and lacking the
check that would arise from a thorough understanding
of these evils, they adopt a strike as a first, instead of
a last resource.　A strike is under any circumstances a great evil to the workmen engaged in it ; it
involves actual loss of wages during the time that it
lasts, and consequent suffering to wives and families ; it
tends to send the home trade to foreign markets,
and by thus sending away work while leaving hands,
depresses the value of labour in the particular trade
concerned, and so reduces the men to the necessity of
accepting a lower rate of wages.　Or it often has the
effect of overstocking and permanently depreciating
the value of skilled labour in a trade, by letting into
it large numbers of " handy labourers"—men of
somewhat similar, but less well-paid trades—runaway
apprentices, and the thousand-and-one other dwellers
on the threshold, who are always found ready to supply
the place of men " on strike," and who, getting " the
run" of the trade during the period of the strike, acquire a knowledge of the little of it that they had still
to learn ; and, finally, strikes invariably tend to demoralize the trades in which they occur.　If, as often
happens, workmen " on strike," after holding out for
a considerable length of time, are at last compelled to
give way from the sheer want and poverty which continued loss of wages inevitably brings, the masters,
partly from the bitterness of feeling engendered by the

strike, and partly with a view to recouping themselves for *their* loss, often impose harder terms than those against which the men had struck, and the men return to their work sullenly, and secretly resolved to " pay off," or " be straight with," the masters, at the earliest possible date.   While, if the masters have to " knock under," they often " keep it in" for the men, so that one strike frequently lays the foundation for others, and creates a distrustful, unsympathetic, and bickering tone between employers and employed, from which the latter are ultimately the greatest sufferers.   And if working men generally could only be induced to calmly weigh these obvious considerations, instead of allowing themselves to be influenced by the clap-trap of professional strike-mongers, to whom a strike is " a paying concern," and who stand in the same relation to workmen " on strike" as the boys did to the frogs in the fable, strikes would become much less frequent occurrences than they are at present, and working men would, in the long run, be the gainers by the change.   In the present day, too, all working men should, for their own sake, remember that England is no longer the absolute autocrat as a manufacturing nation that she has been ; foreign countries are running her close, and nations that less than a generation ago were almost entirely dependent upon her for many of the most important descriptions of manufactured goods, now not only supply themselves with those classes of goods, but are formidable competitors with her for supplying the foreign, and even the home, markets.   There has certainly been considerable exaggeration with respect to the extent and character of this foreign competition ; but *all* the recent talk about it has not—as many working men flatter themselves is the case—been got up for political party purposes.

There has been some mere political and alarmist " cry" on the subject, but there is also undoubtedly a good deal of " wool" in what has been said. " Foreign competition" is an established fact, and to all dependent upon or connected with English manufacturing industry, a most important one, and as such, and on the principle that delays are dangerous, it should be grappled with. But while foreign nations have made, and are still making, rapid progress in the manufacturing arts in which England formerly reigned supremely dominant, England can yet give " a start and a beating" to the best of her competitors, if all whose fortunes are cast in with her manufacturing boat will pull together ; but it is only by the proverbial long pull, and strong pull, and pull all together, that she can any longer hope to maintain her still decided lead in the manufacturing race. And while English workmen are to be commended for endeavouring to obtain the highest market value for their labour, and a legitimate share of the wealth they help to create, they should be careful that the means they adopt to gain their ends are not of a suicidal character. They should bear in mind that whatever may be done in matters of detail, it is only by a cordial co-operation of English capital and labour that foreign competition can be beaten off. In short, the time has now arrived, and capitalists and workmen are alike called upon to recognise the fact, when of capital and labour, in connexion with English manufacturing industry, it may be said, with literal truth, united they stand, divided they fall—fall before competitors their own inferiors in everything save unity of action.

SOME NON-BENEFICIAL CUSTOMS
OF BENEFIT SOCIETIES.

" SUFFICIENT unto the day is the evil thereof," is a text in which, when the evil days come, most people are disposed to believe thoroughly. They are *then* generally of opinion that *more* than sufficient for the day is the evil thereof; and it is this feeling which prompts most men to lay by out of the passing good a portion wherewith to neutralize or alleviate so far as may be the evil that may come at any time. Of the evil days that come to man, the day of sickness is the most general, and the most unavoidable. Under the most favourable circumstances, and viewed merely in the abstract, sickness is a great evil. It involves positive physical suffering: the negative pain arising from the withdrawal from the ordinary pursuits and enjoyments of life; the handing over of yourself to the control of doctors and nurses, and the swallowing of horribly nauseous compounds, which, but for your pains or fears, you would willingly throw to the dogs. But to those men who are the bread-winners for themselves or others, and whom sickness incapacitates from labour, the contemplation of the disastrous results consequent upon enforced idleness is often more painful than sickness itself. And it is particularly incumbent upon such men as these, and more especially upon those of them who, in the more literal sense of the phrase, earn their bread by the sweat of their brow, and are known to other sections of society as " the working classes," to be prepared, as far as possible, for the adverse results incidental to sickness.

Such were the thoughts that passed through my mind as I reflected upon my position on reaching man's estate, and finding myself " out of my time," and for the future solely dependent upon my own exertions as a working mechanic for a livelihood. I was young and confident, had—to use a stock phrase—a good trade in my fingers, and the world before me where to choose. And despite all that I had heard concerning the exceeding wickedness of the present generation, I hopefully believed that there was still much that was good and pleasant to be found in the world that was before me, and had every prospect of being able to earn, in my position in life, a good living. But still I remembered sickness might come at any moment ; the vigorous health of youth might be shattered, the strong arm rendered weak, or the skilfully-trained hand lose its cunning ; and against the dire consequences of such possibilities it behoved me, as one who valued " the glorious privilege of being independent," to be prepared, by making some provision out of the fruits of the good days, for the evil and unproductive days that would almost certainly come.

The only principle upon which working men can to any considerable extent and in a reliable manner be provided to meet the contingencies arising from sickness is that of mutual assurance ; and of the many institutions founded upon this principle Friendly or Benefit Societies are the best adapted to their incomes and requirements. This being the case, I determined, with a view to carrying out my prudential resolves, to join The Ancient Order of Good Fellows, one of the first established and most extensive of the benefit societies supported by the working classes. On mentioning my wish to two of my fellow-workmen who were members of the society, they at once offered to propose and second me in their "lodge." I accordingly gave them my proposition fee, and in due time they informed me that I had been accepted, and would be "made" on the following lodge night.

When that night arrived I duly appeared at the lodge (which was held, as are all lodges of the large benefit societies, in a public-house) in company with my proposer and seconder. On reaching the door of the club-room, one of my companions gave a complicated series of knocks upon it; a small slide in the door was then withdrawn and an *ear* appeared at the opening; and he who had knocked whispered something into the ear, and was then admitted. My other companion called out, "Brother Jones without the word," the proprietor of the ear repeated, "Brother Jones without the word," and a voice from the top end of the room then said, "Admit Brother Jones." Brother Jones was then admitted, and I was left alone in my misery; for all this mystery fully impressed me with the notion that, after all, the tales about red-hot pokers and other instruments of torture necessary to the initiation of members into these societies, were no myths. After waiting for some minutes, during which there was a great shuffling of feet and jingling of glasses going on inside the room, the door was again opened, and I was invited by him of the ear to walk in. I had been instructed as to how I was to salute the Noble Grand and his subordinates in office, and having got through this form of salutation successfully, and being somewhat reassured by seeing no indication of the hot poker, I ventured to take a survey of the room. At the upper end the Noble Grand, with the scarf of his office around his grand and noble body, was enthroned under a canopy of blue silk, and was supported on either side by officers second only to his noble grandship in rank. At the lower end the vice-grand was enthroned; and at two tables that extended the whole length of the room were seated about a hundred and fifty of the brethren, each with his pot or glass before him. Some of the brethren, it was evident from their stupefied stare and maudlin gestures, were already " gone ;" others were " getting on," and there was a general disposition among them to be noisy. The walls of the room were emblazoned with flags, mottoes, and official scarves, and above the throne of the Noble Grand was fixed a roll of fame in the shape of a board, on which were written in letters of gold the names of the past noble grands of the lodge.

By the time I had noticed these particulars, the initiating officers were prepared to receive me. After answering a number of questions, and repeating after one of them a long and senseless rigmarole which was in effect an oath not to reveal the secrets of " the order" (which, by the way, there is little danger of my doing, as, independent of a moral obligation not to do so, a sense of shame would keep me silent about the senseless mummeries which constitute *the secrets* of " the order"), I was pronounced fully made. Where-upon the whole of the brethren rose to their feet, and holding their charged glasses above their heads, after the manner of bacchanalian choristers in an opera, or the " supers" who represent the pirate horde carousing in nautical melodramas, shouted as one man, "Long life and happiness to our new brother !" and emptied their glasses. How I was expected to acknowledge this unexpected honour I knew not; but I was speedily relieved from my embarrassment upon this point, by my proposer suggesting in a stage whisper that

I should "stand something." I asked how much it would be necessary for me to stand. He put it to my conscience, that, considering the number of brethren who were present, I could not well stand less than a gallon of ale; and a gallon of ale I accordingly "stood," and as many of the brethren as got their glasses replenished from this supply of ale again toasted their "new brother."

My initiation being now fairly completed, I took my seat at one of the tables, and for some time there was a cessation of all business save that of drinking. But presently arose Brother Smith; who, when he had secured the attention of the noble grand, proceeded to make a statement, to the effect that Brother Mansell—whom he frankly described as a drunken old vagabond—who was then "on the box" (that is, receiving the sick benefit of the society), had been seen going about the streets in a state of intoxication; and it being against the laws of the society to get drunk while on the sick list, he called upon the officers of the society to punish Brother Mansell by confiscating his sick pay. The instant Brother Smith had finished his statement, Brother Williams (a brother-in-law of the denounced Brother Mansell), who was so far "gone" that he had to support himself by clinging to the table, staggered to his feet, and in a fierce, spluttering tone, intimated that he did not believe a word that Brother Smith had said, that only he (Brother Williams) could not afford to be fined, he would there and then "knock his" (Brother Smith's) "two eyes into one." To which Brother Smith responded, by saying that if Brother Williams attempted to hit him, he would make him (Brother Williams) look nine ways for Sunday. Brother Williams was about to make some threatening, and, probably, from the suggestive manner in which he turned up his coat sleeves, practical rejoinder; but at this interesting point the Noble Grand, who had been engaged in " bottoming" a pot of porter, interposed his authority by saying, " Now, chaps, you mustn't get fighting here, you know, or I shall have to fine you both." Upon hearing this, Brother Williams, who seemed to have a particular horror of a fine, sank into his seat, and was speedily sleeping the sleep of the drunken, and the investigation into Brother Mansell's transgression was quietly allowed to drop.

By this time it was ten o'clock (I had gone to the lodge at eight), and the brethren, some of whom showed by their staggering gait that they had " got their load on," began to disperse, and by a little after eleven the last man had departed. And so ended the night of my initiation, the proceedings of which gave me anything but a favourable idea of the mode of conducting the society's business.

" The social glass " is in its proper sphere no doubt a pleasant and admirable institution, but there can be equally little doubt that the glass which cheers but *may* inebriate is not in its proper place in a meeting of an avowedly business character, and at which subjects that affect the individual or collective welfare of those present have to be discussed, or matters of a semi-judicial nature—such, for instance, as the granting or withholding of the sick pay of any member of the lodge who may have declared on " the box " under what are considered suspicious circumstances, or the nature and extent of the penalty to be inflicted upon any member who may have transgressed against the laws of the society—have to be argued and decided upon. Even in a small friendly circle the members of which were acquainted with each other, drinking would be out of place during a business meeting; and it is more emphatically out of place in a miscellaneous gathering of a hundred or two or three hundred, as the case may be, of working men, of various trades, opinions, and dispositions, met together for business purposes. The unrestricted drinking not only permitted but in many cases practically enforced at the meetings of members of benefit societies, is at all times detrimental to the business interests of the societies, and frequently leads to most unseemly proceedings when any matter upon which there is an antagonism of feeling or interest is under discussion. Thus Brother Bloggs of our lodge, than whom when sober there is no quieter or civiler man breathing, after he has had his third pint of ale on a club night becomes pugnaciously quarrelsome, and has a decided and irrepressible leaning to the blasphemous in expressing his drunken and contradictory opinions. And when his views upon any club affair are opposed he exhibits those objectionable peculiarities, by calling those who venture to differ with him, sanguinary liars, and threatening to punch their sanguinary heads; and even dares to talk of " warming " the Noble Grand, when that distinguished individual fines him, as by virtue of his grand and noble office and the laws of the society he is bound to do, for swearing in the club-room. Again, Brother Perkins, a small, and in his sober moments a particularly meek-spirited man, whose wife has been twice fined by the local police magistrates for husband beating, will—urged thereunto by the half-and-half that he has consumed—whenever he finds himself in a minority in a club division challenge the whole of the majority to fight; and inform them with curses loud *and* deep that he " can lick the lot of them one down the other come on." On the other hand, Brother Morgan, who is usually as melancholy as a

clown off the stage, will when he has " got his load
on" utter ribald jests, the question at the moment being
—how we can best give something beyond the specified
" funeral money " to the widow of a late brother who
has been killed in an awfully sudden manner. If there
is any difficulty, Brother Jones, our oldest member, has
to be roused from the sleep of the drunken, in order
that we may ascertain whether he is aware of any
precedent for what is proposed. Nor are such direct
evils as the impeding and complication of business,
and the impossibility of a fair and dispassionate
consideration of any question that may be brought
forward, the only ones that arise from the drinking
practices associated with the present system of benefit
society management. I have frequently heard and
read that married ladies in the upper ranks of society
look with great disfavour on their husbands' clubs ;
but these ladies have, I fancy, much less cause to be
opposed to club proceedings than the wives of many
working men who (the men) are members of benefit
societies. For the loss to a working man's wife of the
portion of her husband's scanty and perhaps precarious
earnings, which is spent in the society's club-room, or
through the reckless spirit engendered by the drink
imbibed there, may and often does mean an insufficiency
of food and clothing for herself and children. And it
is no unusual thing to see a number of poorly clad,
anxious-looking women waiting outside of a club-house
on a " lodge night," in order to try and catch their
husbands coming out, so as to induce them to go home
without indulging in " the parting glass," to which the
drinking in the club-room leads men of a convivial or
"spreeing" disposition. I do not propose the abolition
of the drinking customs that at present obtain in benefit
societies as an " universal remedy " for drunkenness,

though such abolition would have a decided tendency to lessen the certainly decreasing but still unhappily too prevalent evil of drunkenness among the working-classes. For this club-room tippling induces drinking habits in some young men, confirms them in others, and affords convenient opportunities for indulgence to those who are already confirmed " lushingtons." But apart from all social, moral, or domestic considerations, and looking at the matter merely from a business point of view, it must be obvious that these drinking customs are amongst those that would be " more honoured in the breach than the observance." This drinking in club-rooms is in all cases officially sanctioned, and as I have already said, in the majority of instances practically enforced; for in most lodges there is an unwritten but perfectly understood and rigidly enforced law to the effect that each member *must* spend something " for the good of the house." And even where this is not the case no man of merely ordinary strength of mind can screw his courage to the point of maintaining a state of drinkless blessedness while surrounded by a hundred and fifty or two hundred brethren, each with glass before him, and with a waiter reproachfully or indignantly eyeing him (the would-be drinkless one), and significantly announcing the most obvious fact that he (the waiter) is in the room. At least in all my large acquaintance among members of benefit societies I have only met one who successfully withstood that ordeal; and that he was a person with peculiar tastes, and endowed with more than ordinary strength of mind where regard for the actions or opinions of a majority was concerned, is proved by the fact that he made open application for the office of executioner at a local hanging; and afterwards expressed an emphatic hope that he would live to have the hanging of a number of the brethren who ventured to suggest that such an application upon his part was likely to bring discredit upon " the lodge."

After the drinking customs, the most objectionable feature in connexion with the management of benefit societies is the absurd and degrading manner in which the demonstrations and *fêtes* organized for the delectation of their members are carried out. I know from my own experience that " all work and no play makes Jack a dull boy," and though personally I do not care about taking my pleasure in crowds, I believe that demonstrations and *fêtes* would, if they were planned and conducted in a sensible manner, be highly beneficial to the class of men who are members of benefit societies. But while an occasional day's play may do good to Jack, who is a hardworking bricklayer or blacksmith, it can only degrade Jack and bring him into contempt to march him through the streets bedizened with gaudy scarves and ribbons, in a style that would be considered *outré* in an African chief, or to send him to a place of public resort " got up " in a fancy costume that gives him the appearance of a veritable guy, and that causes him to be the observed and contemned of all observers. Nor does the evil attending the demonstrations of benefit societies terminate with degrading those who take part in them, as in addition to having that anything but desirable effect, they involve the societies in their corporate capacities, and the members individually, in unnecessary and *unjustifiable* expense.

A few months after I had joined the society to which I belong, some of my elder brethren—in a society sense—informed me in a tone of jubilation that the A. M. C. (Annual Moveable Committee) was to be held in the town in which our lodge was situated, and that the various lodges of the district had resolved to celebrate the meeting of the committee by a demonstration, to consist of a grand procession of "the order" and dinners at the various club rooms. Our lodge was noted for its splendour in affairs of this kind, and the officials of it convened a meeting of the members, to decide upon the position we were to assume in the coming demonstration. This meeting I attended; and on learning that our " incidental expense fund " (from which is paid the lodge expenses arising from demonstrations, and other proceedings that do not come under the head of any of the specified benefits of the society) was already more than 25*l.* in debt, I respectfully suggested that as one lodge would not be missed in so extensive an affair as a district demonstration, we should take no part in it at all. This notion was indignantly scouted as subversive of the glory of " the order." I then proposed that since we must take part in the demonstration, we should, in consideration of the unsatisfactory state of our fund, do so as economically as possible, and in this I was supported by some of the brethren; whereupon a fierce discussion as to whether or not we should have a band ensued, and at last terminated in an adjournment until the following lodge night. At the next meeting the bandites mustered in great force, and after a short but hot discussion, in the course of which Brother Bloggs, whom I had ventured to contradict, informed me that he would " hit me like a horse kicking " when he got me outside, and Brother Patrick Murphy threatened to rive the earth up if a fine that had been inflicted upon him for attempting to " smashivate " one of the brethren was not remitted, they carried their point. In the meantime every available band in the town had been engaged by other lodges of our order, and it became necessary for us to send a delegate to " the black country "—where bands formed by the workmen from the mines and ironworks are numerous—to hire a band. A flag bearer had also to be engaged; and all the more respectable loafers in town having been secured by other lodges, we were fain to put up with the services of an individual well known but by no means respected in local police circles as Ferret; who though he might be most admirable as a poacher, was scarcely a desirable standard bearer. On the day of the demonstration the members of the order were early astir, and our lodge met at the club-house at the appointed hour of ten, the officials wearing the decorations of their office, and carrying the regalia of the lodge, and the brethren wearing scarves and such other decorations as their fancy dictated. And now for the first time we saw the band that our delegate had engaged. They had been described to us as a first-class band; but a shabbier, dirtier, more incapable lot was never denounced by Mr. Babbage. They were colliers by trade, and their faces having only had what one of their number aptly described as a " lick and a promise," they looked much fitter for doing the " nigger business " than taking part in even a benefit society's demonstration. They were dressed in a uniform that might at one time have looked gay, but it was now miserably ragged, tarnished, and ill-fitting, and gave its wearers a most grotesque appearance. In explanation of their wretched playing the leader stated that they were a very good lot in a general way, but that just then their best player was unfortunately in gaol for beating his wife, and one of the other members had not been able to come in consequence of his instrument being in pawn. And then the instruments of those who had come were rather out of order. This

last statement at least was correct, for the instruments
were almost dropping to pieces ; and each player had
to carry a supply of putty with which to re-stop any
of the already puttied cracks in them that might open
again.   However, as there was no chance of getting
another band, we were compelled to make the best of
the very bad one we had got ; and after a little delay
—occasioned by Ferret, our poaching standard bearer,
having been detected in an attempt to steal a valuable
dog belonging to the landlord of the club-house,—we
formed in order of procession, and marched, headed by
the unabashed Ferret, who in point of costume was an
artistically harmonized blending of labourer, groom,
gamekeeper, and bargeman, to the place where the
various lodges were to meet.   We were among the
latest arrivals, and had not to wait many minutes
before the grand procession—of which, owing to the
peculiar fame and strange dress of our standard-
bearer, and the remarkable appearance and playing of
our band, we formed but too conspicuous a part—
started on its senseless and objectless journey.   For
two hours and a half we paraded the streets, with the
only effect, so far as I could see, of affording a little
amusement to the idle and juvenile portions of the
population of the town, whose remarks upon the
personal peculiarities and adornments of some of the
processionists were much more pointed than pleasant.
Ferret came in for so large a share of these remarks
that he twice laid down his flag to charge and disperse
the taunting crowd.   After walking through the principal streets, and greatly distinguishing ourselves in
the way of frightening horses and impeding traffic,
each section of the processionists returned to its own
club-house to dine.

Very strict *etiquette* could scarcely be expected at

a two-shilling benefit club-dinner; but when the men who go to such dinners go sober, they generally behave with decent propriety of manner. Upon the present occasion, however, some of the more thirsty souls of our lodge having indulged in "drains" at almost every public-house on the route of the procession, were in a state of more than semi-intoxication when they came to the dinner-table; and their behaviour could be only characterized as beastly. Putting their hands into their own and other persons' food was a moderate part of their proceedings. When the cloth was withdrawn, various toasts to the glorification of "the order" were given, and then general drinking set in with such severity that in less than an hour fighting began—in which, owing to a strong desire upon the part of Brother Bloggs to carry out his threat of hitting me "like a horse kicking," I had much difficulty in avoiding some part. This phase of the proceedings having been exhausted, harmony—if the singing of a number of songs of the "Slap bang" type can be so called—commenced, and was continued until eight o'clock in the evening, when the party broke up.

Later in the evening a number of the brethren got up a supplementary "demonstration," the chief features of which were a bacchanalian dance, accompanied by an appropriate chorus, performed in the high-street of the town at the witching hour of night; and the carrying away of a number of emblematical trade signs, such as barbers' poles and wooden cheeses. Unfortunately for some of those who took part in it, the police authorities could not be brought to see the point of *this* demonstration. The consequence was that about a dozen of the brethren were taken into custody and lodged in the police cells until the following morning, when they were taken before the bench of magistrates, who with an amount of wisdom and leniency rare among " the great unpaid," discharged them, with one exception, " with a caution." The unhappy exception was Brother Murphy, of our lodge, who, having resisted the police and threatened in a wholesale manner peculiar to himself to " have the blood " of the magistrates and all other constituted authorities, and to " burn the town down," was sent to prison for seven days in default of paying a fine of twenty shillings and costs.

The advocates of the present system of benefit societies' demonstrations assert that such demonstrations attract members to the societies. Such *may* be the case, though I am inclined to doubt it, as I know from personal experience that they are the means of keeping many sensible working men from joining such societies, and the cause of others who have joined them, leaving them ; while there can be no doubt that they depreciate the character for manliness, common-sense, and self-respect of the working man in the estimation of other sections of the community. The result of our grand demonstration was, so far as our lodge was concerned, that 15*l.* was added to the arrears of the incidental expense fund ; and when a levy was subsequently laid upon the members for the purpose of paying off the arrears, several of those who had opposed the hiring of the band left the society. I am well within the mark in saying that taking into consideration the loss of a day's wages, the average cost of the demonstration to each member was ten shillings ; and as our lodge mustered in round numbers three hundred members, that gives a sum of 165*l.*, drawn exclusively from working men and worse than wasted ; for it was spent in making them ridiculous in the eyes of other classes of society.

I have no wish to disparage benefit societies, which are, so far as their primary and ostensible functions are concerned, among the best institutions to which a working man can belong, but merely wish to call attention to the fact that there is still much room for reform and improvement in their management. The most pernicious of the evils associated with the present system of management could be very easily remedied. Owing to the establishment of working men's club-houses and similar institutions, there are now in many towns ample facilities for withdrawing the business of benefit societies from public-houses; and where such facilities do not exist, the passing of a law by the executive council of any society making it a fineable offence to introduce drink into a club-room during business hours, would effectually put a stop to the present objectionable drinking customs. And with the great variety of rational modes of amusement at present accessible to all ranks of society to select from, the managers of benefit societies could experience no difficulty in introducing some advantageous modifications in the present system of " demonstrations." Of the childish ceremonials which constitute " the secrets of the orders," and some other minor weaknesses connected with the transaction of the business of benefit societies, I say nothing. They please some and do harm to none, and their retention or abolition is consequently a matter of indifference; but until at any rate the discreditable drinking practices connected with them are abolished these associations will not be fully deserving of their name of benefit societies.

PART II.

WORK AND PLAY.

ON THE INNER LIFE OF WORKSHOPS.

In all phases of life, there is, I fancy, a sort of inner life—a life behind the scenes—that is known only to the initiated. At least, I know that such is the case in respect to the social life of the working classes; and in none of the many phases that go to make up the sum total of such social life is this more fully exemplified than in the life of workshops. To those particularly wise people who believe that one half of the world—the half namely to which they belong—*does* know how the other half live, those embodiments of " all the talents" who arise in the House of Parliament and other public places, and in an I am Sir Oracle strain assert their thorough and absolute knowledge of the wants, wishes, habits, virtues, and vices of the working-classes, life in a workshop will appear a very simple thing indeed. The people of this class would tell you that the be-all and end-all of workshop life was to labour for so many hours a day for a stipulated amount of money, and that all that was necessary to qualify a man for this life was that he should be possessed of a certain degree of technical skill, or physical power, or a combination of both. And it is by no means surprising that this should be an outsider's idea of what consti-

tutes the life of a workshop. At the first glance, it
seems the most natural, and is, *as far as it goes*, a
really correct view of the case; and a view that is
strengthened and confirmed from the circumstance
that when visitors are taken through those "show"
workshops, which naturally form one of the sights of
a manufacturing country, particular care is taken both
by masters and workmen to arrange " the show" in a
manner that must impress sight-seers with the notion
that work, and work alone, is the beginning and end
of workshop life.   But any working man who entered
a workshop with such an idea in his mind, and with
no other qualification than being able to use his
tools, would soon find himself in very evil case.
For him the shop would be "made hot"—so hot, that,
as a rule, he would have to leave it ; and might thank
his planets if he was fortunate enough to escape personal violence. This, however, is only a hypothetical
case, for such a monster as a working man who
considered work, even during his working hours, to be
his being's end and aim is happily for himself rarely
to be met with in the flesh.

There are traditions, customs, and usages interwoven
with, and indeed in a great measure constituting, the
inner and social life of workshops, a knowledge of which
is as essential to the comfort of those whose lot is cast
amongst them, as technical proficiency is necessary to
obtaining or retaining employment. To these unwritten,
but perfectly understood and all-powerful laws of workshop life, all working men—whatever may be their private opinion—must in some degree bow.   The social
phase of life in a workshop—the phase embodied in the
customs and traditions of " the trade"—is generally
the first into which the beginner is initiated.   When
an apprentice enters a shop, he will in all probability

be taught to " keep nix" before he is told the names
of the tools; and though the apprentice, everything
around him being novel, would prefer being enlightened regarding the elementary mysteries of his trade
to being put to keep nix, this merely shows his want
of wisdom. Keeping nix is a really important job, and
one the efficient discharge of which is supposed to imply
the possession of considerable ability on the part of the
apprentice, and which elevates him in the estimation of
those who are to bring him up in the way he should go.
Keeping nix, consists in keeping a bright look-out for
the approach of managers or foremen, so as to be able
to give prompt and timely notice to men who may be
skulking, or having a sly read or smoke, or who are
engaged on " corporation work"—that is, work of their
own. The boy who can keep nix well—who can detect
the approach of those in authority, while they are yet
afar off, and give warning to those over whose safety
he has been watching, without betraying any agitation,
or making any movement that might excite the suspicion of the enemy—will win the respect of his mates;
he will be regarded by them as a treasure, a youth of
promise.   But should he be so slow or so unfortunate
as to allow his mates to be " dropped on" while he is
upon guard, then woe to him !   Curses loud and deep
will be heaped upon his thick head ; a stout stick and
his back will probably be made acquainted ; and from
that time forth, until he has redeemed his tarnished
reputation by doing something specially meritorious in
the nix keeping way, he will be regarded as one
concerning whose capacity to learn his trade there are
grave doubts.

Another accomplishment which an apprentice has
generally to learn before settling down to the acquisition of the art and mystery of his trade, is that of

smuggling drink into the shop in a bold and scientific manner. As drunkenness has for years past been giving way to moderation among the working classes, the practice of smuggling drink into workshops has also decreased. There are now many working men who are not only guiltless of this pernicious practice, but totally opposed to its being carried on by others, and who would, were it in their power, save the apprentices from being implicated in it. For not only does a boy run the risk of being disgraced and punished if he is detected in bringing in the drink, but the " sups" with which he is rewarded on these occasions often lay the foundation of drunken habits. But an apprentice lad in a large workshop is the servant of many masters, and is bound to do the bidding alike of the soberest man and greatest " lushington," who, in virtue of their position as mechanics, are placed in authority over him. And though a boy, of course, *could* refuse to bring drink into the shop for any man, he is, practically speaking, compelled to do so, for he cannot afford to deny a favour to a man upon whose goodwill depends the question as to whether he is to be a good or bad workman. For, though it is nominally the master to whom he is bound, who has to teach him his trade, it is on the goodwill of the skilled workman of the establishment that he has really to depend for being initiated into those little " wrinkles" and specialities the knowledge of which makes the difference between the good and the bad or only ordinary workman. And it not unfrequently happens that the lushingtons, the thirsty souls who towards eleven o'clock in the day find themselves afflicted with a craving for a hair of the dog that bit them over-night, and significantly observe in the hearing of an apprentice, that they could do nicely with a pint if they could get it, and then, upon getting no response to this hint, pathetically ask, " Do you think you could manage it for us, Billy ?" are the cleverest workmen, and the kindest to boys, and the very men whose good graces the fathers or friends of the boys recommend them to cultivate ; and thus a boy is often compelled, against his own better feeling, to turn smuggler. This smuggling calls into action a far greater degree and combination of talent than is required for keeping nix ; and a clever smuggler—that is, one who can conceal a can or bottle about his clothes in a manner that gives little or no indication of its existence, who can deftly scale a wall, or boldly walk out through a workshop gate as though he were bound upon some perfectly lawful errand, who can instantly and unhesitatingly frame a plausible answer should he be stopped and questioned, and, above all, who is prompt in device, and swift and decisive in action, in the way of getting rid of his contraband cargo should he be detected or captured in the act of running the blockade—is regarded by the lushingtons as a gem among boys, who must turn out a first-rate workman ; and to him they will, in due course of time, teach the cunningest trade wrinkles of which they are the masters.

Nor must the young apprentice, however he may be burning to penetrate the mysteries of the trade in which he has secretly resolved to become a shining light, dream of quietly devoting himself to the pursuit of technical knowledge, until he has undergone a further initiation into the nature of workshop life, by having a number of stock tricks played off upon him by the older apprentices. These tricks generally turn upon the new apprentice's ignorance, or only partial understanding of what he sees going on around him, and vary in different trades. A common spirit pervades them, however, and a brief description of some of those practised in the trade to which I belong, will serve to show what manner of tricks they be.

The lads of a large workshop devote the first day or two of the appearance of a new boy amongst them, to questioning him about himself and relatives, and more especially as to his designs about becoming the Stephenson or Watt of his day: in a word, to " taking his measure." Having ascertained his degree of gullibility, their next step will probably be to send him to the most ill-tempered man in the shop, with instructions to address him by some offensive nickname, and ask him for the loan of a half-round square, or some other non-existent and impossible tool: his reception by the man to whom he is sent on this fool's errand, and who is a stock victim of this particular pleasantry, will be both astonishing and disagreeable. After this they will profess sorrow for the trick, and offer to make atonement by teaching him how to handle his hammer and chisel. When they have got him fairly to work, one of them will jerk the elbow of his hammer arm, and by that means cause him to hit his chisel hand. If he knocks a piece of skin off it, that is considered to add piquancy to the joke; and when he pulls a face and wrings his hand, he is told that it *couldn't have hurt him, as it wasn't on him a minute.* Encouraged by success in these preliminary experiments, the more determined of the practical jokers proceed to lay a new and much more elaborate trap for " the new nipper"—a trap into which the doomed boy is, despite the caution which his previous experience may have engendered in his mind, almost certain to fall unless he is warned against it. In all workshops the men frequently get small chippings of iron, or some other material with which they are working, into their eyes, and when this happens they at once go to one of their mates, who, seeing what has occurred, places the patient with his face to the light, turns up the top eyelid—on the inside of which any particle of *cold* matter that enters and remains in the eye is almost certain to be found; with his pen-knife or " scriber" he then takes off the irritating substance.   Many mechanics—but more especially stone-masons, and that class of engineers technically known as " fitters"—attain a remarkable degree of proficiency in cleaning eyes in this manner; and I have more than once seen an ordinary working mechanic take a minute particle of iron—part of a " splash"—or a still more difficult thing to see, a grain of sand from a grindstone—out of eyes that a number of doctors had declared to be suffering from weakness, and *not* from the presence in them of any foreign substance.   This operation an apprentice will probably see performed before he has been in the shop many hours, and the sight of it soon becomes quite familiar to him.   He sees that a steady hand and eye are all that are required for doing it, and that being able to do it is a most useful qualification in the trade to which he is destined, and he probably wonders whether he could do it, and mentally decides that he has no doubt that he could, as he sees other lads successful.   Things being in this state, one of his fellow-apprentices gets into conversation with him, and while they are talking up rushes another apprentice, apparently in great agony, and holding one of his eyes open with his fingers, thus sufficiently indicating that he has got something in his eye.   On seeing this, he who has been talking to the new boy is struck with consternation, and looking at his own hands, which are in a dreadfully dirty state, excitedly exclaims, " By jingo, Bill, here's Harry got something in his eye ; just take it out for him; I can't

touch him with these hands." Eager to at once relieve the agony of his brother apprentice, and try his
own 'prentice hand at a surgical operation, he immediately draws out his penknife, goes up to the suffering
youth, places him in position, peers anxiously into the
eye—and receives a mouthful of water plump in the
face. The successful completion of the plot elicits a
burst of laughter from those who arranged it, and who
have by this time gathered round their discomfited
victim. Occasionally, however, this trick is made to
cut backwards. It is generally pretty well known
when it is going to be played off upon any boy,
and if it should happen that the principal performer in
it—the one who is to fill his mouth with water and
pretend to have something in his eye—is, from being
fast or disobliging, disliked by the men, some of them
will let the intended victim know what is in preparation
for him. He is instructed to go up to the gentleman
who is supposed to have something in his eye, as though
he intended to search for it, and when he gets well
within reach, to give the afflicted youth a sharp flat-
handed slap upon the mouth, and watch the result.
Which result, if the lad carries out his instructions
properly, will be, that his would-be victimizer will be
as nearly as possible choked.

Having by a more or less painful experience obtained
a knowledge of those phases of the inner life of a
workshop that apply more especially to boys, and
having by a fight or two settled which of the *other
apprentices* may or may not venture to fag him, and
having selected a mate with whom to go for walks in
the evenings and on Sundays, and exchange confi-
dences concerning their respective sweethearts (for by
this time he will have learned that in order to be in
any degree worthy of his age and generation he *must*

have a girl—even if he has to invent one)—the young
apprentice may begin to think of settling quietly down
to the study of his trade.   He will now be left unmo-
lested to practise with the simpler tools at this time
entrusted to him, and to wonder within himself whether
he will ever be able to acquire that extraordinary degree
of deftness in handling them which he sees possessed by
the workmen around him; he will be left to learn by observation and inquiry "the ins and outs" of the strange
things that he sees going on around him, and otherwise to generally qualify himself to witch the world
with noble workmanship, and realize his idea of
becoming in time one of the great men of the profession.   For the next two or three years he will go on
pretty smoothly, gradually improving in proficiency as
a workman, and, as a rule, getting " disenchanted " as
he becomes familiar with the intricacies of the trade.
During this period he will get upon terms of equality
with most of the apprentices, and be in a position to
lord it over some of the younger of them, though
himself not as yet allowed to mix as an equal with the
journeymen.   From some of these he will in the meantime receive kind and considerate treatment, while
from others he will get ill-treatment.   Whenever any of
these men abuse him, he will probably console himself by confiding to his chosen companion that he
intends to pay Mr. So-and-so for all this on the day
on which he comes out of his time.   And though
these vows are as rarely kept as the resolution to become the Stephenson of his day, I once did see a young
man fulfil a vow of this kind.   As soon as the clock
struck twelve on the day on which his indentures expired he threw down his tools, and immediately "pitched
into" a workman who had habitually ill-used him during
the first three years of his apprenticeship.   Having

first given the man a sound thrashing, he deigned to
explain his reasons for doing so thus :—" I always
told you when you used to knock me about when
I first came to the trade that I would pay you off for
it when I was out of my time ; and now if I send
anyone to you for my character you can tell that I
keep my word." But though until he is getting into
the last year of his time an apprentice is practically treated as a boy by the journeymen, and is
bound up to the last day of his apprenticeship to do
their bidding, when he has once got through his
greenhorn period he will by means of a little observation, and putting of two and two together, be able to
obtain a tolerably accurate general insight into those
customs and usages of workshop life, a knowledge of
which will be absolutely essential to his " knowing his
way about," when in course of time he has to go out
in the world as a journeyman. Among the first things
that will attract his attention will probably be the
curiosities of smoking as carried on among the men
in a workshop. Most working men are smokers, and
some of them very constant smokers,—an ordinary
allowance of tobacco for many of them being an ounce
a day, some of them use considerably more than that ;
and while all smoke more or less, and the rules of the
shop prohibit smoking during working hours, it is
scarcely a matter for surprise that working men should
find out or make curious holes and corners to which
to repair to " have a smoke " unseen. And so though
a boy may regret this state of things, as it necessitates his being put to keep nix, and being thrashed
if he should allow the surreptitious smokers to be
discovered, he will hardly consider it strange. But
when he sees men going about day after day beg-
ging tobacco of their shopmates, and sees a man

offering one of his fellow workmen his tobacco-box to help himself from, giving another a bit which he takes from the box himself, and evidently weighs by eye and hand, and absolutely denying having any tobacco in his possession to a third, he may fairly be excused for wondering what it all means; but it is only in time and by close observation that he can thoroughly understand the mysteries of tobacco cadging or profit by the lessons they teach. This tobacco cadging in workshops, although carried by some men of sponging proclivities to a most degrading extent, is in its origin and up to a certain extent easily accounted for and perfectly justifiable. In hurrying to his work in the morning a man may forget his tobacco-box, or his tobacco may get exhausted in the forenoon, and he may forget to renew or not have an opportunity of renewing his stock at dinner time, and so may be tobaccoless in the afternoon, or a man who has brought out a sufficient supply for himself in the morning may fall short during the latter part of the day from having accommodated a number of mates with pipesful. And under such circumstances as these it is perfectly legitimate for a man to ask one of his fellow-workmen for a pipe of tobacco. Taking advantage of this state of affairs the spongers have reduced tobacco-begging to a system. They have all the stock excuses of the honest smokers, and expend a good deal of time in inventing new ones. The lender takes especial care not to trust a " cadger" with his box. For when once a cadging smoker gets his will of a box, he will cram his pipe as tight as he possibly can—afterwards drawing the tobacco out and making two ordinary charges of it. Other cadgers keep a special begging-pipe, that is, one with an unusually large bowl. There is an anecdote current

among smokers showing how a Jesuit of the workshop put off the cadgers in a successful manner,
while at the same time saving his conscience from
the guilt of a direct falsehood. " I haven't got a bit
in the world," this personage would say when asked
for a pipe of tobacco, at the same time producing an
empty box in confirmation of his asseveration ; but presently he would be seen in some of the secret smoking-
places calmly enjoying his pipe. This occurred so frequently, that his shopmates began to ask him where he
got his tobacco from, since, according to his own account,
he never had a bit in the world. " I trust to Providence," was his answer. His fellow-workmen could
not, however, bring themselves to believe in such a
visible and continuous manifestation of it, and on his
being strictly questioned, it presently appeared that the
conscientious man kept two tobacco-boxes, one of which
he called the World, and the other Providence. He
only kept tobacco in the latter, and so could always
show that he had not a bit in the world.

One of the customs which forms part of the inner
life of a workshop, with the existence of which an
apprentice will be made aware at the very outset of
his career, but a knowledge of the incidental details
and ceremonials of which he will have to gather from
after experience, is the payment of " footings" (sums
of money to be spent in drink). This is a custom that
would, doubtless, be more honoured in the breach than
in the observance. The call for footings is generally
made at times singularly inopportune for those who
have to pay them, and in those cases where it is the
rule of a shop for each new comer to pay a footing,
the demand for it often amounts to absolute cruelty.
A man may have been out of work for weeks,
or even months, and he may have a wife and children

in want of bread in some distant town, or he may
have been tramping and have pledged or sold all his
clothes except the much-worn working suit in which
he stands ; and from some or all of these reasons
he may be sick in body and mind. And yet out
of his first week's wages he must pay his footing,
must give a part of his earnings to be spent in drink,
while his wife and family are hungry and he is
himself without a second shirt. This is not always
or even frequently the case, nor would it be the case
in any instance, if the men who asked for the footing
saw the matter in that light, and if a man in such a
position had only the courage to say—" Well, I
would like to pay my footing, but I have been out
of work for some time, and my family and myself are
very badly off just at present." If a man when asked
for his footing on entering a new shop would say
something of this kind, the claim to the footing would
be abandoned. But working men, when demanding
this species of black mail, do not look at the matter
in this way, I am sure ; they merely consider that it
is the rule of the shop, that they have paid it, and
that they have consequently a right to expect others
to pay it ; again, no man likes to plead poverty to
those with whom he is associating as an equal ; and
so the new comer gives part of the first money he has
earned for months to be spent wastefully in a public-
house. And perhaps in a few months afterwards, when
he has ceased to think of these things and has " got
his back up again," he will be one of the foremost in
inflicting upon some other new workman all that
he has suffered himself in this respect. Nor are the
sufferings which they *may* inflict upon those who
have to pay them the only evils connected with the
system of footings : the invariable custom of spending

the money in drink has a decided tendency to create
or to encourage habits of dissipation. The footings,
which may range from five shillings to a sovereign each,
are generally allowed to accumulate until they amount
to some considerable sum,—a sum that will give a
rather dangerous allowance of drink to every man entitled to participate in them. When they have reached
what is considered a sufficient amount, those interested
appoint a house and an evening for spending the
money. During the drinking (the landlord of the
house is expected to add to it at his own expense),
the healths of those whose footings have founded
the feast, and other suitable toasts are drank, and
those who are " good company" sing their favourite
songs, give their favourite recitations, and recount
their choicest anecdotes, and by the time that these
matters have been got through all present will be
getting mellow. The exhaustion of the gratuitous
drink brings the proceedings of the evening to a temporary standstill, and some of the steadier men will
avail themselves of the pause to withdraw ; but such a
proceeding as this would be regarded by the lushingtons as a sinful waste of their opportunities, and
they accordingly resolve to cultivate them still further
by making sixpenny or shilling " whips round" among
themselves. Thus the lushingtons fall to their pipes
and glasses again. Those who when in their cups talk
" shop"—and many do, since work is the only subject
on which many of them *can* talk—will begin to display their knowledge now. With no other tools or
material than the stem of a pipe, beer sloppings, and
a public-house table, they will in a few minutes erect
stupendous palaces, construct locomotives and steamers
capable of unheard-of speed, design ordnance of
hitherto undreamt of destructive powers, and otherwise

demonstrate that they could, if they were so minded, revolutionize the mechanical world by merely making known a few of their original ideas. From kindred spirits these talkers will receive the admiration which they consider due to their genius ; but there is often some unappreciative hearer whose impatience of talking " shop " breaks out at last, and then discord comes in. Sometimes, however, the original ground of quarrel will be a charge of not drinking fair. To drink the greater part of a pot which you are asked to share with a man who does not know how good beer is for him, or to claim the first drink at, and as nearly as possible to empty, a pot for which you have tossed and lost, is, according to the lushington code of honour, not only admissible but even commendable; but for a lushington to drink unfairly of beer which is the common and equally paid for property of a number of brother lushingtons, is a thing to be contemplated with horror, and resented as such a dastardly deed should be. But whatever may be the first cause of a quarrel, when a meeting convened for the purpose of spending footings passes the whipping-round stage, it is certain to result in a general row ; of which those engaged in it retain but a dim recollection on the following morning.

But there will not be wanting signs and tokens by which those learned in the ways of workshops will be able to form a tolerably accurate idea of the general character of the past night's proceedings. When one man asks of another, " Well, how do you feel this morning?" and the other answers, " Awful dickey !" and when the first speaker then goes on to ask, in a hesitating tone, " Let's see, Bill, where did I leave you last night ?" and Bill replies, " Why, I'm blest if I know," you may put it down for certain that they and their mates have drunk " not wisely, but too well." And

when you find men with black eyes or damaged noses,
trying to ascertain who they have been " scrapping"
with, or what they have been scrapping about, you will
know that the proceedings of the previous evening
have not been of an altogether pacific nature.   And
the unfortunate younger apprentices know to their
sorrow when there has been a spree overnight by their
being kept hard at work blockade-running during the
morning, and cursed and cuffed by those men whom
an overdose of drink makes ill-tempered.

That the payment of footings is an undesirable
custom is an opinion now entertained by many of the
most intelligent of the working classes, and the
influence of these men has been so far effective, that
it has gradually brought about a considerable cur-
tailment in the number of occasions upon which
footings were at one time paid.   Formerly footings
had to be paid for exceedingly slight causes—such
as obtaining any little promotion in the shop, or
commencing or finishing a piece-work job, or each
time that a child was born unto a man : in some
shops every time that a man put on a new article of
clothing he was expected to stand treat.   But now the
only times at which, as a rule, footings are paid, are
on a man's first entering a shop, or a boy's entering
upon his apprenticeship, and again on his becoming a
journeyman, and on a man's marriage. In many shops,
and throughout some trades or branches of trades,
footings are only asked for on the three last-named
occasions ; the hardship which may be inflicted upon a
man by making him pay a footing on entering a new
shop having in course of time been made apparent to
many of even the least thinking of working men.

But while the payment of a footing with a boy is
never thrown away, the treatment which an apprentice

receives from the men in a workshop will depend in a
great measure upon himself. If he is lazy, ill-tempered,
or impudent, and stands to the letter of the law in
obliging or yielding obedience to the men, he will be
treated accordingly—that is to say, the men will stand to
the letter of the law in teaching him his trade, and complain of him whenever his conduct gives occasion for
doing so. Boys who are at once willing and dull are the
ones with whom men, from a twofold motive of kindness
and a regard to their own credit, take the most pains;
but they naturally have the greatest degree of pleasure
in teaching those who are sharp as well as obliging.
Nor does their concern for the welfare of their apprentices cease on the boys becoming journeymen, as
the " old hands" will continue for years to take the
warmest interest in the progress of those whom they
have taught their trade.   On completing his term of
apprenticeship, and springing at once from a wage of
eight or ten to one of thirty shillings or upwards per
week, the new-fledged journeyman is generally as
eager to pay his footing to those who are now his
brother journeymen as they are to receive it; and a
newly-married man is generally found to be liberally
disposed towards his shopmates.   Indeed it would be
surprising if it were not so, for while a sovereign is
the utmost expected from him, he receives, in the iron
trade at least, an ovation from his shopmates, on his
return to work after his marriage, that would be cheap
at five times that amount.   On the occasion of his
marriage, a working man takes a few days' holiday,
and on the day on which he returns to work does not
come to the shop until after breakfast.   Then he
receives his ovation in the shape of what is technically
called " a ringing in."   Some of his intimates will
know on what day he is to return, and at breakfast

time on that day everything is got ready for welcoming him. Scouts are placed along the road he has to come, in order to signal his approach, and in the meantime the men and boys in the shop stand, hammer in hand, around boilers, plates of iron suspended from beams, or anything else that comes handy that will give out a good ringing sound when struck. The arrival of the subject of the demonstration is duly announced by the scouts; all stand to their posts, and, the instant he enters the shop, strike up, producing a thundering peal. In a large establishment, the Benedict of the occasion may have to pass through several shops before reaching the particular one in which he works. In that case the ringers in each shop, having rung him through their particular department, follow him as he passes out of it, until the whole body of them are assembled in his own shop, and then the peal reaches its grand climax. When it is considered that there are perhaps as many as five or six hundred men, all skilled in the use of the hammer, all hammering their best on high or sharp sounding material, the intensity of the peal may, and indeed *must*, be imagined, since it cannot be described. The ringing-in is continued for about five minutes, and then the proceedings are wound up with a hearty cheer. If such a demonstration as this is not cheap at a sovereign, then nothing in the shape of a demonstration can be cheap at any price.

By acting upon the principle of being seen but not heard, he will be allowed to join the groups of workmen who at meal-times gather together in winter round the workshop stoves, and in summer in favourite shady places, to have a chat. Listening to the conversation that goes on, he hears the travellers' tales of those who have been on tramp, which tales are to the apprentice what

"Robinson Crusoe" and a course of Captain Marryat and Fenimore Cooper are to the schoolboy, and which set him (the apprentice) secretly longing—poor innocent, romantic youth!—for the time when he shall be on tramp, "regularly hard-up," meeting interesting and picturesque companions, and resorting to all kinds of adventurous shifts for his living. He also, to his surprise, hears the great men of the trade—the men whom he has seen belauded in newspapers and books, whose works are among the great achievements of the age, and whose names he has learned to venerate—coolly spoken of as old Billy or old Jacky So-and-so—hears their characters discussed, and their peculiarities descanted upon and imitated as though they were mere ordinary mortals, and finds, in short, that as no man is a hero to his valet, so no master is a hero to his workman. He will hear that old Tom Smith of Boychester (who is one of the greatest men of the day in his profession, and a reputed millionaire) is, although fiery-tempered, "a good old sort" at bottom—that he is a real clever fellow, who has forgotten more than most men in the trade ever knew—that he knows a good workman when he has got one, and will always pay such a workman well, and, in a word, that he is an admirable master. He will hear, on the other hand, that Jemmy Brown— the great Brown of the Patent Works, Hammerton— is a duffer, the Pecksniff of the trade, and that it is to old Scotty, his clever manager, that the credit of the inventions which Jemmy patents in his own name is really due. He will hear that old Davy Robinson's shop is the very worst shop to work in, principally because old Davy goes prowling about the shop all day long, watching his workmen, sometimes standing staring at one man for five or ten minutes at a spell, and thus

flurrying those men whom he does not inspire with
a longing to rush at him and knock him down;
and in connexion with this phase of Davy's character
there is a stock anecdote told.   Seeing a new workman gazing about him, Davy sharply asked him,
" What are you looking for?"   " Saturday night, you
old varmint !" replied the man, never supposing for a
moment that the shabbily dressed old fellow who had
spoken to him was anything more than some over-
officious clerk or time-keeper.   Upon receiving which
answer, Davy took to his heels and ran up the shop,
shouting out to his foreman, " Mills, Mills ! here's a
fellow looking for Saturday night, and it's only Thurs-
day morning !   Sack him ! sack him !"

This kind of talk about tramping adventures, and
the characteristics or peculiarities of masters, workmen, or workshops, is what has the greatest attraction
for the apprentice during that period of his workshop
career in which he is allowed upon sufferance to join
groups of gossiping workmen in the capacity of a
silent listener. As he gets older, however, and begins to
look forward to the termination of his apprenticeship,
his interest in the topics of workshop conversation
begins to centre more in those matters that relate
more directly and generally to his comfortable pursuit
of his trade in the future.   The men of every trade
speak of their trade among themselves as *the trade*,
and this he learns in time to do, and he is taught
both by the precept and example of his mates, that he
must respect the trade and its written and unwritten
laws, and that in any matter affecting the trade
generally he must sacrifice personal interest, or private
opinion, to what the trade has rightly or wrongly
ruled is for the general good.   He will, as he ap-
proaches journeymanhood, begin to listen with interest

to the story of those strikes or locks-out that have
become historical in the trade, and of the proceedings
of those masters or men who distinguished themselves
in them. He will hear, with commendable trade horror,
of the existence of a proscribed and hated race of
beings called nobsticks or black sheep, and he will be
taught, in effect, that whenever he meets one of
these obnoxious creatures—wretches in human form,
who never having learned the craft in a legitimate
manner, are guilty of trying to get a living by working at it, or who having duly acquired their crafts-
manship, presume to exercise it under circumstances
objectionable to the trade—it will be his duty to " strike
the caitiff down." In some districts he will hear
instances gleefully recounted in which nobsticks have
been literally struck down, for personal ill-usage was at
one time invariably resorted to in dealing with these
offensive characters, and is occasionally still practised
towards them, when the means usually adopted by
the more civilized workmen of the present day, of
threatening to strike, has failed in getting them
removed. From the talk of the old hands about
strikes, locks-out, nobsticks, and other kindred subjects, the apprentice obtains an insight into those
technical trade points which are so frequently the
grounds of disputes between masters and workmen.
He will learn at what times and under what circumstances he will be justified in demanding and holding
out for " walking money "—money claimed in consideration of men being sent to work at such a distance
from the shop as necessitates their rising earlier in
the morning and getting home later in the evening
than usual ; or " dirty money "—money demanded by
men who are put upon repairs, or other work that
involves extra wear and tear of clothes ; and on what

kind of jobs it will be advisable to " kick " the master
for " allowance "—allowance being drink or money to
get drink, asked for by men who are employed upon
work requiring an unusual degree of physical exertion,
or that has to be carried on in very hot or very cold
places, or upon the successful completion of any
unusually large or difficult piece of work. He will
learn exactly how far he may go in doing any work
that does not strictly fall within his own branch of
trade ; what rate of payment to demand for overtime
under various circumstances; with whom he may or
may not work ; in what jobs he may demand or object
to the assistance of a labourer, and a variety of other
useful matters pertaining to trade and workshop
etiquette.

And while at this time and in these things he
may see much of the weaknesses and prejudices of
his class, he will during the same period learn things
that will show him that his class, as a class, have their
noble as well as ignoble qualities. He will be taught
to consider the intimation " he's in the trade," an all-
sufficient reason for extending the hand of friendship
to all fellow-craftsmen, irrespective of position and
appearance, and he will find that the greatest kindness is extended to a brother of the craft at the time
that he stands most in need of it—namely, when he is
out of work ; and he will see that whenever special misfortune overtakes a man, his shopmates are always
prepared to enter into a subscription to relieve his
wants, so far as a little money will do so. He will
see men " pitching into " their work in the hardest
style, in order that they may be able to give a hand
to a mate who through illness is unable to do his full
share, but who, from having a family dependent upon
him, must stick to his work as long as he possibly

can; and he will not unfrequently see a young man—
even when trade is at the dullest—voluntarily offering
himself for " the sack," in order to save a married man
from it ; and when, as sometimes happens in times of
dull trade, the men of an establishment are called
together, and it is put to them whether they will all
agree to go upon short time until trade gets brisker,
to save some of their number from being discharged,
he will invariably find the old hands, those who are
sure of being kept, the first to advocate short time.
Apart from such general matters as these, no one
can be long in a workshop without witnessing special
acts of generosity between mate and mate. And upon
the whole, while the apprentice who has entered a
workshop entertaining great ideas concerning " the
dignity of labour," and the superiority of the " intelligent artisan," will as he nears the termination of his
apprenticeship, find that workmen are not all that his
boyish fancy had painted them, he will probably conclude that, all things considered, their virtues outweigh
their faults.

On entering the last year of his time, the apprentice
begins to find himself regarded by the journeymen as
though he were already " a man and a brother." He is
now allowed to " put in his word," or express his
opinion freely among them; he can command the
younger apprentices with equal authority; and although,
being still legally an apprentice, he is generally only
drawing apprentice's pay, he will be doing journeyman's work, and if he should happen to be attached
to a piece-work gang under a liberal leading hand, he
may also be receiving something like journeyman's
pay. Being treated by the men as a man, and being
in everything but law really a man, he naturally
wishes to put away childish things, and would fain

sever the connexion between himself and the younger
apprentices, in those matters in which they still claim
him as their own. Thus, on the days on which the
boys have a half holiday, he would rather not march
through Coventry with them, for their noisy boyish re-
joicings, as they rush whooping out of the shop, and
the comparisons which he imagines will be drawn
between him and the youngest and smallest of them,
grate upon the dignity of his scarcely confirmed manhood. But he knows that he *must* go out, for even the
men who may sympathize with his feelings rule it so,
lest from old apprentices neglecting to take an allowed
holiday, it should in course of time come to be taken
from the younger boys. Apart from this consideration, he knows that were he to attempt to remain in
the shop the boys would return and " smallgang" him,
an operation of which he will by this time have learned
to have a salutary fear. Smallganging is the workshop phrase for an attack by a number of boys upon
some particularly obnoxious man ; and as it is rarely
resorted to except in the case of some brutal ill-dis-
posed fellow, who richly deserves chastisement, it
may be regarded as a commendable institution. To
people of the muscular Christianity persuasion, it
may seem incredible that a number of boys should
with impunity attack, bonnet, and soundly thrash a
big able-bodied man. But ah, Guy Livingstone ! if
you were tackled by a dozen or more strong plucky
boys, who had had a year or two's experience of
workshop life, and were burning under a sense of
injury, you would—improbable as it may appear to
you—inevitably be conquered. You might " sling
out from the hip," and settle one or two of the
attacking party, but in the end they would prove
literally too many for you. There are few who have had

any considerable experience of workshop life who have
not seen this result accomplished upon men of first-rate
build and strength, and as even in its very mildest
form, smallganging is a decidedly disagreeable operation for the party on whom it is performed, working
men have a well-grounded dread of it, which is a
great protection to the boys.

In the last six months of his time the apprentice is—if he is qualified in other respects—eligible
for admission to a trade club—(and it is at that
time that the majority of the men who acquire their
trade by a legal apprenticeship do join such clubs, and
if of a provident disposition they will probably have
joined one of the large friendly societies at a still
earlier date). Thus upon completing his apprenticeship he will enter the world in every respect a full-
fledged journeyman.

The life and education of the workshop, as I have
attempted to show by briefly epitomizing the career
of an apprentice during his "seven long years," is
twofold—technical and social. What a knowledge
of the world is to the man of the world, a knowledge
of the social life of workshops is to the working
man; it will enable him to push through where others
would stick; to make friends readily; to avoid those
whose acquaintance would be unprofitable; to get
mates to put in a good word for him when he is
out of work; and to go on smoothly with those with
whom he is connected when in work. On the other
hand, a man who is ignorant of the social part of
workshop life, or who lacks tact in practising it, will,
although he may be a good man and clever workman,
find the workshop world a harsh, unsympathetic, and
unjust world to him.

SAINT MONDAY—ITS WORSHIP
AND WORSHIPPERS.

Soon after the Prorogation of Parliament every
year, those highly fashionable and exceedingly knowing individuals, the loungers at the clubs, London
correspondents, and other chroniclers of small beer,
assure us that London is more thoroughly empty, and
"everybody" more completely out of town, than
they have been in any previous holiday season ; and
" nobody," who is condemned through want of means
or pressure of business to linger out a hot and unfashionable existence in town, is consequently more
than ever inclined to regard himself as a last inhabi-
tant, and to consider it hard lines that he should be
" bound to the wheel," while everybody is away from
the city's busy hum. Then we have long descriptions
of holiday resorts abroad and at home. Perhaps, if
put to the test, this annual break out of holiday
literature would be found to be simply a substitute
for long letters on specially reserved grievances,
and the "strange freak of nature," "extraordinary
fulfilment of a dream," and "remarkable case of
longevity" paragraphs with which newspapers were
formerly wont to be exclusively padded in the silly
season; but whatever may be the cause of the yearly
abundance of articles upon holiday subjects, we have
them. That this should be so, that holidays as well
as the more serious phases of life should have a literature of their own, is no doubt right and proper; but

that that literature should be exclusively confined to one branch of the subject is, I think, neither right, proper, nor desirable. The holiday proceedings of the fashionable section of society, whose annual migration from London is supposed to leave "the big city" empty, are doubtless of a sufficiently sublime and interesting character to merit the modern prose epics in which they are sung by those comparatively inglorious Miltons' " Own Correspondents ;" but then there is an inevitable sameness about these proceedings which, after the first year or two, causes any description of them to become stale, flat, and unprofitable in the hands of even the most versatile of own correspondents. Were it for this reason alone, it is a matter for surprise that these indefatigable writers do not occasionally strike out a new path for themselves, by describing some of the holiday proceedings of the unfashionable nobody section of society; which proceedings, though they might not be considered so generally interesting as those of the fashionable world, would have at any rate the interest of novelty. Taking society to be roughly divided into fashionable and unfashionable, the unfashionable part is by far the largest, and its holidays by far the most numerous and varied; and of the many grades that go to make up the unfashionable part of society, there are perhaps none whose holiday doings are more worthy of a passing notice than those of " The Great Unwashed"— the body which comprises all who, in the literal sense, earn their bread by the sweat of their brow, and, to use their own phrase, " have black hands to earn white money."

What in fashionable society would be considered a holiday, the general body of the great unwashed, as at present constituted, cannot have. In the first place, the

unwashed ones have not, as a rule, the means for a few
weeks' residence at a fashionable watering-place, or a
trip to some gay or picturesque part of the Continent;
and even if they had the means and had learned the
manner of " doing the Rhine for five pounds," they
could not avail themselves of holidays of that kind. The
man who wilfully left his work for such a length of
time as would be necessary for doing the Rhine, would
certainly be " sacked;" and in addition to that cala-
mity, would in all probability from that time forward
be regarded by his brethren as a sort of natural
curiosity, and a traitor to his class. But though the
unwashed have no holidays in the fashionable sense of
the term, they are according to their own ideas on the
subject much greater holiday-makers than any othei
section of society. That " all work and no play makes
Jack a dull boy," is an adage in the truth of which most
people believe. There are still a few individuals engaged
in the race for wealth who regard the Factory Act,
which prevents children from being systematically over-
worked, as an obnoxious and unwarrantable interference with business, and who look upon the half-
holidays, short-time, and other similar movements, as
indications of the end of all things. But the people
of this persuasion are now, happily, very rare ; and
the almost universal belief is that Jack should have a
share of play as well as work. Of all who hold this
belief the great unwashed themselves are naturally
the most fervent. They have not yet been able to
realize that golden system of Eight, which is looked
forward to as a working man's millennium, and under
which the constituents of every man's day will be eight
hours' work, eight hours' play, eight hours' sleep, and
eight shillings pay ;" but during the last generation
they have made such progress towards it as to make

its ultimate realization appear by no means chimerical. Artisans still young enough to enjoy a holiday are guilty of little exaggeration when they tell their younger brethren that when they (the old hands) were boys, they had to work—with the exception of a few hours for sleep —" all the hours that God sent;" but all that sort of thing—the number of hours that constitutes a day's work being settled by the arbitrary will of a master, men having to hang about public-houses for hours before getting their wages, or having to take their wages in the shape of dear and unwholesome provisions—has been altered. But while improvements in such matters as these have been the most effective agents in producing that substantial improvement in the condition of working men which has taken place during the last thirty years, it is chiefly by the holidays that he has managed to secure that the Jack of the present day shows the earnestness of his conviction in the truth of the proverbial philosophy that awards him a time to play as a means of saving him from becoming dull. The Saturday half-holiday is already enjoyed by hundreds of thousands of working men, and its benefits are slowly but surely spreading. On each of the three great occasions, Christmas, Easter, and Whitsuntide, the bulk of the working classes secure from three days to a week's holiday, holding revel in parks and other public places during the day, and filling the theatres and other places of amusement at night. Then there are local fairs, wakes, and races, over which the unwashed of the districts in which they are held have another two or three days' holiday, and in most establishments in which any considerable number of workmen are employed, the annual " shop excursion"—the benefits of which are frequently extended to the wives and families of the men—is now an established institution, and two

or three days a year may be safely put down
for holidays arising out of special occurrences. But
the most noticeable holiday, the most thoroughly
self-made and characteristic of them all, is that
greatest of small holidays—Saint Monday.

Which portion of the great unwashed first instituted
the worship of this Saint is a disputed point; but to
the tailors, who are amongst its most ardent devotees,
the honour is usually ascribed. The institution is a
comparatively recent one, and its origin is not very
difficult to trace. The general introduction of steam
as a motive power, and the rapid invention of machinery applicable to all kinds of manufacturing
work, gave rise to a numerous body of highly skilled
and highly paid workmen, who soon found themselves
in a position to successfully oppose the employers of
labour on some of the debatable grounds between
capital, and labour, their most notable victories being
the definite establishment of ten hours as the standard
of a day's work, and the securing of an extra rate of
payment for all hours worked above that number;
and also the laying the foundation of the Saturday
half-holiday movement, by obtaining the privilege—
never afterwards abrogated—of leaving work at four
o'clock on Saturdays. These workmen would at the
end of the week put off their working clothes with
a sense of relief, and, thinking far more of how they
should enjoy themselves to the most advantage during
the Saturday evening and Sunday, than of what would
become of the working clothes in the meantime, the
consequence was that on the Monday morning, when
they had once more to appear " with harness on their
back," and awoke at the usual time for donning it, the
harness was not always forthcoming, especially in the
case of those men who were only lodgers. The clean

jacket and trousers or overalls that were supposed to
be on the chair at the bedside would, after an ex-
asperating search, be discovered at the bottom of
the clothes-basket, unaired, and minus some important
button, in consequence of which latter circumstance,
the unfortunate wearer would have to run to work
holding himself together as it were. The coat, which
is substituted for the shop jacket in going to and from
the workshop, and which is an indispensable appen-
dage of the mechanical dignity, would not be found
on its usual nail, for the reason that the landlady had
stuffed it under the sofa with other objectionable
articles that were considered too vulgar or too suggestive of work, to be allowed to meet the sight of
the guests who on the previous day had attended her
genteel Sunday tea-party; and when the coat was
disinterred from its hiding-place, the cap, which was
supposed to be in the pocket of it, would be missing.
Having, however, by this time not a moment to spare,
the unhappy victim to mislaid clothing would dash off,
keeping a sharp look-out to avoid tripping himself
with the flying laces of his unlaced shoes. By running,
the half-dressed and breathless martyr to Monday
morning circumstances would just manage to rush
through the workshop gates as they were closing, but
only, alas! to find that he had forgotten—had left in the
pockets of the clothes turned off on the Saturday—the
ticket, the giving in of which would alone enable him
to start work.*　In consequence of this he would

* The system formerly adopted of workmen giving in their
tickets on going into the works, and taking them out when they
came out, is now reversed in many large establishments, the workmen taking their tickets off a board on passing into the shops and
placing them on the board again as they pass out. This plan is
obviously more convenient for the workmen than the old, and in
some instances still practised plan.

be compelled to return home, cursing his fate at having had his early rising and hard run for nothing, and oppressed with the distressing consciousness of having lost a quarter (of a day) without having the compensatory pleasure of spending it in bed. Driven by their sufferings in this respect to take some bold measure for their own relief, a large number of the operative engineers adopted the practice of regularly losing the morning quarter on Mondays, a proceeding which no other body of workmen would have dared at that time, when steam power and machine work were making engineering *the* trade of the day, to have carried out! and which there can be no reasonable doubt originated the holiday of Saint Monday. The sufferers from mislaid clothing and forgotten tickets having established this custom for their own benefit, others soon began to avail themselves of its advantages. Did a man feel more than usually inclined for a "lie-in" after his Sunday-evening ramble, he would remember him that it was Monday morning, and indulge himself in the luxury of "a little more sleep and a little more slumber;" or did a "lushington" get a drop too much at the suburban inn to which *his* Sunday-evening ramble had led him, he would remember, when he came to "think of his head in the morning," that it was Monday, and have another turn round in the sheets, instead of turning out, as he would had to have done on any other working morning. Then if a man had any business to transact, he would ask for Monday as being a broken day at any rate; and sometimes, when going to work after breakfast, two or three thirsty souls who had been losing the first quarter, would turn into a public-house for a morning dram, and perhaps end in "making a day of it." And so the thing went on, extending in course of time to other trades, until it cul-

minated in the canonization and setting apart of
Monday as the avowed and self-constituted holiday of
the pleasure-loving portion of "the million."   As
frequently happens in more serious things, some of
those who were converted to the doctrines and observances of Saint Monday, after they were established,
became their most enthusiastic devotees; and it is the
strict and steadfast devotion of these "latter-day
saints" to all its observances that has led to the honour
of the institution of the day being ascribed to some
of them.   But who first instituted this day is not,
after all, a very material question; it may have been
the engineers, or it may have been the tailors—each
have their partisans; and though the weight of evidence
is undoubtedly with the former, the merit of enthusiastic observance is as decidedly with the latter.

On Monday everything is in favour of the great unwashed holding holiday.   They are refreshed by the
rest of the previous day; the money received on the
Saturday is not all spent; and those among them who
consign their best suits to the custody of the pawn-
broker during the greater part of each week are still in
the possession of the suits which they have redeemed
from limbo on Saturday night.   Masters make less
objection to a workman not "turning in" on a Monday
than after he had settled down to his work.   Besides,
the remains of the Sunday dinner being on hand, either
to serve as an early make-shift meal at home, or an
economic provision for a day out, and the household
work being at this early period of the week well under
hand, our wives and families are afforded an opportunity of sharing the forms of holiday. And since Saint
Monday has become a recognised institution, each individual worshipper has additional inducements for
keeping his saint's day in the knowledge that he is

sure to meet with numerous other devotees; and that " enterprising lessees" of pleasure-grounds, and other caterers to the pleasures of the unwashed, provide entertainments for his special delectation. And the holiday spirit engendered by the partial holidays of Saturday and Sunday, the sight of the Sunday clothes not yet returned to the seclusion of the clothes-box, produce an irresistible desire to avail themselves of their opportunities in the minds of the pleasure-loving; and so the worship of Saint Monday goes on.

But the Saint Mondayites are by no means of one mind as to what constitutes a holiday, and their modes of spending the day are as various as their opinions upon this point are diversified. Numerous day-trips, at prices suitable to the incomes of the poor, and allowing those who go by them to spend a certain number of hours at the seaside, are run every Monday during a great portion of the year; and these trips, special galas at the holiday resorts of the Crystal Palace class, and " outs" to suburban re-creation grounds and public parks, are largely patro-nized by the more affluent and sedate Saint Mondayites. These, the most rational and healthy of the holi-days, are mostly supported by young mechanics, who wish to give their wives, or the " young ladies" with whom they are keeping company, a day out, as well as by some family men. The younger couples, as becomes their youth, their position towards each other, and the spirit of the times, go out " quite genteel." The young ladies, who are probably mil-liners or dressmakers, or, if in domestic service, call themselves ladies'-maids, will be dressed in the height of cheap fashion; they will put on their most young-ladyish airs; and as they have often pretty faces, good figures and bearing, and some taste in dress, they might sometimes pass for " real ladies " if they would only keep their tongues still. But considering it essential to their gentility to discard the language of every-day life in favour of the long words and flowery periods of the tales in their favourite cheap magazine, and persisting in an artfully artless manner to speak these words *at* other people, by way of impressing them with the fact that they (the young ladies) do not belong to the " commonalty," the result is that they generally make a mess of it. When a young work-girl, who is out with her lover enjoying " eight hours at the sea-side for three-and-sixpence," rapturously exclaims, as she gazes on the sea,—" Oh, 'Arry, *ain't* it beautiful !" there is nothing essentially vulgar or ridiculous in the exclamation; which is more than can be said of it when a young lady strikes an attitude, and delivers the sentiment thus— " Is not it pictures*cue*, 'Enry, de-ah ?" The young men, both on their own account and in order to play up to the ladies in a worthy manner, do all in their power to contribute to the successful doing of the genteel during their day out.

> " They dress themselves with studious care,
> And in their best apparel dight,
> Their Sunday clothes on Monday wear."

They banish the pipe of work-day life, and smoke instead " matchless Havannas " at seven for a shilling; they wear their " unequalled Parisian kids " at 1*s.* 9*d.* per pair, and manfully persist in wearing them throughout the day, notwithstanding the uncomfortable cribbed, cabined, and confined sort of feeling which they give to their hands; for they know that their hands, if left uncovered, will betray them, however genteelly they may be got up in other respects. Then they address the waiters who attend upon

them in eating-houses or tea-gardens in a superb and
authoritative manner, intended to impress those persons with the conviction that they and their young
ladies are members of the aristocracy, who are merely
indulging in a working-class holiday by way of a
novelty. While the younger couples behave so
grandly, the older couples and family parties do the
economic and comfortable with the remains of the
Sunday dinner made into sandwiches, and washed
down with ale.

These latter are the parties who dine comfortably
under a tree in public parks, and exchange jokes
with those who come to see them " at feeding-time ;"
and they are the chief supporters of those establishments in the neighbourhood of holiday resorts, in the
windows of which is displayed the announcement—
" The kettle boiled at twopence a head." For the
matrons, although out for a holiday, are too thoroughly
imbued with the housewifely spirit to patronize, or allow
their husbands or children to patronize, the teas of the
tea-gardens, or of those establishments which supply
" tea and shrimps for ninepence"—which teas these
matrons declare to be iniquitously dear, and of a
quality that would make them dear at any price. So
they. bring their own packets of tea, and a substantial
pile of bread and butter and "bun-cake," and have the
kettle boiled for twopence a head. Thus they are
enabled to enjoy tea at once cheap and good. It
is the females of these parties whose exclamation of
" Law !" varied in its manner of delivery according as
it is intended to express surprise, admiration, or indignation, resounds through the exhibitions and picture-
galleries which the more sensible of the Saint Mondayites visit. And it is these same female holiday-
makers who " take notice" of, praise, and give cakes

to each other's children; and who, when returning home, freely distribute the remains of their stock
of provisions among any of their fellow-excursionists
in the same conveyance who will accept of them, loudly
expatiate upon the pleasures of their day out, wish
they could have such a day every day, and then
console themselves for the impossibility of gratifying
that wish by " dare-saying" that they would in time
become tired even of holidays, and that rich folks
have their troubles as well as other people; finally
branching off into a discourse respecting the heavy
washing they will have to start to in the morning, or
some other equally interesting household topic.

Another section of the Saint Mondayites who
make excursions to open-air resorts is that which
is composed of the more steady, respectable, and best-
paid portion of the " single young fellows "—young
unmarried mechanics, who, immediately upon coming
" out of their time," make for the London district,
or flit about the country to wherever the best
standing wages or most profitable piece-work prices
current in their trade are to be obtained.   Without
encumbrance, even that of a " young lady," they adopt
a style of holiday-making which is a compromise
between the genteel and the comfortable, and which
may be described as the jolly.   Their dress on the
occasion of a Monday holiday is a medium between
the " fashionable attire" of the young gentlemen
and the old fashioned, well-preserved Sunday suits
of the comfortable family men, and consists of their
evening suits; not the evening suits of dress-society,
be it understood, but the strong, useful, well-fitting,
somewhat sporting-looking " mixed cloth" suits, which
they don when going on their evening rambles in
search of amusement after working hours, and which

enable them to pass muster in any society they are
likely to go into, without causing them to feel that
chronic fear of spoiling their clothes which haunts the
working man when dressed in his best.   These single
young fellows · worship Saint Monday in parties of
from four to six in number, and generally select
some place at which dancing is likely to form part
of the amusements of the day, for most of them are
fond of dancing ; and the cheap " hops" which abound
in working-class districts being a prominent feature
in their ordinary evening amusements, they are
generally spirited performers on the light fantastic
toe.   Should the chosen place be within about ten
miles of their homes, they usually drive to it, but
if above that distance they avail themselves of the
ordinary excursion trains or steamers.   When a trip
by road is decided upon, they hire a smart trap,
and the best driver among them is entrusted with
the task of making a dashing start, in order to remove any doubt the livery-stable keeper may entertain
as to their being able to manage it properly.   The
same driver also takes the reins when they are
approaching the public-houses at which they stop ;
but during the intermediate stages of the journey,
and until they are within a short distance of their
destination, the other members of the party try their
'prentice hands at handling the ribbons, and the
journey is considered well done upon the whole if it
has been accomplished without a break-down or upset.
On coming within sight of the entrance of the pleasure-
ground for which they are bound, the reins are once
more given up to the " first whip," in order that
the approach may be made in a dashing style.   Not
that doing the genteel is at all in their line.   They
do not ask in a mincing tone for a glass of bitter

be-ah, or pale ale, and get short measure, and have
to pay a first-class price for an inferior article in consequence, but call boldly for their pot of porter or
" six ale ;" nor does it ever occur to them that it is a
dignified thing to bully the servants who attend upon
them at their eighteenpenny dinners and ninepenny
teas. Indeed, they rather " cotton to " this class of
servitors. They address the females as " my dear,"
and help them in the very process of waiting. They
call the male waiters " mate," and when one of them
comes to take orders, say for dinner, generally leave
it to him in a friendly way, to order it for them.

When dancing commences the single young fellows
begin to " come out." They look for the prettiest of the
girls, and as, in their own way, they have a good deal
of dash both in their conversation and dancing, they
sometimes make such a degree of progress in the good
graces of flirtingly-inclined young ladies as brings
upon them the jealous notice of the lovers. Fights
frequently ensue in consequence, but are generally
put a stop to before any material damage is done by
the interference of friends ; and sometimes when, after
the fight, it is discovered that the jealous lover is a
working man, and not one of those obnoxious individuals, a " counter-skipper," the combatants and
their respective friends become quite fraternal.

After the excursionist section of the Saint Mondayites the most numerous is that which is composed of the
lovers of sport. This section is chiefly made up of young
men of sporting proclivities. They are posted up in
the dates of, and latest betting, upon all important
sporting matters, and discuss the probable results of
" coming events" as learnedly and vaguely as any of
the professional sporting prophets. They are great in
slang, always speaking of the features of the human

face in the technical phraseology of the ring—according to which the nose is the beak or conk, the eyes ogles or peepers, the teeth ivories, and the mouth the kisser or tater-trap.   They are ready to settle all matters of opinion by offering to lay or take long odds upon the question.   They have a great deal of the "make-believe" sort of imagination in their composition, complacently speaking of "lumping it on" or "going a raker" when they have backed their fancy for five shillings, and regarding themselves as daring speculators when they have "put the pot on" to the amount of a sovereign.   And while the events on the results of which their speculations depend are in abeyance, they confidentially inform everybody whom they can get to listen to them that if they "land the pot," it is their intention to "jack up work" and go on the turf; which they believe to be their proper sphere.   Meantime they have their hair cut short, and, when off work, wear fancy caps and mufflers, and suits of the latest sporting cut ; in which they assume the swaggering walk of the minor sporting celebrities whom they are occasionally permitted to associate with and "treat."   As they get older the majority of these young fellows become more sensible.   They give up the more dangerous of their sporting practices, abandon the idea of going on the turf, and confining their gambling transactions to a draw in a shilling workshop sweepstake for the Derby, or wagering half-a-crown on the English representative in any international sporting contest; while to younger young fellows they leave the expensive honour of "standing" drink for the East-end Antelope, or purchasing tickets for the benefit of the Whitechapel Slogger. There are some of them, however, to whom neither increasing years norexperience brings wisdom, and who, instead of seeing and forsaking the folly of their way, go from bad to worse, and finally go to swell the disreputable mob of hangers-on associated with the body known as "the fancy." Others, who have not been able to exorcise the sporting spirit, have sufficient strength of mind to avoid those weaker points of a sporting taste that almost inevitably lead to the permanent degradation of the amateur sportsman—and settle down among those middle-aged married men who have the reputation of being "knowing cards," and who are constantly dabbling in sporting affairs, occasionally winning a few pounds, but as a rule being considerable losers in the aggregate; as their unfortunate wives and families could sorrowfully testify.

The shrines at which the sporting section of the Saint Mondayites principally sacrifice are the "running grounds" situated in the suburbs of the metropolis and the larger manufacturing towns, at which pedestrian and other athletic sports take place. At these grounds, the amusements consist for the most part of races ranging in length from eighty yards to five miles, wrestling matches, and pugilistic benefits upon a large scale, in which a number of the more or less brilliant stars of the ring "show up" in conjunction with pedestrians and wrestlers. But the events in which the sporting Saint Mondayites take the greatest interest are those amateur ones of which they themselves are the promoters, and in which eminent members of their own body are the principals; such, for instance, as the hundred and fifty yards' "spin," for 10*l.* a side, between the Speedy Mason and the Flying Blacksmith, in which the men have been backed by their shopmates. It sometimes happens, both in professional and amateur matches, that one or both parties come on to the ground secretly determined to

" win, tie, or wrangle ;" and as they cannot, of course,
make sure of a win or a tie, it is generally a wrangle
that the losing side in these cases resort to as a
means of trying to save their money.   Even in
cases in which no predetermined resolve to wrangle
exists, wrangles often occur ; and these disputes,
which are always conducted in language so strong,
that the mildest samples of it would be utterly unfit
for ears polite, invariably lead to a number of fights
between the partisans of the principals in the contests
out of which the disputes arise. When fights commence
under these circumstances, the friends of the combatants immediately interfere ; not, however, as in the
case of the excursionists, for the purpose of restoring
peace, but with the directly contrary object of promoting the fight, by forming a ring and encouraging the
man of their choice to " wire in," or shouting to him
to use the left, or upper-cut, or counter.   The Saint
Mondayites of the black country and other districts inhabited by the less civilized portions of the great unwashed, belong almost to a man, to the sporting section;
but their tastes being considerably stronger than those
of the sporting worshippers of Saint Monday residing
in more refined localities, they add to the milder sports
already spoken of a number of those smaller semi-
professional pugilistic affairs which are to be found
recorded in the " ring intelligence" of the sporting
papers under the heading of " Merry Little Mills,"
or " Rough Turns-up."   The doggy portion of them
further diversify their Monday sports by dog-fights and
ratting-matches.   As might naturally be expected,
wrangles and fights frequently take place among this
class of sportsmen, and sometimes these fights are, by
the mutual consent of the combatants, of the kind known
in such districts as up-and-down fights, in which, as the

name implies, the men fight both up and down ; fight,
in short, like beasts rather than men, kicking and biting
each other, when on the ground, with the utmost
ferocity.

Another section of the Saint Mondayites consists of
those who simply merge the worship of Saint Monday
into the worship of Bacchus. The men of this section
are, as a rule, confirmed "lushingtons," who, having
had a "spree" on the Saturday night, and taken
numerous hairs of the dog that bit them on the Sunday without experiencing that benefit which is popu-
larly supposed to result from such a proceeding, avail
themselves of the circumstance of Monday being a
holiday to have an appropriate and characteristic
wind-up of their weekly spree by a day's idling and
drinking. Whatever the amount of money they may
have received on the Saturday night, these worthies
are invariably penniless on the Monday morning.
Some of them, however, have credit at the public-
houses which they delight to honour, and this credit
they pledge for the benefit of themselves, and
those of their less fortunate brother lushingtons on
whose paying of their share of " the shot" upon
the following Saturday they can depend. But when
a knot of this class of Saint Mondayites are seen outside of a public-house door taking off their waistcoats
and neckerchiefs, and handing them to one of their
number, with instructions to " get as much as you can
on them, Bill,". it may be taken for granted that they
have neither money nor credit; but still, so long as
they have any pawnable clothing, they are never at a loss
for raising a shilling. These people commence their
Saint Monday proceedings about eleven o'clock in the
morning ; at that hour they begin to drop in at their
favourite houses of call, where they sit smoking and

drinking and playing dominoes, or discussing the incidents of their Saturday-night sprees, until one or
two o'clock, when the more seasoned vessels go out
to "have a turn round and get a bit of something to
eat," leaving those of their brethren who have already
become muddled, or whose drunkenness is of the
apathetic kind, to await their return about an hour
later, when the consumption of beer and tobacco again
goes on with renewed energy until about six or seven
o'clock in the evening. By this time money and credit
are alike exhausted. Matters being thus brought to
a climax, they go, or, if *quite* helpless, are taken home,
and having thus a long night before them in which
to sleep off the drink, and being used to it, they manage
to appear at work on the following morning.

The last and worst section of the Saint Mondayites
is the "loafer" section—a section composed of lazy,
dissolute fellows who look upon work as a dire and
disagreeable necessity, and avoid it as much as
they can. They have never the means of indulging
in any of the ordinary holiday amusements of the more
respectable portion of the working classes, and stay off
their work on Mondays from sheer laziness, and because they know that employers being compelled to
tacitly acknowledge Monday as an optional holiday,
they can stay from their work on that day without in-
curring the risk of getting " the sack " or a " blowing
up." If they live in the vicinity of any of the places
patronized by the excursionist section of the Saint
Mondayites, or can find any means of reaching such
places cheaply, these gentry hang on to the excursionists as a sort of camp-followers, snapping up
unconsidered trifles in the way of eatables, sponging
upon the more easy-going for drink, and insulting
those who will not be sponged upon, if they think that

they are not likely to show fight.   When they are not able to join any of the regular holiday-makers in the capacity of hangers-on, they loaf about the outside of corner public-houses, smoking, and indulging in horse-play among themselves, and hustling respectable passers-by off the pavement.   Or if half-a-dozen of them can raise " the price of a pot," so as to obtain an entrance into a public-house, they will attach themselves to other parties who may be drinking in the house, and bully or beg as much drink from them as they can ; while, failing all chance of obtaining drink at other people's expense, many of them attend the police-courts, or hang about the outside of them, to hear the results of the Saturday-night charges, in some of which they take a warm interest, owing to members of their own body being concerned in them.   For the great unwashed being generally flush of money and bent upon enjoying themselves on Saturday nights, the sponging and bullying propensities of the loafers become so rampant on those nights that they often lead to rows, and the appearance of the loafers being against them, and it occasionally happening that they are " well known to the police," they are usually the parties seized when the police have to be called in to quell a Saturday-night row.   And it is with a view of showing their sympathy with, and learning the fate of, their captive brethren, that the loafers, when they cannot get drink, go to the police-courts on Monday mornings, and by attending these courts, hanging on to the skirts of legitimate pleasure-seekers, and loafing about public-houses and street corners, they manage to get through the day in a manner that, to any but a thoroughly lazy man, would be hard work.

Individual or occasional worshippers of Saint Monday may sacrifice to the saint in some personal or

peculiar manner, but the proceedings of the four sections of Saint Mondayites enumerated embrace all the
essential and general features of the day, and its worshippers and observances, and afford ample data for
forming a judgment as to whether such an institution
is or is not a desirable one, or one that is likely to
have a beneficial influence upon the working classes.
Fully admitting the truth of the principle involved in
the proverb that " all work and no play makes Jack a
dull boy," I think that when considered in all its
bearings, it is fairly questionable whether the holiday
of Saint Monday, as it at present exists, is beneficial to
the Jacks as a body, or tends to make them bright.
The excursion form of Monday holiday is in itself commendable, and of a beneficial character; it affords those
who are during a great part of each working day
engaged in the necessarily more or less foul atmosphere of a workshop, an opportunity of enjoying a
purer air; the amusements connected with it are, as a
rule, of a perfectly innocent character; and the holiday
usually comes to a conclusion in time to allow those
who take part in it to reach home and get to bed at a
moderately early hour, so that they can go to their
work on the following morning refreshed and invigo-
rated.   But desirable as is the day-excursion form of
working-class holiday, it cannot be ultimately beneficial
to the working-classes as a body, so long as it is indulged
in—as is the case at present—by large numbers who
cannot really afford it, and by whose self-indulgence
in such matters they and their families are greatly im-
poverished.   Many of the better-paid and more provident portion of the working classes are in a position
which perfectly justifies them, so far as the question of
the expense involved is concerned, in occasionally giving
themselves and their families the pleasure of a holiday;

but while they can thoroughly enjoy and appreciate the value of such holidays, it is only *occasionally* that people of this kind, with whom prudential considerations have weight, indulge in them; while, on the other hand, many of the habitual and more enthusiastic observers of Saint Monday are people who, in the more literal and least desirable sense, "take no heed for the morrow;" people who will feast on pay-day, though they run the risk of starving during the rest of the week in consequence; who will and *can* make holiday on Monday, though they know that their clothes must go to the pawn-shop the next day, and that their imaginations will have to be racked to devise plausible excuses for obtaining credit for a loaf of bread before the end of the week; people who sacrifice all higher and general considerations to the gratification of the hour, and who, living from hand to mouth at the best of times, are, when overtaken by sickness or temporary loss of employment, immediately plunged into the most abject misery. And an institution which affords these people an excuse and opportunity for regularly and systematically indulging their extravagant and injurious propensities, and encourages and developes such propensities in those in whom they may be latent, has, it must be obvious, a tendency to act injuriously upon the working classes generally. These improvident Saint Mondayites, whose philosophy is summed up in the chorus of one of their favourite songs, in which they assert that—

> " Let the world jog along as it will,
> We'll be free and easy still,"

though professing to be, and by many believed to be simply thoughtless, good-humoured individuals, are in reality, as a rule, thoroughly selfish beings. The wives and children of many of the most ardent Saint Mondayites have to go short of food and clothes, and endure other miseries, while the means that should go to make them and their homes comfortable are squandered. Besides, as in most workshops of any considerable size some of the labourers employed in the establishment can only work when the mechanics, whose assistants they are, are at their work, it frequently happens that poor labouring men, who are struggling to bring up families on an income of sixteen or eighteen shillings a week, and who have neither the means nor spirit for keeping holiday, go to their work on Monday mornings only to be sent back in consequence of the absence of "mates," who, without any previous notice, either to masters or fellow-workmen, are stopping off work in order to keep up Saint Monday.

TEETOTAL ADVOCATES AND ADVOCACY.

IT is a prevalent idea that in free and happy England the days have long since passed away in which a man was subjected to persecution on account of his opinions; and I can only say, happy are those whose experience justifies them in entertaining a belief in the truth of this idea—mine does not. Whether it is that my case is an exceptional one, and I have been a "martyr to circumstances," or whether the old spirit of persecution is not so thoroughly eradicated from the human heart as is generally supposed, I am not able to determine; all that I know with that absolute certainty which alone justifies a positive and unqualified assertion is, that for some considerable time past I have been persecuted in a manner almost worthy of the good old times, for refusing to be " convinced against my will" that my own opinions upon a subject to which I shall presently refer are utterly erroneous, and those of sundry of my acquaintances infallibly correct.   I am well aware that a man with a grievance is a bore and a social nuisance; and even apart from this restraining knowledge, I would not think for a moment of attempting to " ventilate" a mere grievance; for I scorn the idea of crying out about any of those petty annoyances of every-day life which are exaggerated by grumblers until they assume the proportions of a grievance.   *I* am no grievance-monger.   *I* never wrote to the *Times* on the subject of " The Hotel Nuisance," although I

once had to pay a tavern bill for bed and breakfast
which, in point of extortion, surpassed any transaction
of the " sixty per-centers" of which I have ever heard or
read, and which induced a sporting gentleman who had
been charged a like amount for the same accommodation, to tell the proprietor of the tavern, that although
he (the sporting man) did not know his (the proprietor's)
exact pedigree, he was confident he was full brother
to a robber.   So far, indeed, from being a grievance-
monger, I may say for myself that I am a particularly
long-suffering individual, and have borne, with fortitude
or indifference, annoyances that would have driven any
person of a less philosophical turn of mind than myself
to despair and the police-courts.   I have been importuned and abused by garotter-like mendicants, to whom
I have given alms instead of handing them over to the
police.   I have been threatened and derided by the
coarsest cabmen, with whose demands (generally about
double their legal fare) I have complied, when others
would have taken their number and " made an example
of them."   I have even been taken before a bench of
magistrates upon suspicion of being a burglar ; this
last decidedly unpleasant event occurring through the
stupidity of a policeman, who stopped me as I was
leaving my work late one winter night, carrying the
implements of my trade (which certainly have a strong
resemblance to the implements of a house-breaker) in
a small bag.   Into this bag A 1 insisted upon looking,
and laughed to scorn the explanation which I offered
to him, saying that I must tell that tale to the natives,
and advising me to " come along" quietly, or he would
put " the darbies" on me.   With this inexorable guar-
dian of the night I accordingly went, and was speedily
consigned to a cell in which bed and board were synonymous terms, and from whence I was taken in the

morning to be examined by the sitting magistrates, to some of whom I was fortunately known, and was consequently immediately discharged, thus escaping any of the inconveniences arising out of the " law's delays," while my captor, whose mistake was after all a very natural one, was severely censured in open court ; one of " the great unpaid" going so far as to stigmatize him as a useless blockhead. These, and as many more of the small ills of life as would fill a volume, I have borne without a murmur, already convinced that " such is life."

Having thus, I trust, sufficiently demonstrated that I *can* " suffer and be strong" under the ordinary annoyances of life, and having incidentally mentioned a few of those annoyances that have fallen to my lot, but of which, be it understood, I do not complain, I will now speak of the persecution of which I *do* complain.

To begin, then, I belong to that portion of the community who are sometimes vaguely and collectively spoken of as " intelligent artisans," and I am engaged in the workshops of a firm who employ about five hundred men. Among such a number of working men, it will readily be believed that there are some of almost every degree of intemperance, from the confirmed and frightful-example description of drunkard, to the one who only gets " elevated" upon rare and festive occasions, such as his own or an intimate friend's marriage, or a public banquet, at which he generally insists upon making a speech, proposing a toast, or taking some other active but uncalled-for and unappreciated part in the proceedings. But though it must be admitted that intemperance is but too prevalent a vice among working mechanics, it is by no means a prominent characteristic of the *class*. On the contrary, taken in the aggregate, they are a very temperate body of men, and among them may be found numerous representatives of " total abstinence" in all its extremes and modifications ; from the " total abstainer," who has always been one, never having tasted intoxicating drinks, to the sensation-craving, procession-forming, medal-wearing, pledge-signing, and altogether ignoble " teetotaller," who is generally a recently-reclaimed drunkard of the worst class, and upon whose continuance in his regenerated state but little reliance can be placed.

Now it is some half-dozen of these rabid sons of abstinence who have become the bane of my existence by their fanatical attempts to induce me to sign " the pledge." There is a proverb which says that " there's a medium in all things ;" but then there is another proverb to the effect that " there is no rule without an exception," and so, despite the dictum laid down in the first of these sayings, it is justifiable to conclude that there are things in which there is *no* medium ; and one of them most undoubtedly is, the intolerant spirit with which the disciples of total abstinence seek to enforce their doctrines and practices upon all other members of society. To strive to promote the interests of what you conceive to be a good cause is highly commendable. But to insinuate that those who by reasoning you have failed to convert to *your* opinion will end their career on the gallows or in the madhouse, and that the transition stages to those undesirable consummations will consist of wife-beating, bankruptcy, moral degradation, premature physical decay, and unutterable sottishness, is to show a decided want of that medium which *ought* to characterize discussions of all matters of opinion. And it is this want of medium in the no doubt well-meant endeavours of my persecutors to induce me to sign " the pledge" that has converted what might have been a friendly discussion into a harassing persecution. " Well, why don't you sign it?" asks Bodgers (who is the spokesman and chief of the band), in a tone of exasperation, after ineffectually endeavouring to convince me that a person who partakes of malt liquor, however sparingly, is little, if anything, better than a murderer. " Come, give us your reasons, if you've got any," persists the indignant Bodgers, greatly disgusted that I do not instantly explain myself. In vain, when thus interrogated, I submissively express my conviction that in its place—that is, applied to incorrigible drunkards, or those who are conscious of a want of self-restraint where intoxicating drinks are concerned—the total abstinence pledge is a most praiseworthy institution. In vain I argue that even strong drinks may have their beneficial uses. In vain I urge that I am a man of temperate habits, that I believe the little drink that I do take does me good, and that even if I found it injured me, or I had any other motive for abstaining from it, I could and would do so without signing any pledge. To hear none of these or the other numerous reasons I bring forward in support of my refusal doth the obdurate Bodgers seriously incline. Moderation, Bodgers sententiously informs me, is the mother of intemperance, and to be good yourself, says the same authority, is not sufficient; you must set the example to others, and try to make them good. " So that, you see, you have not got a leg to stand on," remarks another abstainer. " Oh, he knows he's wrong," observes a third, " only he's too pig-headed to say so." And the rest of them give it as their joint opinion that " that (the last remark) is about the size of it," and that I would " have my own pig-headed way if a saint (and only to a saint's do they consider Bodgers' eloquence second) were to come and tell me I was wrong."

Day after day am I subjected to attacks of this kind
—attacks that, in addition to destroying my peace of
mind, are rapidly impairing my digestion, as they are
generally made while I am at dinner, which meal I
take, in common with my persecutors and many others,
in the dining-room connected with the establishment
in which I am employed. To be catechized, to be
spoken to, and spoken *at* in this manner is bad enough,
but the active part of my persecution is by no means
the worst part of it. No ! it is when I consider " what
manner of men they be " who subject me to this treatment that my cup of bitterness becomes full. When
I remember that the abusive and dogmatic Bodgers of
to-day is the same Bodgers who but one short year
before was wont to sneak to his work by circuitous
routes, in order to avoid the threats and entreaties of
a number of publicans to whom he was indebted for
drink,—the same Bodgers who met you in the street,
and noisily importuned you to " stand a glass," or lend
him " the price of a pint," and who loudly, sometimes
blasphemously, resented any attempt to remonstrate
with him upon his disgraceful conduct : when, again, I
remember that Sturge (who calls me pig-headed) is
the same person who a few months ago figured in the
local newspapers under the heading of " an old
offender," or " Sturge again," and whose case generally appeared at the head of Monday's police intelligence in this style :—" John Sturge, a drunken and
dissipated-looking man, well known at this court, was
placed at the bar, charged for the —teenth time with
being drunk and incapable. Police-constable B 4 de-
posed to finding the prisoner, &c., &c.—Fined five
shillings :" when I remember, I say, that these are the
men who assume the part of mentor, and rail not only
against intemperance, but also against the moderate

use of strong drinks, then I become enraged, threaten to thrash Sturge, and challenge Bodgers to pugilistic combat.

My would-be converters were regular attendants at the weekly meetings of a total abstinence society of which they were members ; and to these meetings they were constantly alluding in my presence, remarking to each other in a tone of voice loud enough for me to hear, that Jones (myself) ought to have been at " the meeting," and he would have heard something that would have done him good, and suggesting that I would not go to their meetings because I knew that if I did I would hear that which would compel me to alter my opinion on the subject of the pledge. Goaded to desperation by the continual taunts and impertinences of these persecuting abstainers, I at length, in the hope of obtaining peace, entered into a treaty with them ; the terms of the treaty (which were proposed by themselves) being, that I was to accompany them to three of their meetings, and if after what I heard and saw at those meetings I still failed to see that it was the duty of every right-thinking person to take the pledge, they would, to use the phrase of one of their number, " give it up for a bad job," and cease to importune me any further upon the subject. To these terms I readily agreed, promising upon my part to weigh, without prejudice or partiality, all that I heard, and that I would not allow any feeling of personal opposition to Bodgers or others to interfere with my judgment. In order that I might not be at a loss to understand the proceedings at these meetings, it would be necessary, Bodgers informed me, for him to explain to me the formation and object of the society. From his explanation I learned that the society consisted of about three hundred members, each of

whom paid a small weekly contribution to a fund
established for the purpose of rendering pecuniary
assistance to any of the members whose case required
it. The society had divided the town into twelve
districts, the members in each of which were called a
life-boat crew, and a captain was appointed over each
crew. The duties of a captain were to look after the
members in his district, and prevent, as far as lay in
his power, any backsliding upon their part, to gain as
many proselytes as possible, and to come forward at
the weekly meetings of the society, and report upon
the state of the crew, and the progress (if any) of " the
cause " in the district under his control.

Bodgers, I need scarcely say, was a captain ; and as
in that capacity he was required upon the platform, he
was unable to accompany me to the first of the three
meetings, to which I was escorted by Sturge. The
business of the meeting was to commence at eight
o'clock, and about ten minutes before that hour I
arrived at the meeting-house. The instant I entered
the room I became painfully aware of the fact that I
was regarded as the lion of the evening, for I had
scarcely got through the doorway when a most significant murmur pervaded the room, and several loudly-
whispered expressions of " That's him," " Him with
Sturge," " Here he is," and others of a like nature,
reached my ears ; and I felt that every eye was upon
me as I followed Sturge to a seat near the platform.
When the excitement caused by my entrance had somewhat abated, I ventured to take a glance at the audience
who had done me the honour of looking so intently at
me, and I am bound to say that the result of my
scrutiny was of anything but a gratifying nature.
There were about two hundred persons present, and
among them some highly respectable-looking individuals;

but the predominant characteristic of a great majority of the countenances of the abstainers who formed the audience was dissipation—dissipation of a more or less marked character; and it was an unnecessary proceeding upon the part of the speaker, who in the course of the evening addressed the meeting, to assure his hearers that a great number of those present had once been " slaves to drink," as that was to be plainly seen in dozens of cases, and the emancipation of many of them was evidently of a very recent date.

Having finished my survey of the audience, I turned my gaze upon the platform, just in time to witness the entrance of the chairman and captains upon it. The chairman upon this occasion (a fresh one was chosen each evening) was a stout, coarse-looking individual with a very red face, and a profusion of still redder hair. He was attired in a suit of seedy, ill-fitting black, and wore a rather cloudy-looking white neckcloth; and this dress, and the circumstance that his nose was of an unmistakably " jolly " cast, gave him the appearance of one of the mutes attached to the staff of an economic funeral company. This mutish-looking gentleman, Sturge informed me in a whisper, was Mr. Bidder, the furniture-broker, who once nearly killed himself by drinking, for a wager, a pint of raw rum in five minutes, and who, before he signed the pledge, seldom went to bed sober. Advancing to the front of the platform, the chairman, in a severe tone of voice, cried " Silence !" and having obtained silence, he then gave out the words of a teetotal hymn, which was sung to the tune of " Ole Virginia Shore," and the burden of which was—

"I've done my best, I've done my best, and I cannot do any more,
But I'll carry the seeds of temperance to every drunkard's door."

The hymn being finished, and a short prayer said, the

business of the evening then commenced. Selecting one from a roll of papers that he held in his hand, Mr. Bidder, after again crying " Silence !" and " Order !" proceeded to say that, at the request of a number of the members, the committee of the society had written to that celebrated advocate of total abstinence the Whistling Waggoner, requesting to be informed when he could make it convenient to give one of his entertainments in this town. He now held in his hand the reply of the Waggoner, which was to the effect that he would be able to accommodate them in the course of a fortnight, and they might at once proceed to " bill " him. This announcement was received with great cheering, amid which the chairman sat down. When the applause had subsided, the chairman called out, " Captain of Number One life-boat crew, please to stand forward." In reply to this call, one of " the twelve " left his seat and advanced to the front of the platform, and said that all was going on smoothly in his district, and that the crew of which he had the honour to be captain were one and all steadfast in " the good cause." Captains Two, Three, and Four reported to the same effect, and almost in the same words. This succession of good reports put the audience into quite a happy frame of mind. But human happiness is, alas ! but transitory. The report of the fifth captain completely extinguished, for a time at least, the exultation raised by the four previous reports. The wobegone expression of Number Five's countenance plainly indicated that his report would be of an unfavourable nature, and he evinced great reluctance to face his audience. So slow, indeed, was he in coming to the front, that loud cries of " Time," " Toe the mark," " Come up to the scratch," " Go in and win," and other phrases that are only to be found in

the vocabulary of " our pugilistic reporter," arose from
all parts of the room. Seeing that his hesitation was
producing an unfavourable effect upon his auditors,
Number Five summoned up his courage, dashed to
the front, and abruptly commenced the delivery of his
report. His intelligence, he was sorry to say, was of
a very disheartening nature. They all knew Finigan,
the big Irishman who had joined their society about a
month ago (cries of " Yes, yes "). Well, as some of
them were probably aware, the committee had a few
days since, at his (the captain's) recommendation, advanced the sum of two pounds to Finigan, to enable
him to start in business as a greengrocer; but instead of expending the money in vegetables, Finigan
had got drunk with it. He had then gone home,
turned his mother out of doors, severely beaten his
wife, and attempted to bite a policeman's nose off, for
which series of offences he was then undergoing a
punishment of a month's imprisonment with hard
labour (cries of " Serve him right "). " The worst
part of the business," continued the captain, " is that
there will be no chance of us ever getting the two
pounds back again, and that is what grieves me; for
the last party to whom the committee made an advance, upon my recommendation, cheated them out of
thirty shillings." This recital of the brutal and ungrateful conduct of Finigan, together with the knowledge of the pecuniary loss sustained by the society in
consequence thereof, served to throw a deep gloom
over the meeting—a gloom which the ordinarily favourable reports of the next six captains failed to dispel.
But all joy had not departed from among them : in
the report of the last of the captains was consolation
found. The manner of captain Number Twelve, as he
came forward in obedience to the call of the chairman,

startled the audience out of the sullen calmness into which they had sunk. There was an elasticity and lightness in his gait, and an expression of cheerfulness and triumph upon his countenance, that would have been a positive insult to his hearers unless accompanied by intelligence of an unusually pleasing character ; and, happily for the peace of the meeting, his information was of a nature that fully justified the triumphant manner he assumed in giving it. The reports of the other captains had been made in the briefest possible manner; but Number Twelve, who evidently imagined himself an orator, spoke at considerable length. He commenced by observing that " they had all heard some very discouraging intelligence that evening," and then went on to say that " the ungrateful behaviour of some of the individuals whom the society had assisted and befriended was almost enough to deter them from attempting to reclaim or benefit others. But though," he continued, " their kindness to those whom drink had brought to poverty and want was, alas ! but too often repaid by the blackest ingratitude, and though their efforts to show the drunkard the error of his way had, in many instances, met with ridicule, scorn, and even blows, yet they could point with pride and pleasure to cases in which their humble endeavours had been productive of good—lasting and permanent good." After giving short biographies of several of the " rescued " persons in whom the society had been the means of effecting " lasting and permanent good," Number Twelve proceeded to inform his hearers that, since their last meeting, a name had been added to the list of " the rescued " that few would have ever thought of seeing there, and he was sure that when they heard that name they would feel amply compensated for any disappointment they had experienced when they heard of

Finigan's case. The person whose name he alluded to—he would use the name by which he was best known to the public—was "Fighting Joe!" The utterance of this name created an immense sensation, and the speaker's voice was lost amid bursts of cheering and cries of "No, no," "It can't be," "He'll break," which arose on all sides. When silence was at length restored, Number Twelve concluded his report by repeating most emphatically that, however improbable it might appear to some of them, it was nevertheless true that Fighting Joe had taken the pledge, and he for one firmly believed that he would keep it. The reports of the captains being finished, the chairman again came forward and announced that "one of their most highly-valued members had kindly consented to address them that evening."

The entrance of the "highly-valued member" was the signal for another energetic burst of cheering, which he acknowledged by a bow that showed that that was not *his* first appearance on any stage; on the contrary, as I afterwards learned, he was the crack speaker of the society, and had been specially selected to astonish me. His subject was the "Evils of Moderation," and his discourse soon showed that he had been coached for the occasion by Bodgers. He was evidently bent on converting me by sarcasm, and at each fresh stab that he made at moderation, the abstainers regarded me with glances which said, "as plain as whisper in the ear," How do you like that, my fine fellow? and I could see that it was generally expected that I would show temper under the severe handling of the highly-valued member. In this expectation the disciples of abstinence were, however, doomed to disappointment. I kept my temper perfectly unruffled, which was easy enough to do, since the whole harangue of the speaker was a mere repetition of the proverbs and arguments

I had heard from Bodgers scores of times, and they consequently failed either to anger or interest me. The address on the evils of moderation being concluded, and a vote of thanks awarded to the deliverer of it, the chairman dissolved the meeting, and the audience quietly dispersed.   Outside of the meeting-house I was joined by Bodgers, who immediately began to try and draw me into a discussion, when I reminded him that one of the conditions of our treaty was, that tee-totalism was to be a forbidden subject between us till I had attended the three meetings, but it was not till I had threatened to decline attending the other two meetings that Bodgers relinquished his efforts to " renew the subject."

The next meeting I attended was the one at which the Whistling Waggoner was to give his entertainment. The audience upon this occasion numbered upwards of three hundred, many of the general public being there in addition to the members ; the admission this time being by payment, and the ordinary business of the weekly meetings being dispensed with.   At the hour appointed for the commencement of the entertainment the Waggoner was ushered on to the platform, and was most enthusiastically received.   When the plaudits evoked by his appearance had ceased, the chairman of the meeting introduced him to the audience as " one of the warmest and most able teetotal advocates we have ;" and then modestly retired into the background, leaving the warm, able, and whistling advocate of tee-totalism the observed of all observers.   The Waggoner was, to use the language of my newspaper, " a thick-set and powerful-looking man, somewhat below the middle height," and his plump and sleek appearance testified to his being a good liver.   His face was too fleshy to admit of any expression, while his eyes were so small and so deeply sunk in his head as to preclude

the possibility of catching their expression if they had
any. His "get up" was a decided attempt at the
clerical, and an equally decided failure; his whole appearance and manner being too suggestive of the
waiter at one of those Gravesend establishments that
supply tea and shrimps for ninepence.

The Waggoner's entertainment, of course, embraced
the usual unauthenticated statistics, stock anecdotes,
and pieces of clap-trap oratory of the professional teetotal lecturers. Drink once more destroyed its sixty
thousand victims annually, slew more than the sword,
filled our prisons and workhouses, our hospitals and
asylums, and caused all our disease and poverty; and,
in a word, drink was held up as the origin of "all the
ills that flesh is heir to," and the great bar to human
happiness here below. The old stone-breaker who
drank ale in the summer to cool him, and in the
winter to warm him, was again brought forward.
The man who boasted that he had drunk his bottle of
port every day for forty years was again silenced by
being asked, "Where are all your companions?" and
the prisoner in the condemned cell, when asked what
brought him there, again exclaimed, "Drink! drink!"
"The first fatal glass" was descanted upon at considerable length; and it was, of course, implied that
all who took that glass ultimately came to poverty and
grief, and were fortunate if they escaped penal servi-
tude or the madhouse.

The only original feature in the entertainment was
the introduction of a number of teetotal songs, which
were very well sung by the Waggoner, who possessed
a good though uncultivated voice. These "songs of
teetotalism" were of a wretchedly doggerel character.
Compared with them, even "The Perfect Cure" would
have appeared a sensible and elegant composition :

however, they seemed to please the audience, who joined lustily in the chorus of the two entitled " I'll Drink Cold Water " and " No Alcohol for Me." At the termination of the entertainment, thanks to the crush at the door, I managed to elude Bodgers, who I knew would want to " renew the subject," and I had already had more than enough of it for one evening.

As there was no immediate prospect of another professional teetotal advocate visiting the town, it was agreed that I should attend the next ordinary meeting of the society, more by way of fulfilling the terms of the treaty into which I had entered than from any hope my persecutors now had of influencing my opinions; for when I informed them that the lecture of the Waggoner had in no way altered my views upon the subject of the pledge, they seemed to abandon all hope of my conversion. The chairman at this, the last of the three meetings " nominated in the bond," was no other than Sturge, who performed his duties in a highly creditable manner. The captains, with one exception, were all there, and each reported that all was well in his district. The absent captain was Number Twelve, who was unable to attend, owing to the effects of a severe thrashing he had received from Fighting Joe ; Joe, as we learned from the statement of the chairman, having, in addition to breaking the pledge, broken the nose of, and otherwise maltreated the unfortunate captain of Number Twelve lifeboat crew. Joe, it appeared, had gone to the races, and was returning from them in a state of intoxication, when he was met by the captain, who taunted him with having so soon broken his promise; whereupon Joe instantly assaulted him in the manner described by the chairman. After the reports had been delivered and the absence of Number Twelve accounted for, a number of the members came upon the platform to

give an account of their " rescue," or speak of their
" experiences." Some of them had taken the pledge
because their friends had promised to pay their debts,
procure them employment, or confer some other benefit
upon them if they would do so ; others for the purpose of saving money ; and some for special reasons
affecting only their particular cases ; one man assigning
the novel reason that he had been stung by the ingratitude of a publican whose house he had been in
the habit of frequenting, in refusing to support him
and his wife and family when he was out of work :
nor did it seem to occur to him that the baker with
whom he had been in the habit of dealing would
probably have acted in the same ungrateful manner.

The experiences were as various as the reasons for
taking the pledge. Some of the speakers had " for
years been drunk every night," others had been in the
habit of spending the greater portion of their earnings
in the public-house, and, on some occasions, the whole
of their week's wages had been consumed in the payment of the past week's " shot " and a Saturday
night's " spree." Some had lost good situations
through their habits of intoxication, and one villanous-
looking character gleefully informed his hearers that
he used to get drunk every Saturday night, and then
go home and " whop " his wife, and smash the
crockery ; and, to judge by his countenance, he seemed
capable of doing even worse things. The last of the
speakers, after observing that for many years he had
scarcely ever had a decent rag to his back, and was
often without food, " all through drink," proceeded to
dilate upon the fruits of teetotalism : the fruits in his
case being, to use his own words, " this slap-up suit of
black and this watch, " pulling the latter article out
of his pocket. He entered into a detailed account of

the manner in which he had accumulated the money
to purchase the clothes and watch with, told the price
of each separate article and the cost of the whole,
turned his back to the audience to enable them to obtain a back view of the coat, exclaiming at the same
time, " There's the fruits of teetotalism for you," and
concluded a somewhat lengthy and perfectly idiotical
address by holding the watch above his head and
shouting, " Who wouldn't be a teetotaler ? "

Some of these speakers had, according to their own
confession, broken the pledge two, three, and one of
them even five times ; but the most painful part of
this disgraceful exhibition was the absence of shame
with which these men paraded the disgusting and
brutal episodes of their lives before their fellow-men.
That such men as these should be brought from a state
of habitual and degrading drunkenness to one of total
abstinence from intoxicating drinks is a great blessing,
not only to themselves, but to society at large, and
those who bring about the reformation of such men
are justly regarded as benefactors of their race. But
that such men, while the stamp of their bestial habits
is yet uneffaced from their countenances, should in-
veigh against the moderate use of the stimulants which
they had so grossly abused, is a most impudent proceeding, and one that tends to bring contempt upon
the (in its proper sphere, the reclamation of habitual
drunkards) truly Christian cause of teetotalism. And
even in the case of those conscientious teetotalers who
have never been drunkards, and those who, by years of
unswerving consistency in their reformed habits, have
earned the right to advocate the cause they profess, I
think it an ill-advised proceeding to try to *force* their
doctrines upon those who are, and always have been,
of temperate habits, more especially as there is so ex-

tensive a field for their labours in weaning men from the curse of drunkenness.

On the morning after this last meeting my teetotal foes again made an attack upon me. One of them began by asking me if I still intended to " be stupid," and on my replying that I did not intend to take the pledge, Sturge reminded them that he had told them that I would have my own pig-headed way. Bodgers, however, upon this occasion came to my rescue, and commanded " those of his inclining " to hold their noise while he and Jones reasoned the matter over. Bodgers' reasoning and arguments would have been very good had they been applied to a drunkard, but they were not at all applicable to my case, as Bodgers himself, and even the most fanatical of his admirers, were perfectly willing to admit that *I* never got drunk, never spent my evenings in a public-house, never neglected a.iy duty for the sake of drink, and that I certainly was a temperate man. " Still," urged Bodgers, " you ought to take the pledge, for you are not sure that you will always be able to remain the same moderate man that you now are, and, even if you are, you will still be doing a great injury to the cause of teetotalism, for unreflecting drunkards will point to such as you as a proof that drink may be taken without any evil resulting from it. But, that evil will come of it," concluded Bodgers, emphatically, " is as sure as that eggs are eggs." Although Bodgers spoke with greater sense and moderation upon this occasion than he had ever done before, his eloquence was unavailing, and the result of our discussion was that I told him respectfully, but firmly, that I must positively, and once for all, decline joining a body of men who wore medals, formed processions, and otherwise took credit to themselves for simply doing what was the duty of

every man, namely, keeping sober. This decision by
no means pleased my persecutors, who, despite the
terms of our treaty, immediately renewed, and have
since continued, their persecution of me.

A year has passed since I attended the last of the
three teetotal meetings, and though during that time
Bodgers has returned to his " former habits," and now
exercises his persuasive eloquence in inducing reluc-
tant landlords to give him credit for " just another
pot," and negotiating loans for " the price of a pint,"
and Sturge has several times made his appearance at
the police-court on the old familiar charge of being
" drunk and incapable," those of my persecutors who
have remained true to " the good cause," and the more
recently " rescued " individuals who have joined their
ranks, continue their persecuting efforts with unabated
fierceness. And they joyfully look forward to that
teetotalers' millennium (which, with the fatuity peculiar to bigots and fanatics, they assert to be near at
hand) when the Permissive Bill shall reign supreme.
And that bill once made law, they cheerfully assure
me I must be prepared to bid a long farewell to that
glass of XX which, in the summer months, is often the
only thing that gives me an appetite for the solid food
which, from the hot and laborious nature of my daily
employment, I stand in need of, or which enables me
to continue at my work when, from the effects of the
combined heat of a July sun and a large blacksmith's
shop, I am unable to take a sufficient quantity of food.
My persecutors suggest dinner pills as a substitute for
porter ; but I have an extreme aversion to drugs under
any circumstances, and certainly shall not take them
while so pleasant a black draught as bottled stout has
" the desired effect." They also bring forward a number of total-abstinence theories to show that it *cannot*

be the stout or pale ale that I drink which does me so much good, because (according to their theories) all alcoholic drinks are injurious to health.   As not only doctors, but theorists also, disagree upon this question, I shall not attempt to decide it.   But I may observe, as a matter of fact, that I enjoy as good health as any teetotaler that I have ever met, and better health than the majority of them ; though this may be because the constitutions of many of them are impaired through early excesses, or illness consequent upon a sudden transition from a state of chronic drunkenness to one of total abstinence.   And I have invariably noticed that among working men, those who drink from half a pint to a pint of ale or porter with their mid-day meal, but who rarely touch stimulating drinks at other times, require a less quantity of solid food than teetotalers.   The appetite of a teetotaler often borders on the voracious, and the quantity of bread that some of them eat is " a caution."   This great appetite is one of their proudest boasts, but in my opinion it is a mistaken one, for sick-headaches and the numerous other complaints arising from indigestion, prevail to a marked extent among the teetotalers in the working classes, and the feeling of excessive repletion caused by their inordinate meals often interferes materially with their activity and capability of enduring fatigue.

To conclude, then, my persecutors lead me a terrible life still, but they do not have matters all their own way ; for when one of them " breaks out," or when I can show them the newspaper containing an account of an additional appearance upon the part of Sturge at the police-court, or inform them that the landlord of the " Lame Duck " is waiting outside the workshop-gate to effect the capture of Bodgers, against whom he has " a long chalk," I have my hour of triumph.

AMONG THE GODS.

Among other things theatrical, the gallery, and its occupants the "gods," have often been the subjects of remark, but as such of the remarks upon the gods as reach the public are generally made by those who occupy the lower and more select parts of "the house," I—a god of many years' experience—have thought that a few observations upon the manners and customs of the gods may not be altogether uninteresting if made by one of their own body, and I cannot better illustrate these manners and customs than by giving a brief account of some of my own experiences as a god.

Although a god when in the theatre, when out of it I am a working man, and like the working man in Mr. Hollingshead's farce of "The Birthplace of Podgers," "I rise at six," and from that hour in the morning until the same hour in the evening, I am engaged in a mechanical pursuit that involves a considerable amount of physical exertion. And being of opinion that a man who works hard for twelve hours a day requires and is fairly entitled to some amusement during a portion of his leisure time, and my idea of amusement being the witnessing of a theatrical performance, and my limited income forbidding the idea of my frequenting any of the more expensive parts of a theatre, I am by choice and of necessity a theatrical god. Perhaps I ought to feel very much ashamed of myself for expressing a belief that a working man ought to have some amusement;

the theory I have often been told is a wrong and dangerous, not to say sinful one, but then it is a very pleasant one to the believers therein, and that may perhaps account for it being so difficult to persuade those believers that their theory is a wrong one. I am told that instead of spending my hard-earned money in visiting places of amusement, I ought to imitate my shopmate Jones, who will go home after a hard day's work and employ himself in cultivating his garden, or making or repairing some article of household furniture ; or to take example by Brown, who devotes his evenings to arduous study, and the acquisition of some art or science. But from doing as Jones does I may readily be excused, as I am a single man, and being " only a lodger," I have neither garden or household furniture, or indeed anything else in the " domestic economy " line to exercise my industry or mechanical ingenuity upon ; and as to imitating Brown, I may as well at once confess that I have in my composition none of that determined perseverance and untiring patience that produces " self-made " and " self-taught " men, and so I am compelled to fall back upon the amusement theory, and the theatre, as being my idea of what constitutes amusement.

My earliest recollections of the interior of a theatre are associated with juvenile nights, and Christmas pantomimes, and the beautiful fairies, crystal lakes, transformation scenes, comic business, and the host of other juvenile enchanting things connected therewith. On these memorable occasions I was taken by my parents to one of the theatres royal of the large seaport town in which I was born, and my first visit took place when I was about six years of age, and from that time until I was twelve years old I was generally taken three or four times a year. I need scarcely say

that during that period I entertained an implicit belief
in the reality of all that I saw in the theatre, and was
desperately in love with divers young fairies, and felt
within myself that had any of those fairies asked me
for anything of which I was possessed, even had it
been the almost life-size rocking-horse presented to me
as a birthday gift by a rich aunt, I could not have
found the heart to refuse their request ; nor need I now
stay to dwell upon how I secretly resolved that when
I was a man I would go to the theatre every night.
At this time my pocket-money was all invested in
" characters," and twopenny boxes of paints and
brushes wherewith to colour them, and many were the
thrashings that I received through these same characters.   Sometimes I would be thrashed for not being
able to say my " night lessons," having been so busy
colouring " Mr. T. P. Cooke as ' William,' " as to
forget all about them, or if I managed to find time to
prepare my lessons, I was almost sure to " catch it "
for being too late for school, through loitering at
shop windows to gaze at " Mr. Hicks as ' Dirko
the Bloodthirsty,' "   or " Mr. Macturk as ' The
Mysterious Pirate.' "   And if by great good fortune I
contrived to avoid punishment at school, I was certain
to get my ears boxed at home for daubing my wearing
apparel or some of the household linen with paint.
But this period of my theatre-going career cannot
justly be considered as the experience of a god, since
at that time I was always taken into the pits of the
theatres that I visited.

My career as a " celestial " commenced when I was
a little over twelve years of age, and my " first appearance in any gallery " will always be associated in my
mind with an adventure, or rather misadventure, that
befell me upon that occasion, and through which

I received a most painful illustration of the truth
of the text, " Be sure your sins will find you
out," and which happened in this wise. Among my
schoolmates was one in whom I found, so far as an
intense admiration of things theatrical went, a kindred
spirit. He was about my own age, and he had informed me in the course of one of our·confidential
conversations that he was in love with the lady whom
he had seen playing Juliet on the night that he had
been treated to the theatre by his " big brother," and
that he would never have any one else for a sweetheart.
As our roads home from school lay for a considerable
distance in the same direction, Tommy Davies—for
that was my companion's name—and I generally
walked home together, making numerous stoppages
by the way, to read, admire, and compare the playbills
of the different theatres. One afternoon in the latter
end of the month of October we were going home, when
our attention was forcibly arrested by a bill of an un·
usually attractive character. It was a very large,
very highly coloured, and very profusely illustrated
bill. The central illustration was a representation of
a " terrific combat," in which a stage " tar," with the
usual portable armoury of pistols and cutlasses hanging
about him, was fighting a great number of characters
of the " black-hearted pirate " type, and as the tar was
represented surrounded by heaps of slain, the pirates
were evidently getting much the worst of the combat.
This picture was surrounded by a number of smaller,
though scarcely less vivid ones, representing " the
robbery at the bank," " the escape of the lovers,"
" the midnight funeral," " retribution," and other
stock situations of a melodrama. The letterpress of
the bill informed us that these illustrations were scenes
from a play of " thrilling interest," entitled " The

Guilty Banker; or, the Convict's Return," which was then being played with "immense success" at the Theatre Royal, Ruff Street, the prices of admission into which ranged from two shillings to threepence. How we gloated over this bill, and how, after stopping for half an hour dwelling admiringly on its details, we turned to take "a last fond look" at each of the numerous copies of it that we saw, may be more easily imagined than described. On the following morning "The Guilty Banker" was the all-absorbing topic of conversation between Master Davies and myself, and after a number of dark hints had been thrown out on either side, we found that each secretly entertained the idea of paying a visit to the Ruff Street Theatre, without the knowledge of our parents, who we knew would have forbidden it; for by the respectable inhabitants of the town that theatre was regarded as anything but an eligible place of amusement, and I had frequently heard my mother stigmatize it as "a sink of iniquity." But the desire to see "The Guilty Banker" was strong within us, and we resolved to go at all hazards, and having arrived at this determination, we were not long in arranging a plan for carrying out our purpose. Magic lanterns, and other entertainments suitable for children, had occasionally been given in our schoolroom, and turning this circumstance to account, we agreed to tell our parents that there was to be an exhibition of a magic lantern at the school that evening, and that all the scholars were expected to attend it. Having given this reason for our absence, we proposed to go to the theatre, and by leaving as soon as the first piece ("The Guilty Banker") was over, manage to get home in time to give a colouring of truth to the magic-lantern story. This "strategic movement" we carried out in a manner that would

have done credit to an American general, and at a
little after seven o'clock Tommy Davies and I were
comfortably seated in the gallery of the Ruff Street
Theatre, anxiously waiting for the curtain to rise upon
the thrilling drama of " The Guilty Banker." The
Ruff Street Theatre was anything but an elegant one,
even in the best parts of it, and the gallery was of an
exceedingly early style of architecture, the seats
in that part of the house being simply pieces of
narrow plank nailed across trestles, and rising one
above another, until the heads of those who
occupied the furthest back one almost touched the
ceiling, and the floor being level, there was,
of course, a space under the seats sufficiently large for
parties to walk about in. Two of the three acts of the
drama had passed off in the most satisfactory manner,
and I was leaning forward watching with breathless
interest a scene in the last act, in which two vile
myrmidons of the libertine lord were about to carry
off a virtuous maiden, when my feet were seized
from below, and before I could comprehend the object
of the attack or raise an alarm, my shoes (a recently
purchased pair) were taken off my feet, and the depre-
dators had disappeared in the dark cavern below the
seats. I made a few feeble attempts to draw the attention of some person in authority to my misfortune,
but I was soon awed into silence by the scowling looks
and threatening hushes of the indignant audience ; so I
quietly sat out the play, my feeling of interest in which
was not altogether extinguished, though of course very
much weakened by the sense of my own painful position. I left the theatre in a very unhappy frame of
mind, and on reaching the street found that it had
been raining heavily. I had to walk home through
the wet muddy streets with nothing on my feet but a

pair of thin white stockings which were soon *not* white. On arriving at home, my distressed looks instantly attracted the notice of my mother, who in a tone of alarm asked what had happened to her dear boy, but on learning from my confession what *had* happened, and how it had been brought about, she gave her dear boy such a thrashing as made him ever afterwards retain a very vivid recollection of his visit to the Ruff Street Theatre.

This visit, which, like a melodrama, terminated with the detection and punishment of vice, was the only one I ever paid to the gallery of a theatre during my schoolboy days; but during the term of my apprenticeship I was a regular Saturday-night frequenter of the galleries of the various theatres of the town in which I resided during that time; and since I have been " lord of myself" I have had an extensive experience among the gods in all parts of England. For though I have not exactly fulfilled the terms of the secretly registered vow of my childhood, to go to the theatre every night when I was a man, I have been, and still am, a pretty constant visitor to the galleries of the theatres of the towns in which I have been, or may be, residing or visiting; so that I am enabled to speak with all the authority of experience of the ways of the gods.

The regular frequenters of the gallery may be divided into the roughs, the hypocrites or snobs, and the orderlies. Of these the roughs are the most numerous division; it consists of those who come to the theatre with unwashed faces and in ragged and dirty attire, who bring bottles of drink with them, who *will* smoke despite of the notice that " smoking is strictly prohibited," and that " officers will be in attendance;" who favour the band with a stamping accompaniment, and take the most noisy part in applauding or giving "the call" to the performers. The females of this class are generally accompanied by infants, who are sure to cry and make a disturbance at some interesting point in the performance. The snobs comprise those who will tell you that they prefer the gallery to any other part of the house, and that they would still go into it if the price of admission into it was as high as that charged for admission to the pit or boxes; nevertheless, they seem very ill at ease in the place of their choice, and shrink from the glances of the occupants of the pit and boxes. The snob, also, is of those who stand on the back seats, and while talking loudly among themselves, but *at* the other occupants of the gallery, are at great pains to inform you that they have merely come into the gallery for a "spree," or "just to see what kind of place it is," but who strangely enough are to be found there two or three nights a week, and are amongst the most deeply attentive portion of the audience. The orderlies are those who, while they admit that the gallery is the least comfortable, and it may be the least respectable part of the house, and that they would much rather be in the boxes, go into the gallery because it is the *cheapest* part of the house—because they can go into that part twice for the same amount of money that they would have to pay to go into any other part once.

Considering that the gods are, as a rule, passionately fond of the drama, the majority of them are surprisingly ignorant of all relating to it. Many of them have never heard of Betterton, Garrick, Kemble, or the other great theatrical names of a few generations back. And even since the tercentenary festival, I have sat side by side with a god who, after a thoughtful pause, hesitatingly confessed that he had heard something of a theatrical "bloke" named Shakspeare, and believed he had written

the play of "Jack Sheppard," but could not say whether
he lived in the time of Alfred the Great or George the
Fourth. Sometimes this ignorance on dramatic subjects
comes out in a very laughable manner ; for the gods are
very fond of talking upon such subjects, and will, with
that freedom from the trammels of etiquette which is
one of their characteristics, unceremoniously join in
the conversation of any persons who may be sitting
beside them. Owing to this habit, a god very often, to
use a gallery phrase, puts his foot into it. I remember
upon one occasion I was in the gallery of a theatre in
a populous county town, and between the acts of the
principal piece of the evening, I was speaking to a
friend who was with me. Our discourse turning upon
stage scenery, I said to him—alluding to the act
drop, which was, of course, straight before us—
" That seems a beautiful representation of the City of
Venice." " Yes," said my friend, " it is very good."
I was about to make some answer, when a man who
was seated next to me, and who had, I suppose, been
listening to our conversation, touched me on the
shoulder and said—" I say, mate, was the City of Venice
a theatrical cove ?" " Yes," said my friend, interposing
before I could reply to this strange question, " he was
an actor, and his name was ' City,' he used to play the
principal part in a celebrated tragedy called ' Venice
Preserved,' in the course of which he sung a song
entitled ' Beautiful Venice,' and so to distinguish him
from another and inferior actor of the same name, he
was called the ' City of Venice.' " " I had often heard
the name before," said my interrogator, who was much
pleased and interested by this explanation, " but I
never knew who he was, and so I thought as I heard
you speaking about him I would ask you." Another
time, while on a visit to Manchester, I went into the

Theatre Royal there. In order to secure a good seat, I had gone in half an hour before the time announced for the performance to commence. While waiting for the rise of the curtain, I entered into conversation with the man beside whom I was seated, and from him I learned that the drama with which the entertainments of the evening were to begin had been running for some weeks past, and that he had seen it twice. " What do you think of that ?" asked my new-found acquaintance at the end of the first act. " It's very good indeed," I answered. " Oh, that's nothing !" said he, evidently disappointed by my tone of admiration ; " *the murders haven't come yet.*" " That's cutting, isn't it ?" observed my acquaintance as the curtain descended on the last act of the drama. " Oh, yes," I said, in a slightly indifferent tone. " Well, it made me cry, anyhow," he said, with an emphasis that implied that that was an exceedingly strong and incontrovertible proof of the " cutting" nature of the drama. " Yes, it did," he continued, seeing that I made no reply ; " and so I must go and have a pint of beer ; will you come ?" " No, thank you." " Well, will you mind my seat till I come back ?" " Oh, yes," I said. There was a song and dance between the pieces, and while the dance was on my acquaintance returned. " What's next ?" he asked when he had resumed his seat. " A farce," I answered, looking at the playbill. " A farce," he said, repeating my words in a tone of inquiry ; " what's a farce ?" " Something laughable," I explained. " Oh, then, I don't like a farce," he said. " I like something deep, I do."

And this predilection for " something deep" is a general characteristic of the gods, who at all times prefer a melodrama or tragedy to a farce, however " laughable" or " screaming" the latter may be. But a burlesque, with its grotesque and beautiful dresses, cleverly arranged dances, and parodies on "new and popular songs," often finds favour in their sight; though the few good and the many feeble and far-fetched puns which a burlesque generally contains are quite thrown away upon the great majority of them. That the celestials are often noisy, and are sometimes given to discharging nutshells, peas, orange-peel, and other annoying, though harmless missiles, at the heads of the devoted occupants of the " regions below ;" and that their " chaff" often assumes an unpleasantly personal tone, previous to and during the intervals of the performance, is but too true. But as Falstaff was not only witty himself, but the cause of wit in others, so the celestials, during the progress of the performance, are not only orderly themselves, but the cause of order in others. For instance, when those two stupid-looking and more than half-drunken " swells," who have come into the boxes at half-price time, begin to annoy the audience by talking and laughing in a very loud tone, and making grimaces at and trying to interrupt the actresses, is it not the gods who bring them to order ? The scornful looks and indignant hushes from the pit and boxes have no effect upon them, but when, at the end of the scene, the gods give loud utterance to their well-known war-cry, " turn them out," the effect is instantly apparent. The swells at once subside into silence, and suddenly become very much interested in the perusal of the playbill. And beside materially assisting to keep order during the performance, it is admitted by all who know anything of theatrical matters, that the gods are by far the most lively portion of a theatrical audience, and the witticisms and eccentricities of those in the gallery are sometimes quite as entertaining as any part of the

legitimate performance. Most of the " good things "
of the gallery are, however, so intimately connected
with some local or incidental circumstance, as to lose
much of their wit and point, when heard by or repeated to persons who are unacquainted with those
circumstances, but still there are a few specimens of
gallery " wit and humour " that I have heard, that I
think will bear repeating. And should they appear
dull or stupid to the reader, the fault must be mine,
for they were decidedly " good " when I heard them,
and brought down as much laughter and applause in
the theatres where they were first spoken, as was ever
heard within the walls of those theatres. The incidents connected with the first of these " flashes of wit "
occurred in the principal theatre of an important seaport town, and were the means of fixing a nickname
upon a gentleman well known in that town, which
stuck to him till the day of his death, and by which
he became quite as well, if not better known, than by
his proper name. On the night on which these incidents took place, a then very popular tragedian was
making his farewell appearance in England, as he was
to sail for Australia on the following day. As this
actor was an especial favourite in L——, the theatre
was crowded in every part long before the rising of
the curtain. So great was the crowd that women were
fainting, children were screaming to be taken out, and
the worst phases of an over-crowded assembly were to
be seen and heard. When the performance began, it was
found to be utterly impossible to hear the actors, or
obtain silence among the audience. Many of the
most influential gentlemen in the town were, with
their families, seated in the boxes, and among them
Mr. R——, a well-known police-court magistrate,
who was noted for his severity to those who were

brought before him charged with being drunk or *disorderly*, for on persons so charged he generally inflicted the heavy (comparatively speaking) penalty of "forty shillings and costs." The performance had proceeded for about an hour and a half amidst a noise and clamour that practically converted the tragedy into a pantomime, when suddenly the densely packed audience seemed to have shaken and crushed themselves into something like a comfortable position, and a silence that, compared with the previous uproar, seemed almost death-like, reigned over the theatre. But this blissful state of things had scarcely lasted two minutes, when one of the gods shouted out, " Gentlemen, what is the meaning of all this quietness ? I'll go out !" and everybody beginning to cry " Order, order," the audience were again thrown into a state of uproar, and it was a full half hour before quietness was again restored, and then the same voice again called out, " What *is* the meaning of all this quietness?" But this time no one called order, but those who could manage to turn their heads looked in the direction from which the voice proceeded, to try and discover who this disturber of the peace was, and one of the most scrutinizing of the gazers was Mr. R———. " What is the meaning of all this quietness, I ask ?" the same voice again cried out. "Why, don't you see old forty-shillings-and-costs in the boxes?" shouted another of the gods, in that impatiently contemptuous tone which a person uses when giving what they consider to be a self-evident explanation of any circumstance, to some particularly stupid and obtuse party. This reply, though it put an end to all order for the remainder of the performance, was received with thunders of applause, and cries of " Bravo, gods," from all parts of the house, and the name thus bestowed upon him Mr. R——— was never able to get rid of.

On another occasion I was in one of the metropolitan theatres, on the Surrey side of the water, witnessing the performance of a very exciting " sensation " drama. The actor who played the principal character in the drama, and whom I shall call Bricks, seemed to be a particular favourite with the audience in general, and with the celestial portion of it in particular, and was applauded " to the very echo," whenever he made one of his numerous " points." In the closing scene of the drama, the character sustained by Bricks was killed, after a " terrific combat " against overwhelming odds, and in doing the "dying business" Bricks writhed about the stage in a style that a contortionist might have envied, and groaned in the hollowest and most approved melodramatic fashion, and altogether died so particularly "hard" that it might reasonably have been supposed that he was trying to give a practical illustration of the pain endured " when a giant dies." This hard dying pleased the gods immensely, and when at last Bricks lay still they applauded him most lustily, and when they had finished cheering, one of them, led away by his enthusiasm, stood upon his seat, and putting his hands to his mouth, so as to form a speaking trumpet, roared out at the topmost pitch of a very strong voice, " Die again, my bold Bricks ! die again !" and the cry being taken up by the other gods, was repeated with a frequency and strength of lungs, that proved sufficient to wake the (stage) dead. For, in obedience to the call, Bricks got up and *did* " die again," and the second dying was, if possible, harder than the first ; and if the applause of the gods is any reward for hard dying, Mr. Bricks did not go unrewarded, though I scarcely think he would relish the roars of laughter that succeeded the second burst of applause.

Of the style in which the gods will comment upon a bad performance, I will not speak, as it is well known to all play-goers, while those who are not play-goers have probably read " Great Expectations," and will remember how the gods criticised Mr. Wopsle's playing of Hamlet. When " chaffed " by the gods, actors generally stand on their dignity, and affect to treat the disapproval of the gallery with contempt. But should the derided actor be also a manager, he will sometimes resent the strictures passed upon him or his company by those in the celestial regions ; though as the gods are usually able to " speak for themselves," a manager seldom gains anything by such a mode of procedure, and sometimes gets the worst of the encounter. I was once present in a provincial theatre when a somewhat laughable occurrence of this kind took place. The " enterprising lessee " who had taken the theatre for a season, played " first parts," and was his own stage-manager ; and he was noted for putting his plays upon the stage in such a mutilated manner as to render them utterly incomprehensible to those who had never seen them played elsewhere, and almost unrecognisable by those who had. Of himself, and each and every member of his company, it could be truly said that they were emphatically, and in every sense of the word, " poor players," and breaks-down was the order of each performance. On the night in question, the manager having, despite of the energetic prompting that he received, broken down more frequently and more completely than usual, and the recommendation of the gods to " take him away " not having been complied with, they (the gods) loudly hissed him, whereupon he came to the front of the stage and made an " indignation " speech, in the course of which he attributed the " beggarly account

of empty boxes" that had characterized his term of
management to the malignant influence of the gods.
" It is their blackguard conduct, and nothing else,"
he said, " that has driven respectable persons from the
theatre, for I have done everything that a man could
do to attract the public.   I have introduced stars———"
" Oh, my *stars*, there's a fib !" broke in one of the gods.
" Oh, no, it's not," shouted another, " for he's introduced *star*-vation amongst his company."   " I have introduced stars," repeated the manager, heedless of the
interruption, " and I have introduced pieces."   " We
know you've introduced *pieces*," derisively shouted
another of the gods, " *and nothing but pieces*, for you
have never given a complete play yet ;" and his well-
known abridging propensities making this a palpable
hit, the manager wisely withdrew from the contest, and
assuming his tragedy air and his " I am ready ; lead
on " stride, left the stage.

ABOUT PENNY READINGS.

FEW persons who have had the pleasure of witnessing a performance of that charming and most pathetic little drama " My Poll and my Partner Joe," will fail to remember the amusing character of the old cobbler nicknamed " The Bishop of Battersea," and his cry of " Hear me preach ! hear me preach," with which, when in his cups, he breaks in upon all kinds of conversation. As it is a really life-like drama, and appeals to the hearts, and enlists the sympathies of an audience, My Poll and my Partner Joe has of course been sensationed off the stage, and it is now several years since I last saw it performed, but still I never hear any person volunteering a display of their pet accomplishment, without being reminded of the Bishop of Battersea, and his " Hear me preach."   I meet the bishop, so to speak, under a great variety of aspects.   Thus when my friend Crotchet, the able organizer and leader of our workshop band, who, since he composed what by courtesy was called *the music* to the " inaugural ode," which was sung at the opening of the Boughtborough National Schools, openly expresses his opinion that Balfe is an over-rated man,—when Crotchet, I say, takes me by the arm, and begins to whistle into my devoted and outraged ear a farrago of discordant notes, and at the conclusion of the performance gives me the unnecessary information that it is " a bit of his own," I, in imagination, see the Bishop of Battersea emptying his can of drink, and rising to his feet, and hear him exclaiming, " Hear me preach." Again I am reminded of the bishop, when Jones, the retired grocer, who is the parochial potentate of our neighbourhood, informs me, after any public meeting of the parishioners, that he flatters himself that he has made an example of that fellow Biggins—" that fellow Biggins" being an irrepressible dissenter, who had immortalized himself in the estimation of the dissenters of Boughtborough, by allowing a portion of his household goods to be seized, rather than pay a church-rate of half-a-crown, and afterwards placarding the walls of the town with the text, " I hate robbery for a burnt offering," and who it is notorious is too much in the matter of argument for the self-complacent Jones. And if my friends adopted the Bishop of Battersea criterion, I have no doubt they would be reminded of that personage, when I invite them to hear me recite a few of the most telling speeches from my original blank-verse drama, which I am convinced would sweep sensationalism from the stage, if I could only find a manager sensible enough to bring it out.

Now when my energetic old friend Smith, president of the Boughtborough Histrionic Club, chairman of the local Mechanics' Institution, and the great promoter of all intellectual amusements in the borough, established the Penny Readings, and subsequently saluted me whenever we met, with, " You should come and hear me read," I, while replying, " I shall come and hear you some of these odd times," mentally put it down as another case of Bishop of Batterseaism. But as I began to hear upon all hands that the Penny Readings were " jolly things," and were "drawing immensely," I determined to attend one of the Boughtborough Penny Readings to hear my friend Smith read. Accordingly one Saturday night I wended my way to the Boughtborough music hall, a little before eight o'clock, at

which hour the doors of the hall were to be opened.
The hall was capable of holding fifteen hundred persons, and when I arrived in front of it, there was, so
far as I was able to judge, more than that number of
persons waiting outside.   Seeing that this was the
case, I joined actively in the rush that took place immediately the doors were opened, and after several
times asking and being asked those stock questions of
a rush, Where are you pushing to ? and Who are you
" scrouging ?" I succeeded in getting in and securing
a seat, and had reason to consider myself fortunate in doing so, as every inch of available space
in the hall was taken up, while there were still
many of the more timid members of the original
crowd outside.   The hall having filled so rapidly, the
audience were left to their own devices during a great
part of the half-hour that was to elapse before the commencement of the entertainments.   Those who had
come together, and in the crush were not divided, entered into conversations, which, owing to the shuffling
of feet and other noises arising from the movements of
a crowded audience settling themselves in their seats,
had to be carried on in so loud a tone that they
reached other ears than those for which they were exclusively intended.   Thus a lady who was seated
on the bench before me informed a gentleman, I
presume her husband, that it was a good job she
had not put her steel crinoline on that evening, as it
must certainly have been broken, and then began to
explain the various merits and demerits of steel, whale-
bone, and cane crinolines in general ; two gentlemen
behind me discussed the civil war at that time
raging in America, and speedily arrived at the conclusion that they could have conducted the affairs of
that then distracted country in a much abler manner

than President Lincoln and his cabinet ; while two
silver-voiced young ladies beside me descanted upon
the merits of " Lady Audley's Secret," and a number
of other novels of the same class, in a manner that
was at once rapturous and slangy. All these people
were probably in blissful ignorance of the fact that
their observations were heard as plainly by me and
others in surrounding seats as they were by the parties
to whom they were especially addressed. At least I
hope that it was so in the case of the novel-reading
young ladies. " Oh, talking of books, Bella," said
she who was seated nearest to me, "have you ever read
Shakspeare?" " Well, not exactly," said Bella ; " but
my brother has it." " Have you any idea what sort of
a book it is ?" asked the first speaker. " Well," said
Bella, speaking slowly, and in a doubtful tone, " it's a
very nice book, and full of beautiful plates." " Oh, I
don't mean that : what's it about ?" " It's about a
good many things, I think," said Bella. And then,
seeing that her friend was going to continue her
questioning, she got rid of the subject by cleverly adding,
" but I'll lend it you some day, and then you'll see."

Those of the audience who had no one with whom
to enter into conversation, and of this section I was
one, fell to consulting the programme of the evening's
entertainments, which was as follows :—

Pianoforte Solo .... Mr. Crotchet.

Reading......... { " *The Trial Scene from the* Mr. O. Rater.
Merchant of Venice " (*Shakspeare.*)

Song..................... " *The Gleaner* " ...... Mr. D. Robinson

Recitation ..... { "*The Combat* " *from* " *The* Mr. S. Poulter.
Lady of the Lake " (*Sir Walter Scott.*)

Flute Solo...... *Airs from* " *The Rose of Castile* " ... Mr. Potts.

Reading......... { " *Mr. Pickwick and the* Mr. Smith.
Lady with Yellow Curl (*Dickens.*)
Papers"

Glee ...." *Hail, Smiling Morn* "	Members of the Boughtborough Glee Union.
Recitation .... " *Lord Tom Noddy* "...	Mr. Brown. (*Barham.*)
Song........................ " *Madoline* "	Miss Arline Crotchet.
Reading......... "*The Rioters at the Maypole* "	Mr. Tomkins. (*Dickens.*)
Part Song......... " *The Red Cross Knight* "	Members of the Boughtborough Glee Union.

Precisely at eight o'clock, the chairman for the evening, who was no less a person than the proprietor and editor of the *Boughtborough Chronicle,* was introduced, and after he had made a few of the usual formal observations respecting his pride and pleasure at being called upon to preside over so numerous and respectable an audience, the entertainments of the evening commenced with Crotchet's performance of the pianoforte solo set down for him. As Crotchet was a really good pianist, and did not upon this occasion play " a bit of my own," but part of the overture to " Don Giovanni," his performance richly deserved the plaudits with which it was rewarded. Miss Crotchet's song was a greater success than even her father's solo, and there was an O. P. row upon a small scale in attempting to obtain a repetition of it ; but upon this point the chairman was as inexorable as our programmes, which informed us, in capital letters, that no encores would be allowed. The singing of the glee union was, likewise, a decided success. The readings and recitations, though not so uniformly effective as the musical part of the programme, were, upon the whole, of a highly pleasing character, as none of them were badly given ; while some of them were delivered with no inconsiderable degree of dramatic ability.

The scene from the *Merchant of Venice* was given in a tolerably good style, but I am afraid it scarcely conveyed a just idea of the genius of Shakspeare to the minds of the young ladies whose conversation I had been compelled to overhear, although they listened to it with commendable earnestness. At the conclusion of it, " Bella " merely remarked that Shylock was a " savage old beast," who would have been transported had he lived in England; while her companion made an observation to the effect that Portia's proceedings in enacting the part of the Doctor of Law was "just the sort of thing she would have been up to."

But the great feature of the evening was Smith's reading—the reading to hear which was the chief cause of my being present upon that occasion. The announcement that the next reading would be by Mr. Smith was received by a tremendous burst of cheering, and cries from the *habitués* of the readings of " Pickwick ! Pickwick !" a name which it appeared they had bestowed upon Smith in token of their admiration of the series of readings descriptive of the adventures of that immortal hero which he had given. And as he came upon the platform, his stout comfortable figure, and broad good-humoured face— although such an idea had never occurred to me before —now seemed to me to be the perfect realization of Pickwick in the flesh ; and when he had adjusted his gold-mounted spectacles, I involuntarily began to try and select a representative—Sam Weller, or at least a Mr. Snodgrass—from among the gentlemen assembled on the platform, and felt quite disappointed at not being able to do so. Smith happily proved to be one of those scarce personages—a really good reader ; and throughout his reading successfully maintained the illusion which his appearance had created, and kept his audience in almost continual "roars of laughter." Even his cough, when he was supposed to be hidden behind the bed curtains, had "method in it," and conveyed to those who heard it, as plainly as words could have done, the mingled feeling of horror, and a desire to explain and apologize, which a stout, respectable, middle-aged "party" would naturally be supposed to experience on finding himself in a bed-room with a lady in yellow curl-papers. At the conclusion of the reading I joined heartily in the tumultuous applause which was so deservedly bestowed upon Smith.

From that hour I became an ardent admirer of penny readings. In the course of the pilgrimages which in the pursuit of my profession I am compelled to take, I have attended them in all parts of England, and more especially in the manufacturing districts, and I am glad to find that they are exceedingly popular all over the country. Of the many plans that have been devised for providing the working classes with that amusement of which, it is admitted upon all hands, they stand in need, the penny readings, considered upon the principle of judging a tree by its fruits, are the best. The many thousands of working men and boys who frequent them give unmistakable evidence of their appreciation of them ; and, apart from this consideration, I know, from constantly mingling with the working men of the densely populated manufacturing towns, that the penny readings are immensely popular with them. The low price of admission to, and the intrinsic merits of the various performances to be witnessed at these entertainments are, of course, their chief attraction ; but I find that among working men the fact that there is no parade of special or pecuniary patronage of their class connected with them (the readings) is, also, a great attraction ;

and this seems to be understood by the managers of the majority of the readings, as they are careful to notify in their bills that there are " No Reserved Seats." In an opera-house, theatre, or concert-room, where all ranks of society attend, and where " the talent " is paid for, and the amusements are a speculation upon the part of the " enterprising lessee " who provides them, reserved seats and graduated scales of payment are imperative necessities; but in connexion with penny readings reserved seats are a mistake, as there is no pecuniary necessity for their institution, and they are in antagonism to the social spirit in which the readings were first conceived. In some few cases, where the penny readings have been unfortunate enough to fall into the hands of some petty speculator, or in small towns, which cheap gentility would fain have marked for its own, the name of the readings has been changed from the Penny to the Popular, and the price of admission raised to three-pence to all parts of the house ; but the immediate and decided falling off in the attendance that has ensued in consequence of such proceedings, has, in all cases of the kind that have come within my ken, speedily " put down " this movement, and brought the price to the legitimate penny.

Independently of the attraction which lies in their cheapness, and the absence from them of oppressive patronage, the " Penny Readings " are peculiarly well calculated to draw large audiences of all classes of working-men, save that now fast decreasing section of them whose only amusement is to be found in the pot-house. Thanks to the vastness and variety of English literature, age cannot wither, or custom stale the infinite variety of the selections which may be given at these readings ; and the amateur musician has a world before him where to choose, almost as varied.

The person who does not hear something to please him at a penny reading must have a very exclusive taste indeed; but if it should happen that only some one or two pieces out of a programme of ten or a dozen should be to the taste of some peculiarly fastidious hearer, he will still have the consolation of feeling—unless he is utterly unconscionable—that the one or two pieces are "worth all the money." At these readings the *really* "intelligent artisan" may get a taste of the great authors of whom he has heard, but whose works he has no opportunity of reading, and may listen once more to the beauties of the authors whom he has already read and admired; while the great unread may, in a body, and while sitting at their ease, listen to the wit and wisdom that have already charmed many generations of readers. Those whose knowledge of Shakspeare has been limited to the witnessing of a performance of a mutilated "acting edition" of some two or three of the most popular tragedies, may at a penny reading learn that his works contain manifold beauties which never appear on the stage. They may, if their imaginations be made of penetrable stuff, while in a crowded gas-lit hall, in a busy city, and on a dull, dreary mid-winter night, indulge in a Midsummer Night's Dream, as they listen to the glorious description of the moonlight revels of Titania and her fairy train. Or if they have any appreciation of genuine comedy, they may enjoy a hearty laugh over the humours of the scene in which Falstaff utters his memorable bragging tirade against "all cowards," and learn, by the way, from the fat knight's exclamation, "You rogue, there's lime in this sack," that even in his day publicans were suspected of "doctoring"

their drinks. In the course of the evening the audience of a penny reading may listen to the beauties of
Shakspeare and Tennyson, may have presented to
their mind's eye, by means of the glowing language of
that greatest of all historical word-painters—Macaulay,
some graphic picture of the life of a past time, may
admire the mingled humour and pathos of Hood and
Dickens, the polished wit of Sheridan, and the manly
humbug-smashing, but still truly humorous satire of
Thackeray. But while the readings are, as I have
already intimated, of a widely diversified character,
there are about a dozen favourite pieces, some one or
more of which you are almost certain to hear at any
reading you may chance to go to. These are, in
serious poetry—Tennyson's " Charge of the Six Hundred," Walter Scott's " Death of Marmion," Professor
Aytoun's " Execution of Montrose," Hood's " Eugene
Aram's Dream," and " The Eve of the Battle," from
Byron's " Childe Harold ;" in comic or serio-comic
verse—Barham's " Lord Tom Noddy," Hood's " Mary's
Ghost," and Thackeray's " Jeames of Buckley Square "
(in conjunction with which latter piece, the " indignation letter," in which the outraged Jeames repudiates
the aspersions cast upon his character in the ballad, is
in some instances read) ; in prose, the famous trial of
Bardell *versus* Pickwick, and some one of the " Caudle
Lectures," Sala's " Accepted Addresses," and latterly
of the Artemus Ward " Letters," and " Brown Papers."
The capabilities of those who give their services at
these readings are, of course, of various orders of
merit. Connected with those readings that have been
established for any considerable length of time, there
are generally a few really good readers, who can
always be relied upon to please the audience.
Managers usually secure the services of one or more

of these established favourites for each evening, and
the other performers can generally read in a sufficiently effective style to convey the true sense of what
they read to their hearers (and even this is an accomplishment by no means so common as could be wished).
Occasionally, however, some rash being, whose ambi-
tion has o'erleaped itself, and landed him upon a
public platform, goes through what he has undertaken
to do in a droning, sing-song manner, that irresistibly
reminds you of the " twice one are two-oo-oo " style,
in which the scholars of a National infant-school chant
the multiplication table ; while others roar and rant
until sense is murdered.   The favourite pieces which I
have named above serve admirably to show how really
great and valuable an art is that of being able to read
or declaim well.   At these penny readings I have
heard such spirit-stirring pieces as " The Charge of
the Six Hundred," " The Death of Marmion," and
" The Eve of the Battle," read by some men without
making the slightest impression upon the audience ;
while, when delivered by " other and better men," the
same pieces have roused the hearers to the utmost
enthusiasm.   You could then see by the restless movements and flushed cheeks of those around you, that
they felt " some far-off touch " of the spirit that had
animated the breasts of " the six hundred ;" you
could tell, by the changes of attitude and sparkling
eyes, that they felt " the situation," when they heard
how, upon hearing of the terrible death of Constance
de Beverley, the mortally wounded Lord Marmion

> " Started from the ground
> As light as if he felt no wound ; "

and again, when

> " With dying hand above his head,
> He shook the fragment of his blade,
> And shouted VICTORY."

Nor is it in the delivery of poetry alone that the differing effects of good and bad reading are so strikingly manifest, as by dint of *very* bad reading it is possible to dim the brilliancy of such gems as the trial of Bardell *versus* Pickwick, and Jeames's letter anent the ballad " Jeames of Buckley Square."

The pieces given at a penny reading should as a rule be of a light and popular character. Rhymed verse of a dramatic or narrative kind seems to " take" best, and after that comic or satiric prose gives the most satisfaction ; but poetic prose, or purely picturesque or philosophic blank verse, as yet finds little favour in the ears of the penny-headed multitude. I have frequently heard compositions of that class, even when given by good readers, coughed down, and always listened to impatiently.

But the readings given at these entertainments are only part of the evening's amusements : vocal and instrumental music now invariably form a considerable portion of the programme, and in this department more uniform excellence of execution is obtainable than in the reading. For moderately good, or at least mechanically accurate, amateur pianists, and performers upon the flute and cornet-à-piston, willing and anxious to discourse sweet music to their fellow-townsmen, are always to be found in abundance, and the glee and other musical associations now established in almost every town and village in England, furnish trained singers of fair ability. And it is pleasant to see that such fine old songs as " My Pretty Jane," " The Death of Nelson," and " Tom Bowling," find greater favour than the so-called comic songs of the modern music halls, or the equally senseless namby-pamby ballads that obtain in modern drawing-rooms.

As is the case with all sublunary institutions, penny

readings have their little drawbacks. For instance, I think that the practice of occasionally coughing or stamping down a bad reader, or dry piece, is neither courteous nor fair, for it should be remembered that those who appear upon any penny reading stage are amateurs, are giving their services gratuitously, and have in all probability come forward at the solicitation of the managers. Coming before the public under such circumstances, it must be particularly hurtful to their feelings if either themselves or the pieces they have selected for reading are clamoured down. Such clamorous disapprobation is the more unseemly as it is altogether unnecessary, since by withholding the usual round of applause at the end of the reading, the audience would sufficiently indicate their feeling upon the matter, and at the same time be showing a juster sense of what was due to themselves and the gentlemen who take the trouble of organizing and conducting the entertainments. The matter most generally to be deplored, however, in connexion with penny readings is, that a number of cads—poverty-stricken puppies of the "jolly dogs" class—*will* come to them, and when there, persistently annoy the performers and disturb the respectable portion of the audience, without respect to persons, or the good or bad qualities of the entertainments. These nondescripts are would-be "swells;" they are for the most part do-nothing fellows who sponge upon their relatives, and clerks and shopmen with incomes of from forty to seventy pounds a-year, the greater part of which income they spend in fashionable slop clothing. They are the objects who are to be met any evening, in twos and threes, like male "unfortunates," walking up and down the streets, that being their only way of spending their leisure time; for they are too foolish and frivolous to occupy themselves in any intellectual pursuit, and too poor to " go into company." The extremely low price of admission to the penny readings, and the opportunity of displaying at them their cheap finery, have unfortunately attracted the attention of this, the most despicable section of snobdom, and these " respectably attired " persons manage to get in. They generally remain standing, and group themselves in a conspicuous position; and then, partially because it is their nature so to do, and partially in the hope of impressing the audience with the idea that it is simply for a lark that they have come there, they bawl out all kinds of senseless slang, under the impression that they are wittily " chaffing" the performers. The genuine swell is a being to be admired; the gracefulness of carriage almost inseparably associated with high breeding enables *him* to carry off his " get up " in a manner " that may become a man," and though even among the true swells there are black sheep, they are in the majority of instances, despite their affectations, good men. But your cheap imitation swell— the " gent " of the present generation—is an utterly despicable creature, fit only to be kicked.

Although I have had a tolerably extensive experience among them, and have a large acquaintance with managers of them, I have only met with one instance of anything in the nature of opposition to these readings. But as this case gives an illustration of the manner in which intolerant, unreasoning, religious bigotry *would* interfere in secular matters, if it had the power or opportunity, I may be allowed to cite it. In a town that *is* a hundred miles, and considerably more, from London, and which in most things is as many years behind the times as it is miles distant from the metropolis, but to which a few intelligent and liberal-minded men have found their way, there is a large hall, which was built by public subscription, but the management of which was unhappily invested in the hands of the chiefs of a band of pre-eminently fanatical teetotalers, who were also sense-less bigots. A number of the "men of the time" established a weekly series of penny readings, and hired this hall as the place wherein to give them. The natives flocked to the readings in shoals, and for some five or six weeks all went well. But after that time a rumour became current in the town, that those who had the control of the hall were trying to put down the entertainments, and on the managers of the readings being put to the question on this point, they were obliged to confess that it was " an ower true tale." Those in whom the power of letting the hall was vested, the managers stated, *had* tried to put down the readings, by withdrawing the use of the hall. Finding that they could not do that until the quarter for which they had let it had expired, they had done all that they could under the circumstances—namely, given notice that they would not again let it for penny readings after the expiration of the three months. The cause of this opposition was not occasioned by any sacrilegious visitor to the readings having, after the manner of frequenters of theatre galleries, taken beer into this teetotally consecrated hall, or any bacchanalian vocalist having sung " The Good Rhine Wine," or " The Glorious Vintage of Champagne;" which might have been a comprehensible reason for their proceedings. The fact was that at one of the readings a clergyman of the town had read Shelley's beautiful little poem " The Cloud." Upon hearing this, the orthodox souls of the trustees were alarmed; the works of infidels, said they, were being read in their hall—a state of things which of course was not to be tolerated; and so, with pious indignation at the desecration their hall had sustained, and sorrow for those misguided beings who had complacently listened to the infidel doctrines taught in " The Cloud " (for though ordinary minds may not be able to see anything save a piece of beautiful description in this poem, it must of course contain infidel doctrine, since Shelley wrote it), they rescued the hall from further contamination.

That penny readings are one of the best institutions that have been yet established with a view of affording rational amusement for " the million," and that they have had, and are still exercising a most beneficial influence upon them, no person who is acquainted with the manners and customs of, and accustomed to mingling with the said million, can for a moment doubt. Their cheapness puts them within the reach of every working man, and in their variety, working men of almost every taste find something to suit them, and large numbers of working boys now attend them; who, were they not at the readings, would probably be at some disreputable " penny gaff," or roaming about the streets, getting into mischief, or perhaps, thanks to the pernicious " thieves' literature," which is at present ruining hundreds of boys, planning some scheme for becoming " boy house-breakers" or " boy highwaymen." Nor is the good effect of these entertainments limited to affording a passing hour's amusement, as in many cases within my own knowledge, working men whose reading, previous to the establishment of such amusements, had been confined to the trashiest of the halfpenny and penny serials, have, through attending these readings, been led to become readers of sound authors.

PART III.

SOCIAL AND DOMESTIC LIFE.

———

WORKING MEN'S SATURDAYS.

WHEN " from six to six " was the order of the day for six days a week, working men regarded the seventh with the sentiment expressed by the lover of " Sally in our Alley," when he sings—

> " Of all the days that's in the week
> I dearly love but one day,
> And that's the day that always comes
> 'Twixt Saturday and Monday."

But among those who enjoy the benefits of the Saturday half-holiday, this tone of feeling has been considerably modified; and, indeed, it is now a stock saying with many working men, that *Saturday* is the best day of the week, as it is a short working day, and Sunday has to come; and this latter is a much more important consideration to the working man than to the uninitiated it would appear to be.

The working man has necessarily to defer the trans-acting of many little pieces of business to the end of the week; and when he had to work till six o'clock on Saturdays, by the time he had washed himself and changed his clothes, taken his tea, and got through the deferred pieces of business, he was generally thoroughly tired, and it was near bed-time, and Sunday was upon him before he knew where he was. And though, in point of fact, this did not lessen the material comforts of the day of rest, yet every one knows that the previous contemplation and mind-picturing of pleasures to come is in itself a pleasure of no mean order, in some cases (and the working man's long " lie in " on a Sunday morning is one of these) anticipation not only lends enchantment to the view, but really gives an added charm to the realization of the looked-for joy. On " week days " the working man wakes or is roused from his toil-worn sleep, or from delightful dreams of a new and blissful state of society, in which it is permitted to all working men to lose a quarter every day in the week, about five or half-past five o'clock in the morning, in order that he may be at his work by six. And when awake he *must* get up, however much he may feel disposed to have another turn round, for workshop bells are among the things that wait for no man, and the habitual losing of quarters is a practice that leads to that unpleasant thing—to working men—" the sack," and so, to slightly alter a line from the " Three Fishers," " Men must work, while women may sleep." Early rising *may* make a man healthy, wealthy, and wise ; but there can be no doubt that it is a great bore when it is compulsory, and when the heavy-sleeping working man, or the one who acts upon the plan of gaining length of days by stealing a few hours from the night, reluctantly " tumbles out," he thinks to himself, " I shall be in there again pretty soon to-night." But when night comes, and he has had a good wash and a good tea, he feels like a giant refreshed ; and having settled himself comfortably by the fireside, or gone out for his evening stroll, he feels almost as unwilling to go to bed early as he does to leave it, and thus morning after morning he has to fight his battles o'er again. Sometimes he does not wake until a little after his usual hour; he will then hastily consider whether he can get to his work in time, decide to try it, spring out of bed, huddle on his clothes, and, without waiting to light his pipe, rush off, and just come in sight of the workshop gate in time to see it shut, and to join with two or three equally unfortunate mates in heaping curses loud and deep upon the gatekeeper. But on Sunday morning there is none of this. On that morning, when from force of habit the working man wakens at his usual time— I know several enthusiastic individuals who have themselves "called" on that morning the same as any other, in order that they may make sure of thoroughly enjoying the situation—and for a confused moment or two thinks about getting up, he suddenly remembers him that it is Sunday, and joyously drawing the clothes tighter around him, he consumes time generally, and morning quarters in particular, and resolves to have a long "lie in," and in many instances to have breakfast in bed. And on all these things the working man who benefits by the half-holiday movement can, when taking it easy on a Saturday afternoon, pleasingly ponder.

For only working men can thoroughly appreciate or understand all that is embodied in that chiefest pleasure of the working man's Sunday, "a quarter in bed." To any late-rising, *blasé* gentlemen who may be in search of a new pleasure, I would strongly recommend the adoption of some plan—(if nothing better occurred to them, they might commit some offence against the law, that would lead to a term of imprisonment "without the option of a fine")—that would for a time make rising at a fixed and early hour compulsory, and when the morning arrives upon which they can once more indulge in a "lie in," they may exclaim, *Eureka!* for they will have found a new and great pleasure.

The working half of Saturday is up at one o'clock, and that wished-for hour seems to come round quicker on that day than any other. In a well-ordered workshop every man is allowed a certain time each Saturday for "tidying up," sweeping of the floor and benches, cleaning and laying out in order of the tools. This is completed a minute or two before one o'clock; and when the workmen, with newly-washed hands and their shop jackets or slops rolled up under their arms, stand in groups waiting for the ringing of the bell, it is a sight well worth seeing, and one in which the working man is, all things considered, perhaps seen at his best. He is in good humour with himself and fellow-workman; is in his working clothes, in which he feels and moves at ease, and not unfrequently looks a nobler fellow than when "cleaned;" and is surrounded by the machinery with which he is quite at home. When the bell rings the men leave the works in a leisurely way that contrasts rather strongly with the eagerness with which they leave at other times; but once outside the workshop gates, the younger apprentices and other boys immediately devote themselves to the business of pleasure. They will be seen gathering together in a manner that plainly indicates that there is "something in the wind." The something in the wind may be a fight that is to come off between Tommy Jones, *alias* "Bubbly," and Billy Smith, otherwise "The Jockey," owing to the latter sportingly-inclined young gentleman having openly boasted that he could take Mary Ann Stubbins for a walk any time he liked; Miss S. being a young lady of fourteen, the daughter of a retail greengrocer, and generally regarded as the lady-love of Bubbly, it being notorious that she gives him much larger ha'p'orths of apples than any other boy, and—when her father is not looking—supplies him with roasting potatoes free of charge.   Or the something in the wind may be a hunt after a monstrous rat that is believed to haunt a neighbouring pond ; or perhaps the something is the carrying out of a hostile demonstration against the butcher who rents the field adjoining the workshop, and who has been so unreasonable as to object to their catching his pony and riding it by three at a time.

The first proceeding of the workmen upon reaching home is to get their dinner, which they eat upon Saturday and Sunday only in a leisurely manner ; and after dinner the smokers charge, light, and smoke their pipes, still in a leisurely and contemplative manner unknown to them at other times.   By the time they have finished their pipes it is probably two o'clock, and they then proceed to clean themselves up—that phrase being equivalent among " the great unwashed" to the society one of performing your toilet.   The first part of the cleaning-up process consists in " a good wash," and it is completed by an entire change of dress.   A favourite plan of cleaning-up on Saturday afternoons is—among those who live within easy reach of public baths—to take their clean suits to the bath, and put them on after they have bathed, bringing away their working suits tied up in a bundle.   Some of the higher-paid mechanics present a very different appearance when cleaned up from that which they presented an hour or two before, when we saw them sauntering out of the shop gates.   Working-class swelldom breaks out for the short time in which it is permitted to do so in all the butterfly

brilliance of " fashionably" made clothes, with splendid
accessories in collars, scarves, and cheap jewellery. But
neither the will nor the means to " come the swell" are
given to all men, and a favourite Saturday evening
costume with the mass of working men consists of the
clean moleskin or cord trousers that are to be worn at
work during the ensuing week, black coat and waistcoat, a cap of a somewhat sporting character, and a
muffler more or less gaudy.   Of course, the manner in
which working men spend their Saturday afternoon is
dependent upon their temperaments, tastes, and domestic circumstances. The man who goes home from
his work on a Saturday only to find his house in dis-
order, with every article of furniture out of its place,
the floor unwashed or sloppy from uncompleted washing, his wife slovenly, his children untidy, his dinner
not yet ready or spoilt in the cooking, is much more
likely to go " on the spree" than the man who finds
his house in order, the furniture glistening from the
recent polishing, the burnished steel fire-irons looking doubly resplendent from the bright glow of the
cheerful fire, his well-cooked dinner ready laid on a
snowy cloth, and his wife and children tidy and cheerful.   If the man whose household work is neglected
or mismanaged is, as sometimes happens, of a meek
character, and has been unfortunate enough to get for
a wife a woman who is a termagant as well as a sloven,
or one of those lazy, lackadaisical, *London-Journal-*
reading ladies with whom working men are more and
more curst, he will have to devote his Saturday afternoon to assisting in the woman's work of his own house.
But when the husband is not of the requisite meekness
of spirit, he hastens from the disorderly scene, and
roams about in a frame of mind that predisposes him
to seek the questionable comforts of the public-house,

or to enter upon some other form of dissipation. On
the other hand, the man who has a clever and industrious wife, whose home is so managed that it
is always cosy and cheerful when he is in it, finds
there a charm, which, if he is endowed with an ordinary
share of manliness and self-respect, will render him
insensible to the allurements of meretricious amusements. In no rank of society have home influences so
great a power for good or evil, as among the working
classes. Drunkenness is in many cases, doubtless, the
result of innate depravity, and a confirmed drunkard
is rarely to be reclaimed by home comforts, which to
his degraded mind offer no charm; but at the same
time there can be no doubt in the mind of any person
who is acquainted with the manners and habits of the
working classes, that thousands of working men are
driven by lazy, slovenly, mismanaging wives, to courses
which ultimately result in their becoming drunkards
and disreputable members of society.

There has been a great deal written and said about
what is called modern servantgalism; and while there
could, no doubt, be a good deal said respecting ill-
tempered, ignorant, selfish, and " genteel " mistresses,
there is equally little room for doubt that the complaints against modern female servants are " founded
on facts." To those whose lot it is to employ servant
girls, the combination of vanity, affectation, ignorance,
and impudence, which go to make up servantgalism,
may afford amusement as well as cause annoyance.
But it is no joke when we consider that these
servant girls, and their compeers the shop and dress-
maker girls, are the class who become the wives of
working men and the mothers of their children.
Servantgalish ideas and sentiments are, in a general
way, the result of the universal fastness of the age, of

the all-pervading desire for the possession of wealth,
and the love of display, which developes Robsons and
Redpaths, causes Jones, ex-greengrocer, to publicly intimate that it is his intention to be known for the
future by the name of Fitzherbert, and brings so many
" fashionably attired" young men before the magistrates.
But while the general character of the age we live in
may in a great measure be held responsible for the
vanity, love of dress and high notions which characterize the female domestic mind, and in a still more
remarkable degree the minds of the " young ladies" of
millinery and other establishments, there is a *special*
element which contributes directly to the generation
and fostering of the worst spirit of servantgalism.
That special element is the devotion of those
females to the perusal of the tales published in the
cheap serials, of which they (the class of females in
question) are the chief supporters.   The miscellaneous
parts of these serials, the " household receipts," " sayings witty and humorous," and the " ladies' page,"
may, though dull, be harmless and even instructive ;
nor is there anything immoral in the tales, which
are the chief and most injurious features of these
publications.   On the contrary, it is the tremendous
triumph and excessive reward—of which a rich, titled
and handsome husband is invariably a part—awarded
in them, to virtue, as embodied in the person of a
" poor but virtuous maiden," which is the most objectionable part of these tales; and which, taken in conjunction with the distorted views of life which they
contain, and the exaggerated splendour and luxury of
their accessories, make them the most pernicious of all
works, not of a directly immoral character, that can
be placed in the hands of poor, half-educated, and not
particularly strong-minded girls.   That poor but vir-

tuous maidens occasionally find rich and titled husbands is doubtless true, but still constantly harping on this string, and mingling the sensational adventures of the stock virtuous maiden, and the poor clerk or travelling artist, who ultimately turns out to be a rich nobleman, with splendid carriages, gorgeous dresses, dazzling jewellery, and luxurious boudoirs, is scarcely the way to make the general run of poor but virtuous maidens contented with their position in life. For neither their type of mind, nor the nature of their education is of a kind that fits them for making fine distinctions, and they are wont to argue in this wise, "Are not we, too, poor and virtuous? and should not we therefore also get rich husbands, be dressed in gorgeous garments, and wear costly jewellery, and lounge in magnificently furnished boudoirs?" The discontented and hankering spirit which these stories create in the silly girls who read them, render them particularly liable to become a prey to any "fashionably attired" scamp who can use the high-flown language of the stories themselves. To uninterested observers the ideas of those whose minds are inflamed by these absurd tales may appear simply ludicrous; but to those upon whom they have a direct bearing they have a sad as well as a grotesque aspect. Household duties are neglected in order to find time to read the tales, or discuss with some sympathetic soul the probable means whereby some "lowly heroine" will ultimately defeat the schemes of the intriguing and demoniac Duchess of Bloomington, and marry that mysterious young gentleman with the raven locks and marble brow, at present employed in the shawl department of the West-end emporium at which the duchess deals, and whom she and the reader know to be the true heir to the richest earldom in England.

And when the tale-tainted wife begins to contrast the manners and language of her commonplace husband with those of Lord Cecil Harborough, or the Honourable Algernon Mount Harcourt, the result may be imagined. In short, these publications pander to a very dangerous kind of vanity. I am fully aware that the labouring classes have benefited largely by cheap literature, but at the same time I am bound to say, speaking from an extensive experience among those classes, that the particular class of cheap literature of which I have been speaking exercises a most injurious influence upon them, and is frequently the insidious cause of bitter shame and misery, as well as a potent cause of the squalor and mismanagement so often found in the homes of even the higher-paid portion of the working classes.

Taking it for granted that the representative working men have tolerably comfortable homes, their methods of spending their Saturday afternoons will then depend upon their respective tastes and habits. The steady family man who is " thoroughly domesticated " will probably settle himself by the fireside, and having lit his pipe, devote himself to the perusal of his weekly newspaper. He will go through the police intelligence with a patience and perseverance worthy of a better cause, then through the murders of the week, proceed from them to the reviews of books, and " varieties original and select," take a passing glance at the sporting intelligence, and finally learns from the leading articles that he is a cruelly " ground-down " and virtually enslaved individual, who has no friend or well-wisher in this unfairly constituted world save only the " we " of the articles. This is generally about the range of a first reading. The foreign intelligence, news

from the provinces, answers to correspondents, and
" enormous gooseberry " paragraphs, being left for a
future occasion. By the time such first reading has been
got through tea-time is near—for an early tea, a tea to
which all the members of the family sit down together,
and at which the relishes of the season abound to an
extent known only to a Saturday and a pay-day, is a
stock part of a working man's Saturday. The family
man, whom the wives of other working men describe
to their husbands as " something like a husband,"
but who is probably regarded by his own wife as a
bore, and by his shopmates as a mollicot—will go
marketing with or for his wife, and will consider his
afternoon well spent if he succeeds in " beating-down "
a butterman to the extent of three-halfpence. The
unmarried man who "finds himself," and who is of a
scraping disposition, or cannot trust his landlady, will
also spend his afternoon in marketing. Many of the
unmarried, and some of the younger of the married
men of the working classes, are now members of
volunteer corps, workshop bands, or boat clubs, and
devote many of their Saturday afternoons to drill,
band practice, or rowing. When not engaged in any
of the above pursuits, the men of this class go for an
afternoon stroll—sometimes to some suburban semi-
country inn, at others " round town." In the latter
case, they are much given to gazing in at shop windows—particularly of newsagents, where illustrated
papers and periodicals are displayed, and outfitters,
in which the young mechanic who is " keeping company " with a " young lady," and upon whom it is
therefore incumbent to " cut a dash," can see those
great bargains in gorgeous and fashionable scarfs
marked up at the sacrificial price of 1s. 11¾d. Those
men who are bent upon improving their general

education, or mastering those branches of learning—
generally mathematics and mechanical drawing—
which will be most useful to them, spend their Saturday afternoons in reading.   Other men again, who
are naturally of a mechanical or artistic turn of
mind, and industriously inclined, employ their Saturday afternoon in constructing articles of the class
of which so much has been seen during the last
two years at industrial exhibitions; or in making,
altering, or improving some article of furniture.   But
whatever may be the nature of their Saturday afternoon proceedings, working men contrive to bring them
to a conclusion in time for an early (about five o'clock)
tea, so as to leave themselves a long evening.

Burns' " Cotter's Saturday Night," though one of
the best of his many fine poems, and an enchanting
picture of natural and *possible* " rural felicity," and
probably a truthful description of the *best* pastoral life
of the period, would be in no respect applicable as
a description of the Saturday nights of the present
generation of working men and their families.   How
cotters of the agricultural labourer class spend their
Saturday nights I am not in a position to say, but it
is quite certain that if compared with the model cotter
of the poem, the artisan class of the present day would
show a decided falling off in moral picturesqueness.
The " intelligent artisan " (I merely state the fact)
does not spend his Saturday night by his ain fireside,
or devote it to family worship, and however " hale-
some parritch "—" thick dick " he would call it—
may be, he would emphatically object to it as a Saturday night's supper.   The lover of the modern Jenny,
when going courting on Saturday night, will *not*
rap gently at the door, but will give an authoritative
ran tan upon the knocker; and on being admitted

will not be " sae bashfu' and sae grave." On the
contrary, he will have a free-and-easy, almost patronizing manner, will greet Jenny in an off-handed style,
and tell her to look sharp and get her things on; and
while she is dressing, he will enter into familiar conversation with her father, incidentally telling him to
what place of amusement he is going to take Jenny,
and perhaps informing him that he has put a crown on
the Cheshire Nobbler for that pugilistic celebrity's
forthcoming encounter with the Whitechapel Crusher.
When Jenny is ready he will take his departure with
her, merely observing that he will see her home all
right, and feeling proudly conscious that he has fully
impressed his parents-in-law that are to be with the
fact that he is a young man who " knows his way
about." In other words, he is not a Scotch cotter,
but an English mechanic.

After tea those men who have been out during
the afternoon generally stay in for an hour's rest before
setting forth on their evening ramble in search of
amusement, while those who have been at home, go
out in order to get through any business they may
have on hand before the amusement begins. Saturday being the only time at which working men can
safely indulge in any amusement that involves staying
out late at night, and being moreover a time when
they are flush of money, and when they can get to
the entrance of any place of entertainment in time
to take part in the first rush, and so secure a good
seat, they avail themselves of this combination of for-
tuitous circumstances, and hence the crowded state of
theatre galleries on that night, and the notice on
music-hall orders that they are not available on Saturdays. The theatre is the most popular resort of
pleasure-seeking workmen, and the gallery their

favourite part of the house.   Two or three mates
generally go together, taking with them a joint-stock
bottle of drink and a suitable supply of eatables.
Or sometimes two or three married couples, who have
" no encumbrance," or who have got some neighbour
to look after their children, make up a party, the
women carrying a plentiful supply of provisions.   To
the *habitués* of the stalls and boxes the eating and
drinking that goes on in the gallery may appear to be
mere gluttony, though the fact really is that it is a
simple necessity.   There is scarcely a theatre gallery in
England from the back seats of which it is possible to
see and hear with any degree of comfort, or in a manner
that will enable you to comprehend the action of the
piece without standing during the whole of the performance, and standing up in a gallery crowd is a thing
to be contemplated with horror.   In order to get a
place in the gallery of a well attended theatre on a
Saturday night from which you can witness the performance while seated, it is necessary to be at the
entrance at least half an hour before the doors open,
and when they do open you have to take part in a
rush and struggle the fierceness of which can only
be credited by those who have taken part in such en-
counters.   And when you have at length fought your
way up the narrow, inconvenient, vault-like staircase,
and into a seat, and have recovered sufficiently to reconnoitre your position, you find yourself one of a
perspiring crowd, closely packed in an ill-lighted, ill-
ventilated, black hole of Calcutta like pen, to which
the fumes of gas in the lower parts of the house
ascend.   It is not unlikely, too, that you find yourself
seated next to some individual who has been rendered
ferociously quarrelsome by having been half strangled
in the struggle at the doors, and who, upon your being

unavoidably pressed against him, tells you in a significant manner, not to " scrouge " *him* whoever else you
scrouge. To endure this martyrdom some substantial
nourishment is absolutely necessary, and the refreshments of the gods provided by the theatrical purveyors
of them, being of a sickly and poisonous, rather than
an ambrosial character, consisting for the most part of
ale and porter, originally bad, and shaken in being
carried about until it has become muddy to the sight
and abominable to the taste ; rotten fruit, and biscuits
stale to the degree of semi-putrefaction ; those gods who
take a supply of refreshments with them when they
go to a theatre, display, not gluttony, but a wise regard for their health and comfort. After the theatres,
the music-halls are the most popular places of Saturday night resort with working men, as at them they
can combine the drinking of the Saturday night glass,
and the smoking of the Saturday night pipe, with the
seeing and hearing of a variety of entertainments,
ranging from magnificent ballets and marvellous
scenic illusions to inferior tumbling, and from well-
given operatic selections to the most idiotic of the
so-called comic songs of the Jolly Dogs class. Music-
halls being practically large public-houses, it is not,
as a matter of course, permitted to take refreshments
into them. The refreshments supplied in these halls,
however, are generally moderately good, but at the
same time more than moderately dear, while the
waiters, who, in accordance with the usage of these
establishments, have to be pecuniarily " remembered "
each time that they refill your glass or bring you the
most trifling article, haunt you in an oppressive and vam-
pirish manner if you venture to linger over your drink ;
and, all things considered, it is not too much to say that,
notwithstanding the comparatively low prices of admis-

sion to them, music-halls are about the dearest places of amusement that a working man can frequent. Next to the theatres and music-halls, the shilling, sixpenny, and threepenny " hops " of the dancing academies and saloons which abound in manufacturing districts, are the amusements most affected by the younger and more spruce of unmarried working men. And it is at these cheap dancing *academies* (which, not being connected, as the *saloons* generally are, with public-houses, are looked upon as exclusive and genteel establishments) that unfortunate working men generally make the acquaintance of those young ladies of the millinery and dressmaking persuasion, who entertain secret hopes of one day marrying a gentleman ; but who, unhappily for society in general and the working classes in particular, become the slovenly mismanaging wives of working men. Other men spend their Saturday nights at public-house " free-and-easies," from which they will come home happy if the comic or sentimental song—the learning of which has been their sole mental labour during the past week—has been favourably received by their free-and-easy brethren.

Of course there are some of my class who prefer above all things to spend a quiet Saturday evening in a reading-room, or at a working man's club, though the members of these clubs are by no means so numerous, nor is the success of the institutions themselves so great as might be supposed from so much having been written and said about them. But, however differently working men may spend the bulk of their Saturday night, it is an almost invariable practice with those of them who are not teetotallers, to " drop in " some time during the night at some house of call, in order to have a pipe and glass in company with the friends or shopmates who frequent the house. For though drunkenness is happily giving way to "manly moderation" among the working classes, they have not yet reached the bigoted stage of anti-alcoholic belief that would decree that because they are virtuous, there should be no more pipes and ale.

And while the men of the artisan class (the class that has chiefly benefited by the Saturday half-holiday movement) now look upon Saturday as in many respects the best day of the week, their wives and families also regard it as a red-letter day. For on that day Mrs. Jones, the blacksmith's wife, gets the new bonnet or dress without which, she assures her husband, she is not fit to be seen out of doors ; or the new article of parlour furniture, lacking which—since she has seen a similar piece of furniture at her neighbour Mrs. Brown's house—she is, she tells Jones, quite ashamed when any decent body calls to see them. On that day, little Billy Jones gets the new jacket, and his sister Polly the new frock, which will draw upon them the envy or admiration of their companions at Sunday school on the following day, and each of them will on Saturday receive the penny which is their weekly allowance of pocket-money, but which, owing to the promptings of their "sweet tooth," and the advice of not altogether disinterested, though for the time being extraordinarily affectionate playmates, they will spend a few hours after they have got it, and experience in consequence much remorse whenever during the ensuing week they see a great bargain in the way of toffee. On Saturday night too Billy and Polly are indulged in the dissipation of sitting up late, in order that they may have a share of the hot supper, which, like a tea with relishes, is also a characteristic of a working man's Saturday.

That the Saturday half-holiday movement is one of

the most practically beneficial that has ever been in-augurated with a view to the social improvement of "the masses," no one who is acquainted with its workings will for a moment doubt. It has made Saturday a day to be looked forward to by the working man with feelings of pleasurable anticipation, to be re-garded as the day on which he can enjoy many things, which but for it he would not have the opportunity of enjoying; and do many things tending to his own improvement, or the comfort of his family, to the doing of which he had formerly to devote that portion of his Saturday night which he can now spend in some re-creation.   It enables them to view their relative posi-tion in a rosier light than that in which they were wont to regard it, and to see that though they may often have to work whilst others play, they can also sometimes play when many others have to work : and disposes them to think that, notwithstanding that there are many hardships incidental to their station in life, they are not *quite* so " ground down," robbed and oppressed, as sundry spouters and writers who live on and by them would have them to believe.

But there is one aspect of the Saturday half-holiday movement in which those sections of the working classes who have benefited by it have been weighed and found wanting.   They have not as a body given the practical aid which, without any inconvenience to them-selves or their families, they might have done, and which as working men they ought to have done, to the extension of the movement among the less fortunate sections of their own class.   In the manufacturing trades the Saturday half-holiday is an almost general thing, and many of the largest employers of labour in those trades—both companies and private firms—now pay their workmen on Friday night, with an ex-

press view to facilitating early shopping and marketing
on Saturdays. And yet it is notorious that the late
shopping of the artisan class is the sole means of keeping thousands of shops open till eleven and twelve
o'clock on Saturday nights, and consequently of keeping tens of thousands of shopmen and assistants at work
till those late hours; thus making Saturday the worst
day of the week for them, and compelling them and
their families in many instances to do their shopping *on
Sundays*. Workmen of the artisan class are disposed to
entertain a rather contemptuous opinion of " counter-
skippers," but they should bear in mind that even
counter-skippers are men and brethren, who feel all
the irksomeness of confinement, and are doubtless
endowed with bumps that cause them to long for,
and would enable them to enjoy, a half-holiday.

It would be simply absurd to suppose that the sections of the working classes who already enjoy the
Saturday half-holiday could by any act of theirs *at
once* extend the movement to other sections, but still
it is in their power to do much towards it. If the
men in those trades in which the holiday is established
would follow an understood law, to have all Saturday marketing and shopping incidental to the requirements of themselves and families finished, as a general
rule, by four o'clock, the result would be that thousands of young men would be released from the bon-
dage of the counter some hours earlier on Saturday
night than they are at present. It is in the power of
the working classes to do much in this way, and the
thoughtlessness and indifference of many working men
on such points as these must often give additional
pain to those of their own class who suffer by it. And
I am sure it must have brought something of shame
as well as sorrow to the minds of many thoughtful

working men when, in the early part of 1866, the
clothiers' assistants in the large clothing establishments at the East-end of London brought their grievance (that of having to work seven days a week, and
ninety-four hours for a week's work) before the public,
and appealed to " the workmen of London to give them
one day's rest out of seven, by not shopping at clothing
establishments that continue to keep open on Sundays."
Occasions frequently arise in which large sections of
the working classes, and sometimes even the general
body of them, stand in need of the good opinion or
friendly assistance of other sections of society, and it
behoves them to show themselves deserving of assistance when their hour of need comes, by showing such
brotherly kindness and consideration for each other
as may be in their power, even if they *should* have to
make a little alteration in their habits to do so. And
of the matters in which it is in the power of some
sections of the working classes to render material
assistance to others, the extension of the Saturday
half-holiday movement is one of the most prominent,
and one in which aid may be given with little or no
self-sacrifice upon the part of the givers.

WORKING MEN'S SUNDAYS.

I.

MORNING.—SUNDAY DINNER.

APART from its religious aspect or the question of its
divine origin, Sunday is to the great majority of civilized mankind a most blessed day. To all classes of
society its calm and quiet, and comparative relaxation
from the bustle and labour of the business of life—the
clamour and weariness of which penetrates beyond the
immediate circle of the toilers and spinners—must
bring something of joy and contentment. It is a day
on which many of the wicked cease from troubling,
and the weary are at rest—a day which brings happiness alike to the truly religious, who regard it as a day
more specially devoted to the service of their Master;
to the dressily religious, who look upon it as a day, and
the church or chapel as the most fitting place, for
the triumphal inauguration of new bonnets or new
dresses; and the church-courtshiply-religious, who,
in church or on the way to or from it, manage to
exchange at least glances and signals with the beloved
beings from whom an unkind fate, in the shape of a
limited income or a stern parent, or something of
that kind, wholly divides them on other days; but
to none does it bring greater happiness than to
working men, and by none is it more eagerly looked
forward to, or keenly appreciated. To them it is lite-

rally a day of rest—a day but for the existence of which the portion of the primal curse that decreed that man should earn his bread by the sweat of his brow would to them be a curse indeed ! It is the greatest of all boons to labouring humanity, the brightest of the flowers that has been left them since the Fall, and is regarded by them as an inestimable treasure, even though the trail of the serpent is over it, inasmuch as the joys of the day are somewhat dimmed by the sad reflection that Sunday comes but once a week, and that in this uncertain climate of ours, those disastrous events, wet Sundays, are of frequent occurrence. But, taken with all its imperfections, the day is still itself alone, and stands out in joyous pre-eminence from the other six commonplace days of the week. It will naturally be supposed that those modern working class institutions, the Saturday half-holiday and the holiday of Saint Monday, have tended to dim the once all-exclusive glory of Sunday, and to a limited extent and in certain senses this supposition may be correct, since, much as they esteem the day, it is questionable whether the present generation of working men are capable of feeling that intense consciousness of its joys, and cheering and renovating influences, which *must* have been experienced by their less privileged and less well-cared-for brethren of former generations, to whom Sunday was the one sole break in the monotonous, wearying round of toil. Still this is only supposition ; and, so far as personal observation showeth, any tendency which these and other modern holiday institutions may have to detract from the high estimation in which Sunday is held, must have merely affected the longing for and ideal contemplation of the day. Viewed merely in the commonplace light of a weekly holiday, Sunday stands out superior to all others. The Saturday half-holiday is, as its name implies, only a partial holiday in respect to time, and its benefits have as yet been only partially extended, and its general effect among those who have benefited by it is chiefly to pave the way to a more thorough enjoyment of the Sunday, as sundry little things, the doing of which had at one time to be deferred to Sunday, can now be better and more appropriately done on Saturday.

However radical may be their ideas and practices upon other points, working men are undoubtedly conservative with respect to the chief joys and observances of their Sunday. No man can remember, nor is there the slightest tradition pointing to a time when working men did not take a pride in having, and look upon as necessary to the proper enjoyment of the Sunday, that outward and visible sign of working class respectability and prosperity, a Sunday suit; and "Susan's Sunday out" was a recognised institution generations before it became the theme for doggrel music-hall song, and when "The Kitchen Miscellany" and "The Scullery Journal," which, in conjunction with the example of the let-us-be-genteel-or-die classes, have developed modern servantgalism into "a thing to shudder at, not to see," were yet in an unimagined future. And Sunday clothes and servants' Sundays out—on which latter depends a great deal of that "keeping company" which among the working classes is the preliminary to the formation of a matrimonial partnership—still continue, and seem likely to continue to be the principal features in working-class Sundays. The opportunity of indulging without self-reproach in the luxury of "a long lie in," is the earliest and most universal of the delights of a working man's Sunday. It is believed that there are working men who often, and especially in the summer months, rise as early

upon Sunday mornings as they do on other mornings,
but such men are regarded as a sort of Wandering
Jews—men of evil conscience or bad digestion. There
are also well authenticated instances in which
unfortunate men who have been brought wholly under
" the wife's dominion," are habitually compelled to
rise at a comparatively early hour on Sunday mornings
and make the fire and tidy up the place before their
lazy and masterful or lazy and lackadaisical wives
come down, and it also occasionally happens that
comparatively early Sunday rising becomes a necessary
part of the arrangements for some special mode of
observing the day. But these cases form the exception to the rule ; and a " long lie in " in the morning
is an almost universal feature of a working man's
Sunday.

As the other standard and characteristic customs
of the day are also, practically speaking, universal ones,
a general idea of the manner in which the day is
passed among the working classes, and its influence
upon them, will perhaps be best conveyed by recording in a somewhat dramatic form the Sunday life
of an illustrative household—a household the Sunday
life of which is a type of the Sunday life of tens of
thousands of working class households in all parts of
the country. We will take a family of the working
class branch of the omnipresent Joneses. Some men
of a Sybaritish or sleepy-headed turn of mind, and those
who have not gone to bed till about the hour at which
on other mornings they are thinking of getting up,
indulge in the extravagance of breakfast in bed, and
those worthies after breakfasting again address themselves to " lying in " till eleven or twelve o'clock in the
day, just rising in time to have a leisurely wash and
dress and enjoy a comfortable pipe, and otherwise get

themselves thoroughly awake before their one or two o'clock dinner. The breakfast in bed section is, however, a very small one, and the great majority, in which our friend Jones is included, begin to turn out between nine and ten o'clock. By that time the reactionary, too-much-of-a-good-thing kind of feeling begins to set in, and morning, considered from a sleeper's point of view, begins to be made hideous by the noise and bustle which even, or rather *especially* on Sunday mornings, characterizes the working man's household. Mrs. Jones will have been up some hour or so before to make the fire, and prepare an early breakfast for her younger children, who have then to be arrayed in all the glories of their Sunday clothes, and started off to Sunday school. These proceedings involve a considerable amount of running up and downstairs, and of other noises which are however as soothing music compared with the sleep-murdering roars of the itinerant purveyors of breakfast "relishes," who shout with redoubled energy on this, their greatest trading day ; for extra relishes are a so universal and well understood part of a working man's Sunday breakfast as on that day to be scarcely regarded as relishes. First comes the cries of those who are going round with the various mixtures called milk ; this is immediately followed by "Watercresses ! all fresh-gathered watercresses ! two bundles for a ha'penny ;" while the watercress dealer pauses for a moment, the recitative of the shrimp man comes in. "Fine fresh Gravesend shrimps, fresh every day! penny a pint, shrimp O !" Then come " Fine Yarmouth bloaters, fine fresh Yarmouth! Prime smoked haddock!" and other cries, which only give way to be taken up by the yells of the costermongers who deal in dinner vegetables. But Jones, hardening himself against the disturbing influence of the cries of the relish merchants,

is preparing to have " another bit of a snooze " before
tumbling out, when his preparations are arrested by a
noise downstairs, of the cause of which he has from previous experience a pretty good general idea. His sons
Harry and Tommy, aged respectively fourteen and
twelve, though at work, have not altogether put away
childish things, and have on the night before spent part
of their weekly allowance of pocket-money in eatables,
Harry bringing home two or three sausages, and Tommy
a rasher of bacon, and they are now quarrelling for the
right of precedence in cooking these, the relishes of their
choice. Tommy founds his claim on the grounds of
being already in possession, and having been downstairs first ; Harry on the ground that he is the
elder. " O ay," says Tommy, " wouldn't you like to !
I shall shift when I'm done, and not before ; I was
here first, and I shall cook my bacon first, so I tell
you." " Well," exclaims Harry, " it's a nice go this is,
that you are to come it over me ; if I'd been that cheeky
when I was your age, I'd have known of it pretty
quick. But I tell you what it is, our Tommy, if you
don't shift with being told civil, I'll shift you in a way
you wont like." " Will you, our Harry?" says Tommy,
defiantly ; " you *wont* though, and you'd better not try
either. If you want to cook your old sausages, your best
plan will be to leave me alone, for the more you don't
get on with me, the more sooner I'll be done ;" and he
doggedly goes on with his cooking. But presently he
half shrieks, half cries, " Oh mother, just look here !
our Harry has been and sopped up all my bacon liquor
with his bread." " Well, you should shift, then," says
Harry, sulkily. " I'll shift your ear for you, my gentleman, if I come down to you," roars Jones from his
bedroom, and this produces a brief silence, which is
broken by a loud yell, the cause of which is explained

by Mrs. Jones calling upstairs, " You really must
come down to these lads ! here's Harry made Tommy's
nose bleed again ! " " He shouldn't have bit a lump
off my sausage, then," shouts Harry. " Only you
wait till my nose stops bleeding," replies Tommy, who,
attended by his mother, is bathing his nose. " You'd
better stop where you are," says Harry, threateningly.
" Ah ! you think you can cock it over me," answers
Tommy, " but Bill Smith is the boy for you, and he ain't
yer size, either." " It's a lie ! " roars Harry, " I'll
fight him one hand, any day." " Well, you'll see,"
shouts Tommy ; and then there is a sound of rushing
and scuffling, and Tommy is heard crying, " Let me
get at him," and Harry replying, " Yes, let him come
on, mother, and see what he'll get." Jones, hastily
descending, is met by the sight of a tableau of Tommy
armed with a soap-box, and affecting to be desperately
struggling to break from his mother's restraining
grasp, in order to rush upon and annihilate Harry,
who, with the remains of his sausage in one hand,
stands on the defensive in a Tom Sayers' attitude. The
appearance of the father upon the scene at once restores order, and then Mrs. Jones completes the preparations for the substantial family breakfast. But
just as she is chipping her egg, she bethinks her of
her lodger, a young journeyman employed in the
same establishment as her husband, and who has
lodged with her ever since—on coming " out of his
time," two years back—he came up to " the big city "
to get the London polish and London wages ; and
for whom, as he is a civil easy-going young fellow, a
pretty good sample of the rising generation of " intelligent artisans," she has something of a motherly
regard. Besides—as is often the practice of lodgers
of this class with their landladies — he calls her

mother; and he strikes her as being like what her
first-born boy would have been had *he* lived to be
three-and-twenty. " Do you know whether Charley
came in last night ?" she asks her husband. " I
don't know whether he came in *this morning*," replies the husband, smiling in a manner suggestive
of there being very little danger of Charley having
come in while it was yet night on a Saturday ;
" you'd better go up and see." Mrs. Jones accordingly goes upstairs, and will probably find either
that Charley has *not* come in, or that he has not
only come in himself, but brought some fellow-wan-
derer of the night with him. The latter happens to
be the case in the present instance, and after a minute
or two's hard knocking, Mrs. Jones succeeds in
awakening the heavy-slumbering Charley, who calls
out, " Holloa, mother, what time is it ? " " Ten
o'clock, Charley," replies Mrs. Jones ; " will you come
down to your breakfast, or shall I send it up ? " " Oh,
I'll come down ; I've got a mate with me," he answers.
" And mother," he calls, as he hears her turning away,
" do us some herrings, and make the coffee strong,
that's a good sort, and cut any quantity of bread, for
the fellow that I have got with me is an awful character to eat. Just send Tommy up with about a
bucket of water, for we are a couple of thirsty souls
this morning, and no mistake." " Ah, Charley," replies his landlady, reproachfully, " merry nights make
sorrowful days, remember." " No, upon my word,
mother," he cries—but Mrs. Jones cuts short her
lodger's defence by going downstairs. In a minute
afterwards Tommy takes up a jug of water, which
Charley eagerly seizes, and takes a long pull at,
then giving his companion, who has by this time
fallen asleep again, a dig in the ribs, hands it

over to him, saying, "Now sleepy-head, here's the water you've been making such a noise about." Then turning to Tommy, he asks, "How do I look this morning?" "Rather barmy," replies Tommy, smiling knowingly. "No, but *do* I, though," says Charley, in a dubious tone, which implies that he thinks and hopes that it is possible Tommy may be chaffing him. "Oh, you *do*, and no kid about it," Tommy repeats; "anybody could see you'd had your load on." "No, it ain't that," says Charley, "I didn't take what would have hurt anybody if it had been good; it's the quality not the quantity that's done it; we got some awful stuff, but we'll be all right when we've had a wash. What time was it when we came home, do you know?" Tommy replies that he does not know. "Oh, well, it don't matter," says Charley; "just take our shoes down and give them a brush, will you, that's a good chap; I'll give you threepence." Upon hearing this, Tommy, who has been spending his week's pocket money with the prodigal rashness of youth, seizes the boots and hastens downstairs; where he is heard telling Harry, to whom by this time he is perfectly reconciled, that Charley is going to give him threepence, and that now he will go in the raffle for Bill Smith's rabbits. When Charley and his companion, the latter looking rather sheepish, come down, Mrs. Jones, after good mornings, and the customary commonplaces respecting the weather have been exchanged between herself and husband and their lodger's guest, asks, "Will your friend wash in hot or cold water, Charley?" "Cold will suit you best, wont it Dick?" says Charley. "Rather!" replies Dick, and they go off to the wash-house, and come back looking considerably fresher. By this time the family breakfast has been concluded, and the breakfast table reset for Charley and his friend, who now sit down to it, the former, as he takes his first herring, apostrophizing it in a frequently quoted line from a forgotten poem of some inglorious Milton of the realistic school,

> " Oh, herring red,
> Thou art good with 'tatoes or with bread."

" I feel all the better for that lot," says Charley, when he has finished his breakfast ; " now I'll have a pipe, and then I'll be all right.   We were at the theatre last night, mother," he continues, when he and his friend have got their pipes fairly going, and have joined Jones in literally blowing a cloud.   " Oh, were you," says his landlady ; " which one did you go to ?" " The Adelphi, to see this ' Rip Van Winkle,' " answers Charley.   " What sort of a piece is it ?" asks Jones.   " Is it deep ?" asks Mrs. Jones.   " Yes, towards the end," answers Charley.   " You know, mother," he goes on, seeing that she is interested, " Rip is a drunken happy-go-lucky sort of a fellow, that wont stick to his work, and is always getting on the spree, and, of course, his wife can't see the beauty of it, and is always jawing him, and one night she turns him out in a dreadful thunderstorm, and he wanders into the mountains, and there he meets with the spirits of a lot of pirates, and they give him a glass of drink that brings on the sleep of twenty years.   Then, in the next act, you see him waking, an old white-headed man ; but he doesn't know it, for he thinks he's only been out all night, and when he gets back to the village everything is changed, and nobody knows him, and they think he's some silly old fellow ; but at last his daughter, that he had left a little girl, recognises him, and then comes the cutting part ; don't it, Dick ?"   " Yes," answers Dick ; " and he

does it splendid; you wont see many dry eyes in the
house then, I can tell you." By the time Charley
has finished his epitomized version of " Rip Van
Winkle," his landlady has washed up and put away
the breakfast things, and is commencing her preparations for dinner. For the Sunday dinner is by a long
way the most important culinary affair of the week;
and though its preparation and cooking is to the
managing and industrious housewife a labour of love,
it is also a labour of time, and must be started
pretty soon after breakfast, if dinner is to be on the
table at the fashionable working-class dining hour of
half-past one. A good plate of meat and potatoes,
with bread and cheese *ad libitum* to follow, is not a
bad " week day " dinner, even for so distinguished an
individual as " the intelligent artisan," but it must not
be compared with his Sunday one. The bill of fare
for a working man's Sunday dinner, will often include
a roast and a boil, three different dishes of vegetables,
and two different puddings, or pudding and tart, with
bread and cheese and celery, and plenty of beer.
Nor is it merely in the greater variety of meats
that warmly furnish forth the dinner table, that
the Sunday dinner is an important affair; it is eminently important as a social institution, and as a
means of beneficially influencing the manners and
customs of the working classes generally, from the
more or less elaborate and polite style in which it is
laid out and conducted. It is set out in the best
room, and on the best table, covered with the best
table-cloth, and the family plate, consisting of a plated
cruet-stand, a gravy-ladle, and pair of tablespoons,
and a salt-cellar and salt-spoon, with, of course,
the best set of knives and forks—the set which, save
on Sundays and such high days as Christmas-day and

Good Friday, are wrapped in a cloth, and carefully put
away among the family linen.   The carving, the helping to the various dishes and passing round of the
plates are gone through with all due forms and observances, which forms and observances, though trivial
matters in the abstract, are, like most other things,
useful in their place, and have undoubtedly a refining
effect upon men who for six days in the week have
neither the time, means, nor inclination for practising
those ceremonies which pertain to dining as a fine art.
Lastly, though by no means leastly, the Sunday dinner
is, with the exception of "Christmas time," the sole
vehicle for special family or friendly re-unions, and
express interchange of social rites and courtesies.   It
is true that there is generally a larger number of guests
at the Sunday tea than the Sunday dinner; but the
gathering at tea-time is of a miscellaneous and acciden-
tal character, while the dinner visitors are strictly
select, and join the family party by special invitation.
Any friend who may be passing your house about tea-
time, may, without the least impropriety, "turn in,"
and any mere acquaintance who may call during the
afternoon, is usually asked to stay and take a cup of
tea.   But any person who, without having some very
sufficient reason, was to drop in about dinner-time,
would be considered guilty of an impertinent intru-
sion; while no breach of hospitality is involved in
allowing morning callers to depart without hinting
at their staying to dinner, or even offering them that
back-handed kind of invitation which is perfectly understood to be given only that it may be declined, and
consists in coldly observing, as you are seeing your
visitor to the door, that you suppose he *wont* stay to
dinner.   In short, the Sunday dinner, and the customs
connected with it, are, socially considered, perhaps the

most important features, not only of the working man's
Sunday, but of his household life generally; and if
some of those "highly accomplished" middle-class
ladies, whose accomplishments, however, unfortunately
for their husbands, do not include any knowledge of
housekeeping or the management of servants, could
only see the style of Sunday dinner which "managing" wives of steady regularly employed mechanics,
of whom our Mrs. Jones is an example, turn out, they
would be very much, and not very agreeably surprised. Everything about the dinner is scrupulously
neat and clean, the general arrangement of the table,
as, with its equipment completed, it awaits the company, is harmoniously effective, and every dish is
well dressed. For Mrs. Jones has been a gentleman's
cook at a time when "flashing," "nobbling," and
"milking," now unblushingly resorted to by many
of the competitors in the race for wealth, were comparatively unknown, and when a really "good plain
cook" was sufficient for all the culinary requirements of a moderate establishment; and Mrs.
Jones "wont turn her back on any one at turning
out a plain dinner, though she says it as shouldn't.
None of your baker's dinners for her, thank you;
meat burnt to a cinder outside, and red raw inside;
and pies with scorched crusts and uncooked insides,
may do for your thriftless, know-nothing, dressmaking bodies, that don't know how to boil a potato,
but they wont suit her book, not to mention the toll.
Bakers with five or six children are all very well, but
when the mother doesn't lay in any meat of a Saturday, and the customers' joints come home on a Sunday with hardly any gravy, and the marks of slicing
to be seen on 'em, for all the basting and browning,
and the print of the knife that has been used in lifting

the tops of the pies, in order to toll the inside, are there to be seen, it looks suspicious to say the least of it. People may think it sharp to say that a baker who can't keep his family on toll, don't know his trade, but she don't believe in them keeping either themselves or their families at her expense; and, independent of that, she likes to do her own cooking, if you please." And the well-served, well-prepared, and abundant dinner, on the cooking of which Mrs. Jones thus discourses, costs, even with butcher's meat at cattle-plague prices, but ninepence per adult head; make a note of that, ye who are debating the marriage upon three hundred a year question. Of course the cost of the viands placed on the table would come to considerably more than ninepence a head per dinner; but then, after furnishing the Sunday dinner, these same " viands " will serve for supper, and warmed up they will also supply Monday's dinner, while what still remains of them after that, will, with a little helping out, do for the cold washing-day dinner of the Tuesday. But that ninepence a head defrays the expenses of the Sunday dinner proper is shown by the fact that that is the price charged to the single young men lodgers, who, even when they " find themselves," generally dine with their landlady's family on Sunday, and that the lodgers conscientiously endeavour to eat the worth of their money is well known.

And now, as, on our illustrative Sunday morning, Mrs. Jones proceeds to carry out her principle of doing her own cooking, her sons kindly volunteer to assist her, by peeling the apples, and shelling the peas; but this apparently disinterested offer is promptly and significantly declined; for their mother has found, by unprofitable experience, that somehow or other such

things as apples and peas do not go as far as usual
when they have undergone the preliminary preparations for cooking at the hands of Masters Tommy
and Harry. These young gentlemen, finding their
offers of service declined, and having been detected
and defeated in a joint attempt to steal some of the
apples, go out for a walk. Charley and his companion having smoked out their pipes, and finished
dressing (in their " second best " or night suits), also
prepare to go out. " Are you going to bring your
friend back to dinner with you, Charley?" asks his
landlady as he is going; for Charley, forgetful of the
proprieties, had on one or two occasions, without
giving any previous notice, brought such friends as
Dick with him to dinner, supposing, he said, that his
landlady would have taken it for granted that he
would do so. Such, however, is not his intention
upon the present occasion, for he answers, "Bring him
to dinner, eh! don't mention such a thing, I don't
want to see you eaten out of house and home."
" For shame, Charley," says the good-natured landlady ; " but don't you mind him, sir ; he gets on
with everybody, but I dare say you know him."
" What he says don't trouble me," replies Dick, whose
looks, however, scarcely bear out his assertion ; " the
fact is, ma'am, he's chaffing you ; he knows I'm a
small eater, and he asked me to stay to dinner,
but they'll be expecting me at my own place."
" Oh, well," says Charley, " cheek is everything, but
I wouldn't like to be a round of beef in his way all the
same." " Get along with you, do," says Mrs. Jones,
trying to get up a look of commiseration for Dick. As
Charley is getting along, she calls after him, " Be sure
you come in in time ; Jones's nephew and his girl are
coming, and dinner will be ready exactly at the half-

hour." "All right, mother," shouts Charley, "we are only going up to the barber's, and then for a bit of a turn round; I'll be home in lots of time."

Being now at full liberty, Mrs. Jones begins to bustle about in earnest, and Jones finding himself in the way in the kitchen, fills and lights his pipe afresh, and, taking *The Banner of Freedom* with him, retires to the parlour, and devotes himself to a second and more careful perusal of the weekly epistle of the terrific "EAGLE EYE;" who is constantly informing his readers, in a general way, that every beneficial measure passed by the Houses of Parliament, during the last quarter of a century, has been solely owing to his sleepless watchfulness of the various governments, and the awakening power of his letters. In his letter of this week he proves to demonstration that unless the working classes collect a sum of ten thousand pounds among themselves, and place it at the uncontrolled disposal of "The United Howlers Spouting League," of which "Eagle Eye" is treasurer, they (the working classes) will, in the course of a few months, be taken from their homes, and bought and sold as slaves by a bloated and bloodthirsty aristocracy.

When Charley and his friend get out of doors the latter is inclined to be sulky, but being, apart from his genteel notions, a good sort of a fellow, he is soon restored to good humour, when they get into a general conversation with some of their mutual friends whom they find in the barber's shop. Sunday morning is always an exceedingly busy time in a barber's shop in a working-class neighbourhood. Many of those who only shave once a week habitually choose Sunday for the operation; others, who usually undergo their weekly shave on Saturday, will sometimes, if they find the shop full when they call on that day, or are them-

selves very busy, or not going out till dark or something of that kind, defer the shaving till the next
morning.   Some again, who have been shaved on
the Saturday, but who are rather particular about
their personal appearance, have another "scrape" on the
Sunday-morning, in order to be " all of a piece," when
dressed in their Sunday clothes ; while the swellish-
inclined, who have already put on their Sunday suits,
and are going out for the day, come to have their hair
brushed and " done up." Again, numbers of men
who do not care about dressing to go for a morning
walk, and yet do not wish to be hanging about the
house while the cooking operations are going on,
take a shave or a brush-up as an excuse for joining
in the lively conversation and newsmongering of the
barber's shop.   There is a supply of the cheap weekly
papers on the seats, and those who are waiting their
turn, actively discuss and comment upon things in
general as recorded in these papers, local events and
character as known among themselves, and the performances at the various places of amusement they have
attended on the previous night.   " Have you seen this
'ere new piece at ' The Vick ?' " asks one of those who is
waiting his turn, as the advertisement of that theatre
meets his eye.   The question is put to the company
generally, and some one who has not seen the piece in
question replies to that effect, and asks what sort of a
piece it is.   " Stunning," says the first speaker warmly.
" I never see a better piece in my life.   It's very deep
all the way through.   There's three or four murders in
it, and Slogger's got a nobby part, ' Red-handed Ralph,
the Bloodhound of the Seas.' He makes you shiver
when he's doing the murders ; he looks so *gashly*
pale, and grinds his teeth so when he says, ' Now
for the bloody deed.' And Miss Howard, she's got

a good part too—she's Lady Clara Loamland, and
her father wants her to marry a villanous lord; but
she wont have anything to do with him, because she's
in love with Harry Lister, her father's gamekeeper,
and so the lord, he gets a gang of poachers to carry
her off to Red-handed Ralph's vessel. 'And now
my young lady,' he says to her, when he'd got her
aboard, 'I have ye in my power, and ye shall learn
what it is to scorn a De Melville.' 'O spare me !
spare me !' she says. 'Never,' says he, 'a De Melville never spares.' 'Then my blood be on your
head,' she says, and snatches up a dagger, and is just
going to stab herself, when a voice calls out, 'Hold,
Lady Clara, stay thy rash hand;' and down into the
cabin jumps the gamekeeper, and them as De Melville
had thought was poachers, but who were Harry's
friends in reality, because he had got to know the
lord's little game, and had took this way to put the
double on him. And then there's a terrific combat,
and Harry kills De Melville, and the pirates are taken
prisoners, and then it comes out that Harry is the
right Lord De Melville, only he had been stolen when
he was a child; and so he marries Lady Clara, and
gets the estate." "I'm blow'd if I don't wish I had
gone there," says the gentleman to whom this description has been more especially addressed, "for the
performance at the Borough was up to nothing. I
could play better myself than the duffer they've got
for the leading character. He's neither use nor orna-
ment; for he can't act a little bit ; and, as to the comic
character, I'm blessed if I don't think he's off his head—
he neither knows what to say or what to do with himself, and he goes wandering about the stage like a cat on
hot bricks." Personal, *very* personal banter of some
one or more of their number, is a usual mode among

the Sunday morning frequenters of barbers' shops of
enlivening their proceedings ; and a diversion in that
direction taking place at this point, the severe strictures upon the company of " The Borough " are cut
short. A young man of the would-be-if-they-could
type of swelldom has just taken his seat in the ope-
rating-chair, and to the barber's question of, " a
brush or a shave," replies, " A brush, and part it
down the middle." " Well," observes a gentleman
whose own personal appearance would be materially
improved if there was a little more of the swell and
less of the slouch about him, " Well, if I had such an
October cabbage as yours, I'd try if I could'nt brush
it at home." " Ah, now that's your nastiness, Bill,"
says another ; " if his head is big there's nothing in
it." " Now, you two fellows," says a third speaker,
" are only crabbed because you see that he's been to
' The Lane' this morning, and got another seven-
and-sixpenny coat." " Ay," adds a fourth, " and because he's got his gold guard from his uncle's, in
Lombardy." " His uncle's ?" says Bill, sarcastically ;
" you don't catch uncle taking in that sort of stuff;
why you can buy them kind of guards in Birmingham
at half-a-crown a bushel, and a basket in to carry
them away." " Do you mean to say it's not gold ?"
asks the previous speaker. " Gold !" repeats Bill,
sneeringly, " ay, the same sort of gold as brass candle-
sticks are made of." " Now, you know, Bill, you are
going on in that style, because he told Polly Roberts's
father he was a draughtsman," says our friend Charley.
" And so he is a draughtsman," replies Bill, who is
great in stock witticisms, " a full-sized draughtsman—
he draws a hand-cart." Each hit at the working
swell is followed by a burst of laughter, and, amid the
roar elicited by this last joke, he escapes, and the spirit

of chaff being now in the ascendant, another victim or two are tackled and discomfited. A rather sullen-looking personage, who comes in as the swell is going out, and who is known to pride himself upon the imperious manner in which he rules his very meek wife, is greeted with " Holloa ! what makes you look so like two pen'orth of God-help-us this morning? has your wife been beating you *again ?*" and the cue thus given, the chaffing goes on merrily.

But, " sweeter than this, than these, than all," than the discussion of general news or local events, the criticising of dramatic performances, the chaffing of acquaintances or the generally pleasant whiling away of an hour, is the Sunday morning attraction to some barbers' shops in the shape of various cunningly concocted " revivers," which are euphemistically styled medicines, and are privately retailed at threepence per dose to those with whom the barber is personally acquainted, or patients who are introduced by persons on whom he can rely. The disease for which these medicines are supposed to be specifics is that known as " Hot coppers," and it generally supervenes upon having had a drop too much overnight ; or in the case of working men having, while in a state of thirst, drank even a moderate quantity of the " Saturday night particular," sold in and about cheap places of amusement. Its symptoms are a more or less violent headache and unusual thirst. The medicines dispensed by barbers on Sunday mornings, for the remedy of this complaint, really to a certain extent act as revivers, and instead of producing wry faces and exclamations of abhorrence from the sufferers, give rise to lip-smacking and sighs of pleasure. Patients will often, of their own accord, call for a second dose immediately after taking the first ; a state of things sufficiently accounted for by the fact, that in taste the medicines are curiously like sweetened and spiced rum or brandy ; or should the patient prefer to have a colourless draught, gin or whisky. From some or all of these reasons Sunday morning is the busiest and most entertaining time in the establishments of those barbers who ply their craft on the chins and heads of "the working man." The proprietors of these establishments will do more trade between ten and three on a Sunday than they will do on any other day ; and, with the exception of Saturday, more than they will do in any three days of the week. For five days in the week the barber will be able to do all his business himself, and have a considerable amount of time to spare for the making and repairing of such articles as fishing-rods and bird-cages ; on Saturday, which is his busiest "week day," he will manage to get through his work with the aid of a boy to act as latherer ; but the run of trade on Sunday morning is so great as to necessitate the employment of two or three assistant shavers.

Having, in the course of about three-quarters of an hour, had a shave and a " reviver " each, Charley and his friend leave the barber's to go for a " bit of a turn round," and have not got far when they come upon and join company with three of their shopmates, who are also going for a turn round. Presently one of these three, a well-known lushington, dolefully observes that he is almost dying for a glass of beer, and proposes that they should go to " The Bird in Hand," as he knows he can get in there. What do they say ? Well, they don't care much about it, but still they don't mind, and so they direct their steps to the bye-street in which " The Bird in Hand " is situated. On reaching the back entrance of that not over-reputable hostelry the beer-

craving lushington gives a signal knock, and they are
at once admitted into a dimly-lighted kitchen, in which
about a score of men are already seated smoking and
drinking, and conversing in a low tone. As soon as
they are inside, the lushington calls for a pot of
porter, which he and his companions empty in the
first round ; and, having thus had what the lushington styles a " squencher," a second pot is called for.
They then seat themselves to drink at their leisure,
as they listen to the narrative of a gentleman who is
entertaining the company with a graphic account,
plentifully illustrated by appropriate action, of sundry
astonishing exploits that he professes to have performed when " tight " on the previous night, and
which led to his getting those honourable scars, which,
in the shape of a black eye, and broken nose, disfigure
his not particularly handsome visage. But while he
is yet in the midst of the description of the " terrific
combat," in which single-handed he had defeated a
band of fierce marauders from the slums, whom he
believed to have entertained a felonious design upon his
watch ; his story is brought to an abrupt conclusion
by the son of the landlord, who has been stationed
at an upper window which commanded a view of
the full length of the street, rushing downstairs
with the alarming intelligence that a " bobby " is
visible. In an instant all is confusion among the
group of drinkers. " Drink up," cries the landlord, and pots and glasses are rapidly emptied and
thrust into a closet, from the shelf of which the landlady takes down a large breakfast-tray, with a half-
consumed breakfast artistically arranged upon it, and
places it upon the table, which a minute before had
been covered with pots and pipes. A number of the
lushingtons, who know the " runs " of the house,

meanwhile betake themselves to places of conceal-
ment. These dispositions for the reception of an
enemy completed, the landlord hastens upstairs to
the look-out station to reconnoitre, and a pause of
anxiety ensues. In about a minute, which seems to
be at least ten, the landlord descends, and restores
peace of mind to his alarmed customers by saying,
" It's all right, there is a ' blue,' but he is one of the
right sort," which latter phrase being interpreted
means that this particular " blue " is one of that
tolerably numerous sort, who, provided a publican
tips them a " bob" occasionally, and is liberal in the
matter of drops of something short when they are on
night duty, will not see any Sunday-drinking that
may be carried on in his establishment, so long as it
is done with a decent show of secrecy. Reassured by
this information the drinkers resume their seats, and
have their pots and glasses re-filled. But not being
much used to, or caring about, this way of passing a portion of their Sunday morning, Charley and his friend
leave the house.

Having arranged with Dick to meet him at three
o'clock at a point at which those of the set of young
fellows to which they belong are in the habit of
assembling in the afternoon, Charley returns to
his lodgings, where he arrives about one o'clock,
so that he has time to change his clothes before
dinner; " dress " for Sunday dinner consisting of
the trousers and waistcoat of the Sunday suit, and
shirt sleeves—coats being regarded as impediments to
that freedom of action necessary for comfortably and
profitably plying a knife and fork. On coming downstairs after dressing, Charley is informed by his landlady that " Bill and his girl are in the parlour ; " and
being very friendly with Bill, and in consideration of

his being honoured with Bill's friendship a great favourite with "his girl," Nelly Edwards, Charley immediately enters the parlour, and warmly shakes hands with Bill and his sweetheart, asking the former how he is getting on, and how trade is with him, and telling the latter that she looks more killing than ever. To which Nelly replies, " If you get going on in that style, Master Charley, I shall have to tell Polly of you." " I don't suppose Polly cares anything about what I do," answers Charley, speaking with affected uncon- cern, but getting rather red in the face. " Well, no, I don't suppose she does much," says Nelly, smiling wickedly at her lover, who, seeing the hit, bursts out laughing, and says, " You had better leave her alone, Charley, she's one too many for you." " It's well she is, for it would be a bad job if a woman couldn't beat *any* fellow with her tongue; wouldn't it, Nelly?" " Well, as far as that goes, I daresay it would," replies Nelly; " but you've no need to cry out, you can use *your* tongue pretty well." " I don't know about that." " If *you* don't," replies Nelly, promptly, " Jane Brown does." " Jane Brown !" echoes Charley, trying to look surprised. " Yes, Jane Brown," repeats Nelly; " you needn't try to look so innocent over it, you was making love to her the night that you saw her home, when she had been here with Bill and me, you *know* you was, Charley." " Make love to her," answers Charley, smiling, " why, of course I did ; but you should have been the last to have told me about it, for it was seeing Bill cuddling you in the passage, when he was pretending to put your cloak on, that set me going." " Oh ! after that, *I'll* be going," says Nelly, running out of the room, and tucking up her dress as she goes along, so as to be ready to assist "mother," as she too calls Mrs. Jones,

in serving up dinner. In a few minutes she returns bearing a leg of mutton, which she places in
the centre of the table which has previously been laid
out. Jones follows immediately afterwards with a
large rabbit-pie, and is succeeded by Mrs. Jones with
a large dish of potatoes, while Nelly, who has again
been to the kitchen, returns a second time with the
peas and early cabbages, which dishes complete the
first course. While dinner is being brought in, the
opening and shutting of the street door, and a cry
of " Now just you drop it, our Harry, or else you'll
be made, and pretty sharp too," proclaims the return
of Harry and Tommy. These young gentlemen, on
their mother putting it to them whether they will
take their dinner with father, or in the kitchen with
their younger brother and sister, immediately decide to
go to the kitchen—the observance of dinner etiquette
and the supervision of " father " not being conducive
to their idea of comfortable dining. This point being
settled, the parlour company seat themselves.

Bill Johnson, Jones's favourite nephew, is in his
way a rising man, for though not yet thirty years of
age, he is already under-foreman to the large building
firm by whom he is employed, and has a salary of two-
pound-ten a week, and being a stalwart, healthy,
intelligent, and tolerably good-looking young fellow,
is upon the whole an exceedingly good match for the
plump, handsome Nelly Edwards, with whom he had
fallen desperately in love some six months before,
when superintending some repairs in the West-end
mansion in which she was in service as a housemaid.
Indeed, when the Joneses, who are Bill's nearest
living relatives, first heard of his engagement, they
were inclined to think that he was " throwing himself away ; " but when they came to know the merry,

kind-hearted, lovable Nelly, they soon altered their opinion, and assured Bill that he was lucky in meeting with such a girl, an opinion in which Mrs. Jones was further confirmed on finding that Nelly " was clever with her needle, a rare 'un at house-work, took up cooking wonderful, and had none of your faldaral notions about her." And Nelly being shortly to become one of the family, and being regarded by the members of it as though she were already one of themselves, and Charley being in more than a lodger-advertisement sense " treated as one of the family," the dinner party of the Joneses may upon this occasion be considered virtually a family one. For this reason some of the stricter and more melancholy of the formalities that would have been observed, had strangers been at table, are dispensed with. When dinner has fairly commenced there is not much conversation going on, and what does occur is of dinner dinnery. "That's a fine bit of mutton," says Jones. " It ought to be, too," says his wife, " it cost a fine price, I can tell you." " It's just done to a nicety, too," observes Charley. " Yes," chimes in Nelly, " you don't catch mother turning out any bad cookery, I shall come and take lessons from her when——" and then she hesitates and blushes; upon which Jones exclaims, " When you and Bill are married; out with it, we all know what you meant." At this they all laugh, and Bill getting confused knocks the treasured salt spoon off the table, upon which Charley calls out, with an air of mock concern, " Oh, hang it, Bill, mind the family plate, whatever you do." Presently Jones, who has in vain been trying to pick a rabbit-bone with his knife and fork, exclaims, "Well, excuse me, but fingers were made before knives," and putting aside the modern instruments as he speaks, he takes the bone

in his hand and falls to work to polish it with his teeth.
"Oh, well, if that's it," says Charley, "I'm with you,
or else I shall never be able to eat my ninepen'orth ;
and if that was to happen, I would never forgive
myself," and he too puts down his knife and fork
and takes a bone in his fingers. "They talk about
this and that not paying the old woman her ninepence," he goes on, "but it's very certain it'll never
pay the lodger *his* ninepence to stop to use a knife
and fork to his Sunday dinner while his landlord uses
his fingers." Finding that they are falling behind, and
seeing the example set them by their host, the other
members of the party also betake themselves to their
fingers ; and then the first course is speedily finished.
Mrs. Jones, assisted by Nelly, promptly and with very
little bustle, clears away the remains of the first course,
lays fresh plates and brings in an apple-pie and a rice-
pudding. "Which will you take, Bill ?" asks Mrs.
Jones when she is ready to serve. "I'll take a bit of
apple," he answers. "And you, Nelly ?" "The same,
please," says Nelly. "Apple for you too, Charley ?"
asks his landlady, when she has served Nelly. "No,"
answers Charley, "I'll have rice, it's nice and light, and
I must think of my constitution." "And so must I,"
says Jones. "Yes, you're a couple of delicate creatures,
I've no doubt," says Mrs. Jones, and having served them,
eating and conversation are resumed. The third and last
course, which consists of small preserve tarts, as a sort
of dessert, is eaten in a much more leisurely manner
than the two preceding ones, and the conversation over
it becomes more general. While they are chatting and
laughing and nibbling their tart, Harry and Tommy,
who have finished their dinner, are heard going out, and
negotiating a fifty per cent. loan transaction as they go
through the passage. "Lend us a penny, will you, Tommy,"

Harry is heard saying. "O-ay!" exclaims Tommy, in a tone intended to indicate that he is intensely astonished at the mere mention of, and utterly repudiates such an idea. " I'll give you three halfpence for it on Saturday if you will," urges Harry. "Yes! so you *say*," returns Tommy, doubtfully. "Oh, I will upon my word," Harry assures him earnestly. " But then I want to go into the raffle for the rabbits," Tommy observes. " Well, Bill 'll trust you a penny till Saturday, if you give him the other twopence," says Harry. " Do you think he will ?" asks Tommy, still doubtful. " I'm quite sure he will," replies Harry, emphatically. " And you're certain you'll give me the three halfpence on Saturday as soon as we're paid?" questions the unrelenting fifty per center. " Yes, upon my word and honour," replies his brother. "Say in double deed," persists the money lender in the tone of one administering some terribly binding oath. " In double deed," repeats Harry, solemnly. " Well, here you are then," says Tommy; "but mind you, if you don't pay me I'll tell father." " Oh, honour bright, what I say I'll do," answers Harry, pocketing the penny, and then they open the door and rush out whooping and yelling, and rattling on the railings as they pass.

While they have been listening to this, the party in the parlour have finished the tart, and Mrs. Jones and Nelly, after clearing the table, retire into the kitchen—a movement equivalent to the " society " one of the ladies retiring to the drawing-room, and leaving the gentlemen to their wine; which, seeing that they have neither drawing-rooms nor wine, is about as near an approach as people of the working classes can be expected to make to the observance of this the concluding part of the dinner ceremonial.

II.

AFTER DINNER.—GENERAL OBSERVATIONS.

WHEN left to themselves after dinner, the men charge and light their pipes, and enter into desultory conversation upon things in general, and the all-pervading Reform question is naturally the first topic touched upon. Jones refers in eulogistic terms to " Eagle Eye's " letter, and expresses his opinion to the effect that Eagle Eye is the boy for them—" them " being the supposed opponents to reform. Charley does not know so much about that ; men who knew Eagle Eye when he was at work, before he got to the delegate and spouting business, tell him (Charley) that he was a mischief-making fellow that could do nothing but talk. Bill believes that Eagle Eye is " the boy " for his own pocket. But Jones falling asleep, as is his custom of a Sunday afternoon, the subject is dropped, and Charley and Bill talk over the past week's races, the progress of a workshop brass band, and other matters, till Charley announces that he has to go out, and they then go into the kitchen, leaving Jones to the enjoyment of his forty winks. Bill joins the ladies, while Charley passes upstairs to get his coat and hat. " Will you be in to your tea ?" asks Mrs. Jones as he goes out. " I daresay I shall," he replies. But as he passes Nelly, that young lady whispers to him, " You know very well you'll be in ; Polly's coming." In a few minutes after Mrs. Jones goes upstairs to dress her hair and put her best cap on, and Bill embraces the opportunity —and Nelly—to snatch a kiss. When Mrs. Jones returns to the kitchen, Nelly praises her cap, and this leads to a rather technical conversation be-

tween them upon the subject of fashion and dress,
Bill being occasionally appealed to as to how *he* likes
some particular fashion. While this talk is still going
on, Jones, who has had his nap, joins them, and being
in his turn appealed to for an opinion upon the merits
of some of the fashions upon which his wife and Nelly are
discoursing, expresses views adverse to modern fashions
generally, and begins to talk of the time when he was a
boy, and is still holding forth upon that delightful period
when the conversation is broken up by the arrival of
his daughter Polly, the Polly to whom Nelly had
alluded when chaffing Charley, and who, it being her
Sunday out, has come, accompanied by one of her
fellow servants, to take tea with her parents. When
Polly and her friend have been welcomed, and
have taken their things—that is, their bonnets and
shawls—off, the whole of the party go into the parlour,
where comfortably seated they pass the interval till
tea time, in gossiping upon such subjects as chance or
the conversational powers of the company may bring
on the carpet.

In the meantime Charley has reached the place of
appointment, where he meets some half-dozen friends
and acquaintances. Greetings are exchanged, and
then the general body make one of their number
unhappy by glancing meaningly at a new coat that he
has got on, and telling him that it " fits him too much,"
that it is "like a ready-made shirt, fits where it
touches," and much more to the same disheartening
effect. Having got through these preliminaries they
start for " a stroll down the road," (as we are supposed to be in London, let us say that " the road " is
the Commercial or East India-road : a walk up or down
those roads being a favourite Sunday afternoon stroll
with work people of the East-end). As they go

sauntering leisurely along the road, they nod and are
nodded to by passing acquaintances, and one or other
of them occasionally drops behind for a minute or two
to speak to some more intimate friend ; and they have
not gone far before one or two of their number meet
their sweethearts, and turn back with them.

Further on they meet one of their shopmates, accompanied by his wife and two children, all looking
cheery and comfortable. After acknowledging their
respectful good afternoon, Mrs. Robinson passes on,
leaving her husband with a child in each hand to exchange a few words with his friends, who assure him
that he "looks all a father," and declare there is
no mistake about the young 'uns being Robinsons.
Then Charley, addressing the eldest child, a bright-
eyed four-year-old boy, as "Blacksmith," asks him
if his mother has got any more like him, whether
he thinks he could fight that chap (his father) if he
'would pull himself down to his weight, and finally,
whether he thinks he could eat a cake, and gives
him a penny ; then seeing that Mrs. Robinson has
come to a standstill, they say good afternoon to her
husband and stroll on. "Well, I only hope that
I shall be as comfortable as Bill when I'm married,"
observes one of them when Robinson is out of
hearing ; "there's no mistake about him having a
tidy wife, and they are about one of the happiest
couples in England, I should think. When that break-
down job came in last week, and Bill had to work till
ten, he asked me to call and tell his wife as I went
to my tea, and I'm blest if the house wasn't like
a little palace, and there was his tea laid out and
her nicely cleaned up, and everything regular first-
rate ; it was enough to make a fellow wish he was
married." "Ay," observes another of the party,

on the conclusion of this rather rhapsodical speech,
" Bill has got a different style of wife from poor
Joe Thomas.   Lord forbid that ever I *should* get
such a trollop as Joe's for a wife.   " Oh, so you
say now," observes one of his companions, " but
if ycu had her to deal with, and was spoony on her,
as Jce is, you would very likely do pretty much as
he does."   " I shouldn't, though," answers the other ;
" if my meals were never ready for me when I went
home, and the children were running about in the
gutter, unwashed and in their night dresses, when the
men were going home at dinner time, and remarks made
about it afterwards in the shop, it would soon take
the spooniness out of me, and I should say to myself,
' Joe, the best thing you can do is to slope.' "

The company now turn back and saunter home-
wards in the same leisurely way.   As they near the
point from which they started, they begin to drop
away in ones and twos, and Charley goes home to tea.
There he hopes to see, and does see, Polly, and with
an affectation of off-handedness, shakes hands with
her and asks her how she is getting on.   To this she
simply replies, " Oh! tidy, Charley, how are you?"
but it does not require any particularly acute observation to perceive that their hand shaking is a meaning
one, and that their eyes as they meet " look love
to eyes that speak again."   For Polly, with her
rosy cheeks, ripe lips, soft brown eyes and hair, neat
figure, and " winning ways," has palpably made a
conquest of Charley, and knowing this she scarcely
cares to conceal either from herself or others that
" the smite " is mutual.   Polly had been in the
country when Charley had gone to lodge with her
parents, but the family with whom she was in service
having come to live in London a few months

since, Polly had of course become a frequent visitor
to her parents, and always spent her Sundays out
with them, and she had soon, as Charley confidentially expressed it to his friend Dick, "put the stunners
on him." And though they were not as yet formally
engaged, "the situation" was fully understood by all
parties concerned, and the Joneses knew that Charley,
although still given to going to the theatres occasionally, and coming home late on Saturday nights, has
been "on the steady" almost from the first day of his
meeting Polly, and is saving money as hard as he can.

When the slight bustle caused by the entrance of
Charley has subsided, Mrs. Jones lays the tea
tray, and the bread-and-butter having been previously cut and the tea made, they are soon seated
at Sunday afternoon tea, the most formidable
appliance of the match-maker of working-class society,
and a really powerful means of promoting courtship
and matrimony among the working classes. The
gathering at tea-time is, as has already been noticed,
a larger, more promiscuous, and less ceremonious one
than the dinner party. Such eligible young men as may
call in the course of the afternoon to see fathers or big
brothers, or "our lodger," can be asked to remain to
tea without giving rise to suspicions of any ulterior
designs being entertained; at tea-time the women are
dressed in their best, and in the preparation and dis-
pensing of tea, female arts are supremely dominant.
Then the meal itself is of such a light, cheerful, cosy
character, and affords such unequalled opportunities
for the display of prettiness of manner. Teetotallers
talk of the victims to strong drink, and sing the
praises of tea as being the cup that cheers but
not inebriates, but could the number of "intelli-

gent artisans" who annually fall matrimonial victims
to Sunday afternoon tea be ascertained, the so-
called statistics of the teetotallers would become insignificant beside them.   "*Do* take another cup, now,
Mr. Brown," says Susan to young Jack Brown, who
had called to see her brother Tom, unconscious at the
time that Tom's sister, of whose existence he had
vaguely heard, had come home " out of place."   " Half
a cup now, come, just to keep me company," she continues, and without further parley she seizes his cup
and fills it again, smilingly asking as she prepares to
sweeten it, whether he is *quite* sure that the last cup
was "to his liking."   On being assured that it was
beautiful, she hands the cup to him, and their
hands accidentally touching, a thrill seizes Jack, and
Susan blushes.   Under such circumstances as these, a
cup of tea becomes a cup that *does* inebriate.   It sends
Jack into the seventh heaven of delight, and causes him
to be firmly impressed with the idea that if there is an
elysium on earth, it is this ! it is this ! it is to drink
tea on a Sunday afternoon in company with and under
the guidance of Tom Stokes's neatly-dressed, and flat-
teringly and tenderly attentive sister.

As upon this occasion there is no one at Mrs. Jones's
tea to be specially assailed, it serves principally as a
means of promoting social small talk and those banter-
ing allusions to love and matrimony which " in company" are indulged in by or at the expense of those
who are known to be already engaged, or supposed to
be progressing towards the engaged state.   Although
the Sunday tea is regarded less as a meal than as a
vehicle for pleasant social *réunions,* Mrs. Jones places
a plentiful supply of edibles, consisting of piled-up
plates of toast and bread-and-butter upon the table,

while Jones tells his guests there is plenty more in the
cupboard. Mrs. Jones fills the cups, and Polly grace-
fully hands them round. When Nelly has taken a few
sips, she pronounces it to be beautiful, and asks Mrs.
Jones how much per pound she might have paid for the
tea. " Five shillings, my dear," replies Mrs. Jones.
" I tried some of the cheap sorts as they talk so much
about, but, bless you, I couldn't get a good cup out of
it, however much I put in the pot." After the third cup,
the men cry enough, and Jones and his nephew keep
to their decision despite the entreaties of the ladies.
Charley, however, shows signs of weakness, and the
man who hesitates in refusing " another half-cup" at a
Sunday afternoon tea-party is lost. " You can manage
half a cup more," says Polly in reply to Charley's
reiterated " I've done." " Well, I don't like to say
no to a good thing," says Charley, " but really——"
" But really you'll take another cup," says Polly, and
he is martyred forthwith, and so the entertainment
closes. Mrs. Jones and her daughter then clear the
table, and prepare a second tea in the kitchen for
Harry and Tommy, who come in soon afterwards, and
as they have had a long walk, and regard tea in its
merely material aspect, looking upon any unnecessary
conversation during its progress as a culpable weakness,
they soon make a happy despatch of basins of tea and
large quantities of toast.

The boys being disposed of, Mrs. Jones and Polly
return to the parlour, and that apartment being very
small, and the centre table comparatively large, the
party are compelled to take close order, and in carrying out this movement Charley contrives to get beside
Polly on the sofa, and his love-making, which both he
and Polly fondly imagine to be unperceived, becomes
so manifest that Nelly believes she can see unmis-

takeable indications of Charley coming to a point that
night. When they are all comfortably fixed, conversation sets in. Mrs. Jones remarks upon the smallness of
her parlour, and this gives rise to Bill entering into a
glowing description of a mansion which their firm are
building for a City man, at the conclusion of which
Nelly takes up the conversational ball by recounting
some of the more notable incidents of a party that
her master had given in the preceding week. Then
the talk turning on amusements, Charley favours
the company with a much more elaborate account
of the plot of " Rip Van Winkle" than he had given
in the morning, and the ladies generally agree that
it must be a very nice play—Polly remarking that
it just puts her in mind of a part in " The Trials
and Triumphs of a Young Domestic," which is
coming out in the " Kitchen Miscellany." At seven
o'clock, Bill Johnson and Nelly take their leave, as
the latter has a considerable distance to go; and at
eight o'clock Polly, who has to be in at nine, also
takes her departure, Charley, of course, going to see
her home. And the fact that Polly did not reach her
master's house till a full half-hour after her time, and
that Charley looked very solemn on returning to his
lodgings, justify the supposition that Nelly's anticipa-
tions that Charley would wind up his proceedings on
this particular Sunday by " coming to the point" have
been fulfilled.

Thus, by chronicling the sayings and doings of a
representative set of people, I have tried to picture the
Sunday at home spent among the general run of the real
working classes, the steady-going, regularly-employed
artisans and labourers, and their wives and families.
There are of course infinite variations in matters of
detail. An artisan who has a less efficient helpmate

than our friend Jones, may have his Sunday dinner
badly cooked, and served at irregular hours, but even
under these circumstances it will be an incomparably
grander affair than his probably ill-cooked week-day
dinner, and those intimates whom he invited to it will
be welcomed as sincerely as though every dish were
" done to a turn," and placed on the table with in-
fallible punctuality. The labourer cannot of course
afford so extensive a bill of fare for his Sunday
dinner as the higher-paid mechanic (though there are
both labourers and mechanics who adopt the feast and
famine principle of living " high " during the two or
three days for which their week's wages last them,
and " hard " for the remainder of the week) ; but in
his degree he duly observes the customs, ceremonies,
and hospitalities incidental to the all-important institution of Sunday dinner. Again, the workman of the
smaller provincial towns is a more subdued individual
than the workman of great cities. Though he is substantially independent of the genteel powers that be, he
scarcely cares about flying in the face of their social
bye-laws, and would, for instance, be aghast at the
idea of his being seen in the streets on a Sunday
morning negligently dressed, and with a pipe in his
mouth, while the gentility of Tattleborough was on
its way to church. Such variations in details as these
are inevitable, but the substantial and characteristic observances of the day, the morning " lie in,"
the " extras " at meals, the gathering together of
friends and acquaintances at dinner and tea, the
servants' Sundays out, Sunday courtship, and most of
the other customs noticed in the chronicle of the
Sunday of the Jones household, are general.

" Outings " are a prominent feature in the working
man's Sunday. Once or twice in the course of the

season—especially if he has been doing pretty well in the way of overtime or piecework—Jones may take his wife and children for a Sunday trip to Brighton and back, and sometimes him and his family are asked to go and spend the day, and more frequently the afternoon, with some friends, and occasionally he will dine early, and, starting out immediately after dinner, take " the missus " to one of the parks, or for a trip down the river. Then Charley sometimes " makes one in four " for hiring a boat or trap for the day, and on some of Polly's Sundays out he will take her down to Greenwich, and insist upon being extravagant in the matter of standing eighteenpenny " teas with whitebait," and sixpenny donkey rides round Blackheath ; and these outings necessarily cause considerable alterations and modifications in the proceedings which characterize the Sunday at home. The arrangements for outings are generally made beforehand, and with the proviso " weather permitting," for a rainy day is fatal to " outing," and as " the rain it raineth every day," those by working people dreaded and objurgated events, wet Sundays, will occur. The worst case of all, however, is when, after a bright or comparatively fair morning—a morning that fully justifies the putting on of Sunday clothes—rain comes on in the afternoon, when the " outing" parties have reached their destination. Rain, under these circumstances, is a serious matter indeed, for then it not only breaks up parties and sours tempers, but also does material damage to the treasured Sunday clothes. At one fell sweep Jones' " superfine black," Mrs. Jones' new dress, and the bonnet and shawl on which Susan has expended the whole of her last quarter's wages, are made " not fit to be seen." The least disastrous form of wet Sunday is the *very* wet one, the one which begins before you rise

in the morning, and gives every indication of being
"set in for the day." It is of course grievously dis-
appointing, but still in this case you know the worst at
once ; and so, after giving vent to your disappointment
by making the usual remarks, that it's *always* raining
on a Sunday, and you're bless'd if ever you saw such
weather, you quietly accept your fate. And out of the
evil of these very wet Sundays there cometh good, for
" on such a day as this " the working man generally
works off some of his arrears of correspondence. " The
working man" is not a good or regular correspondent,
and thinks himself fortunate in not having much correspondence to do ; nor is this to be wondered at, for,
from the nature of his employment, his hands are often
so hard and stiff, that the mere mechanical operation of
writing is a laborious or even painful one to him, and
then he chronically labours under the serious disadvantage of not knowing what to say, when his say has to
be said on paper. If he thinks that by writing a letter
he can help any friend or former shopmate who may
be out of work to a job, or do them some substantial
service of that kind, the working man will screw his
courage to the writing-point with much promptitude ;
but in the way of general correspondence he is greatly
given to procrastination. When experiencing a guilty
consciousness of his remissness in this respect, he will
observe from time to time, in a tone of self accusa-
tion, that he *ought* to answer So-and-so's letter, and
then, as time goes on, and he still " leaves undone
that which he ought to have done," he adds to the
observation that he ought to write, the statement that
he *will* write—next week. But the next week comes
and goes, and still So-and-so's letter remains un-
answered, and the work of correspondence is finally
deferred to some decidedly wet Sunday. He then gets

out the writing materials, resolutely dates his letter, and gets in one of the stock commencements about " these few lines " leaving him well at present. Then comes a pause, during which he bites the head of his penholder, and scratches his head. These inspiration-producing proceedings not having " the desired effect," he presently observes to his wife, or whoever it else may be by, that he's blow'd if he knows what to say now that he *has* made a start, to which the person thus indirectly appealed to replies, in a careless tone, implying that writing a letter would be no trouble to them—" O, tell him how you are getting on, you know." This advice, though vague, produces a line to the effect that he, the writer, is " getting on like a house a-fire." Having said so much, he thinks he deserves to have a pipe. He then lights his pipe and gives himself up to smoking and contemplation till such time as he bethinks him of another item of news, when he again sets to work ; and inspiration coming by degrees under the soothing influence of tobacco, he finishes the letter.

There are of course numbers of the better-educated men of the working classes, to whom writing a letter is little more trouble than it is to an educated man in the higher ranks of life—men who are capable of " knocking off " a well-written epistle in any style, from the rhapsodical, quotation-loaded love-letter, to the formal kind of document in which " Dear sir " is informed that his favour of yesterday's date is to hand, and in reply the writer has to inform him, &c. But these are the exceptions. Generally speaking " the working man " is a poor correspondent, and regards letter-writing as a soul-depressing business, fit only for the gloom and involuntary confinement of a wet Sunday.

With their mode of observing Sunday, the question

of the religion or irreligion of the working classes is
intimately connected, and though any lengthened observations upon a religious question would be out of
place in the present volume, a few remarks upon
this subject may perhaps be permitted. Numbers of
working men regularly attend some place of worship
on Sundays, some in a spirit of true religion,
and others because they are fanatics or hypocrites.
But the greater bulk of the working classes do not
attend places of worship, and hence those people who
confound religion with the due observance of its outward forms and ceremonies, argue that the working
classes are irreligious. This deduction is, in the main,
as incorrect and inconclusive as it is uncharitable.
It would be mere affectation to speak of the working
classes as being *actively* religious, or as being religious
at all in a ritualist's, or revivalist's, or Young Men's
Christian Association sense of the word; but, on the
other hand, neither are they actively or avowedly
irreligious. They neither question nor deride the
teaching of religion, and show no special lack of the
charity, brotherly regard, and toleration which are
prominent characteristics of all true religion. There
are many reasons to account for a working man's not
attending a place of worship on Sundays. The day is
to him literally a day of rest. It is the only day of the
week on which he can enjoy social intercourse in the
generally understood and civilizing sense of the term ;
and if he does not feel disposed to attend a place of
worship from some higher motive, his humble position
frees him from the necessity of attending it merely as
a sacrifice to the proprieties, while the church itself is
calculated to repel rather than attract him. To a
man who has witnessed an Alhambra ballet, or a
magnificently-mounted burlesque, or sensation drama

overnight, the mummeries of ritualism have little
attraction ; and a working man suffers as severely
as any other from the intliction of a dull, droning
sermon, the greater part of which is to him often un-
intelligible into the bargain. And if a working man
whose appearance makes it evident that he *is* a working man, does go into a church, he is put into a free
sitting, where he probably finds himself in company
with a lot of sniggering children, while any well-
dressed individual who enters the church, and who
has no greater claim upon it than the working man,
is obsequiously shown into a pew. This, though in
itself an insignificant thing, touches the working man
on a tender chord—-a chord that is always kept up
to concert-pitch by the harping of his friends, the
agitators who are never tired of telling him that
recondite truth, that it is not the coat that makes
the man, and that *they* never despise a man because he wears a ragged coat. And when these
considerations are fairly weighed, I think it must be
evident that it is doing an injustice to the working
classes to take their non-attendance at places of worship as constructive evidence of any *specially* irreligious feeling existing among them. A favourite
" notion " in tract literature, and among the Exeter
Hall school of religionists, is, that the general body
of working men are in the habit of scoffing at, and
subjecting to social persecution any man of their
class who may be religious in the ordinary sense of
the term ; but this notion is not only untrue, but it
is directly opposed to the truth. Working men do
not scoff at religion, either generally or as embodied
in individuals. On the contrary, they entertain a
high respect for any member of their own body who is
truly religious, and whose actions bear out his pro-

fessions. The presence of such a man has a most beneficial influence in a workshop. His reproof or his advice is always listened to respectfully, and is frequently productive of good. His presence invariably acts as a check to ribald conversation; while any scruples in connexion with workshop affairs which his religious feelings may cause him to entertain, are strictly respected :—for instance, when a workman is known to have religious objections to working on Sundays, under *any circumstances,* both foremen and workmen will, generally speaking, do all in their power to save him from having to take any share in it, when a necessity for Sunday work arises. What working men do scoff at is not religion, but self-righteousness, fanaticism, or hypocrisy, calling itself religion. Men who tell every person who differs in opinion from themselves that they are going to hell, and who excuse themselves from giving a trifle to a workshop subscription for the benefit of the family of some distressed fellow-workman, on the ground that the man on whose behalf the subscription is being made is " one of the ungodly ;" men who having been great drunkards or blackguards, are, from being brought " nigh unto death," or by the force of brimstoney admonition, suddenly converted, and then take to addressing their steady shopmates as their " sinful companions ;" men who run about the workshop groaning out that they are *so* happy now they know the Lord, and throw off texts, and reply to questions respecting their work by singing snatches of hymns ; men who are religious when working for religious masters, and irreligious when working for irreligious ones, or when they find that thrift does *not* follow fawning ;—such men as these are scoffed at, and held in contempt in the workshop ; and I can only say that

I sincerely hope that such will always continue to be the case.

With respect to the disposition at present existing for giving a more secular character to the Sunday, the working classes should be very careful—careful not only as to how far they go themselves, but also to watch that they are not used as tools by others who may have personal or party interests in the question. As music is generally to a certain extent a labour of love to the performers, and is seldom "discoursed" for more than two or three hours at a stretch, Sunday bands in parks may be regarded as a commendable institution, as they afford pleasure to thousands, and are the means of drawing them to places where they get the benefit of fresh air. At the same time it ought to be borne in mind that any material secularization of the Sunday, any movement that tends to detract from its general character as a day of rest, must ultimately tell against the working classes. Any movement of this kind *must* necessitate work, and the work will of course have to be done by people of the working classes; and of Sunday work there is already enough, and to spare. The employment upon Sundays of some classes of workmen, such as furnacemen in the iron trade, and railway servants, is an unavoidable necessity; but in working-class neighbourhoods there is at present—as numbers of shopmen know to their sorrow—a great deal of work on Sunday for which no real necessity exists, and which is occasioned solely by the improvident habits and want of consideration of a portion of the working classes. And, all things considered, I think it would, as the women say, " look a good deal better on 'em " if those of the working classes who have their Sundays free, would see about getting the same privilege to their less fortunate

brethren, before joining " leagues " having for their
object the opening of places of amusement on Sundays.
Looking at the scope he already has in the way of
" outings," I think the working man might very judi-
ciously leave the day to be the day of comparative rest
and quiet that it still is.

THE ISLE OF DOGS.

THE books that under a variety of titles have been written on " London life " would, in point of number, form in themselves a respectable library. We have had works descriptive of London by day, London by night, London in ancient times, and London in modern times; of London in all its aspects of wealth and luxury, poverty and crime, of its noble charities and hideous profligacy, of London, in short, in all those many phases of life, action and passion, which, as the wealthiest and most densely-populated city in the world, it must present. But, notwithstanding all that has been written about it, the subject of London life is an ever fresh one, since, practically speaking, it is inexhaustible, for the chances and changes that must inevitably occur, and the life dramas that are being constantly enacted in " the city of extremes," will always afford matter for contemplation and remark to the observant mind.

But however much may be written and read upon this subject, no one person will ever be able to thoroughly comprehend the infinitely varied modes of existence which go to make up that gigantic aggregate called London life. Strictly defined, the name London is applicable only to the City, but in point of fact, and in the general acceptation of the word, London is the generic name for all places embraced within the postal district of " London and twelve miles round," and in that area are localities which, save by name, and by their immediate inhabitants, the policeman on the beat, and a few individuals of an exploring turn of mind, are as little known as the interior of Africa. An interesting volume might be written on the manners and customs appertaining to these localities, and added to the already extensive literature of London life. These localities are chiefly those which may be called the manufacturing districts of London—districts which are to manufacturing industry what Paternoster Row and Fleet Street are to the bookselling trade—districts in which are made many of the articles which are taken to the remotest parts of the civilized world, and which we daily see and use, without thinking that the ingenuity and labour employed upon them have materially assisted in making England great among the nations of the earth. As there are no public buildings or places of holiday resort in these districts, they offer no attractions to the general or pleasure-seeking visitor, and owing to the absence from them of any portion of that " high life " accessible only to " the upper ranks of society," and those interesting phases of low life, which can only be safely studied under the guidance of a police inspector, they afford very little opportunity for " smart " or sensational writing, and hence they remain comparatively unknown.

One of the most interesting, and in many respects *representative* of these little known districts, is the Isle of Dogs. " The island," as it is familiarly called— although properly speaking it is a peninsula—is not very pleasant in its physical features. It is situated about six miles below London Bridge, and lies considerably lower than the level of the river, which is only prevented from overflowing it by strong embankments. As owing to its exceedingly low level it cannot be efficiently drained, it is very marshy; broad ditches of filthy water running on each side of its main road. To a casual observer it would appear that a visit to the island could only be interesting to persons who wished to study a peculiar style of dwelling-house architecture, the effect of which is that a dissolution of partnership takes place between the wood-work and brickwork of the lower stories before the upper ones are built; or to antiquarians desirous of seeing what the roads of England were like before Macadam was born or commissioners of paving created. And while its slushy, ill-formed roads, its tumble-down buildings, stagnant ditches, and tracts of marshy, rubbish-filled waste ground make the outward appearance of the island unpleasant to the sight, chemical works, tar manufactories, and similar establishments render its atmosphere equally unpleasant to the olfactory sense. Nevertheless, there is much that is interesting in the Isle of Dogs. I have somewhere seen this district described as the Birmingham of London; but I think that the "Manchester of London" would convey a much more accurate idea of the kind of place the Isle of Dogs really is.

The mere mention of Birmingham in connexion with manufacturing art conjures up visions of imitation jewellery and small ware goods made expressly to sell their purchasers—of gimcrack goods manufactured in the cellars and attics of private houses by "the piece," of glass beads, idols, and harmless rifles for the African market—in short, visions of all that is most glittering and least real in that class of manufactured goods known under the comprehensive head of hardware. But in the Isle of Dogs, as in Manchester, the articles manufactured are large, important, and of an eminently utilitarian character. On "the island" is centred the iron shipbuilding and marine engineering of the Thames. There are more than a dozen ship and marine engine building establishments upon it, amongst them being the gigantic one in which the operations of the Millwall Iron Works Company are carried on, and in which the *Great Eastern*, the large Government armour-plated ram *Northumberland*, and many other of the largest merchantmen and vessels of war afloat have been built. Here, too, a great portion of the armour-plate with which our own and foreign nations are encasing their ships of war, and with which the coast defences and other fortifications of Russia are being strengthened, is manufactured. The works of this company alone employ on an average 4000 men and boys, and the other ship and marine engine works on the island employ from 2000 to 100 men each. It would be within the mark to say that the shipbuilding and marine engineering of the Isle of Dogs gives employment to 15,000 men and boys; and, in addition to these shipbuilding establishments, there are on the island tar, white-lead, chemical, candle, and numerous other factories, which afford employment to a large number of men. There are two townships on the island—namely, Cubitt Town and Millwall, and it is in the latter place that a major portion of the manufactories of the island are situated; and Millwall is the place usually indicated when " the island " is spoken of by the inhabitants of the locality.

Any person having a practical acquaintance with the construction of iron ships would naturally expect to find a sprinkling of Scotchmen among the inhabitants of the island; for the mechanics who learn their trade in the shipbuilding establishments of the Clyde are among the most proficient workmen in " the trade," and the wages paid to this class

of mechanics being as a rule considerably higher
in England than in Scotland, it follows as a natural consequence that many Scotch mechanics come
to London. The expectation to meet with the
Scottish element in the Isle of Dogs is more than
realized, for one of the first things that strikes the
visitor is the *preponderance* of this element, as mani-
fested by the prevalence of the Scottish dialect and
Christian names. " Do ye no ken sting'n the wee
boy, ye ill-faur'd limmer, ye ?" were the first words that
greeted my ears on landing on the island on the occasion of my first visit to it, the exclamation having been
uttered by a pretty little Scotch lassie about eight or
nine years of age, who was in pursuit of a wasp under
the impression that it was the same one that had on
the previous day stung a " wee boy" whom she had
been nursing. As I journeyed into the interior of the
island the striking, distinctly-marked Scotch accent and
phraseology continued to strike on my ear at almost
every step ; for owing to the sharp ringing noise caused
by the riveting hammers which are at work in all
parts of the island for many hours in the day, the inhabitants acquire a habit of speaking very loud when
in the streets. And thus the broadly-accented " How
are ye ?" and the "Brawly, how are ye ?" which the gude
wives exchange when they meet, and the invitations to
come awa' in (to a public-house) and have " twa penny-
worth," or " a wee drap dram," reach my ears. During
meal hours, and the early part of the evening, when the
workmen are passing through the streets, the ascendancy
of the Scottish tongue is still more apparent, and Sandy,
Pate, and Andrew are the names that are most frequently exchanged as the men from the various workshops salute each other while passing to and from their
work. At these times a good deal of chaffing goes on

among the workmen, and in this species of encounter, the dry humorous Scotchmen have very much the best of it. But as the burly Lancashire men on whom the Northern wit is chiefly exercised, are as good-tempered as they are big, and the dapper, sprightly Cockneys who occasionally join in the encounter are unable to realize the idea that they are getting the worst of a contest of wit with *countrymen*, the unpleasant consequences to which chaffing often leads are obviated here.

Of course, in a locality so favoured by Scotland's children, there is a kirk, and a very comfortable little kirk it is, and equally of course the patriotism of the "whisky" drinkers is appealed to by such public-house signs as "The Burns" and "The Highland Mary;" and it must be confessed that on the island the public-houses are a much greater success than the kirk.

Life in the Isle of Dogs commences at a very early hour, and that "horrid example" in sluggards who always wanted a little more sleep, would have had great difficulty in obtaining it after five o'clock in the morning, had it been his fate to live on the Isle of Dogs. At that hour a sound of hurrying to and fro begins, heavily nailed shoes patter over the pavement, windows are thrown up, and shouts of "Can you tell us what time it is, mate?" or "Do you ken what time it is, laddie?" are answered by other shouts conveying the required information; while knockers are plied by those who are "giving a mate a call" with extraordinary energy and persistence. By a quarter-past five the sound of footsteps has increased until it resembles the marching of an army, and from that time till ten minutes to six it continues unabated. It then rapidly decreases and becomes irregular. At five minutes to six the workshop bells ring out their summons, and then those operatives who are still on the road change their walk into a run. In the midst of all this bustle rise shrill cries of " Hot coffee a ha'penny a cup," "Baked taters, all hot," and "Cough no more, gentlemen, cough no more," this latter being the trade cry of the vendors of " medicated lozenges." Before the hubbub raised by " the gathering of the clans " of workmen has fairly subsided, the sharp ringing of the riveting hammers, and the heavy throbbing sound of working machinery commences ; and by half-past six life on the island is in full swing. At half-past eight the workmen come out to breakfast ; and at that time the gates of the various large work-shops are surrounded by male and female vendors of herrings, watercress, shrimps, or whatever other breakfast " relishes " are in season. The instant the breakfast bells ring the workmen rush out through the workshop gates, some hastening to their homes, and others into the numerous coffee-shops in the immediate neighbourhood of the yards. A good breakfast of coffee, bread and butter, and an egg, can be got here for fourpence-halfpenny. Forty minutes are allowed for the discussion of the morning meal. During dinner hour, which is from one till two, and from half-past five till half-past six in the evening (in the workshops that are closed at one on Saturdays the men work till six in the evening on the other five working days of the week, in those where they work till four on Satur-days they leave off work on other days at half-past five), the streets of the island are again alive with the crowds of hurrying workmen. But during work-ing hours the streets are comparatively deserted, save by children, and the numerical force of the juvenile

section of the inhabitants of the island does great credit
to the papas and mammas, for though the island is
generally considered a very unhealthy place, the children as a rule appear to be robust.

There is no place of amusement on the island, but
in the winter months popular lectures are delivered
in the dining-hall attached to the establishment of
the Millwall Iron Works Company, and these lectures
are generally pretty well attended. As the islanders are, almost to a man, admirers of muscular
Christianity, much of their leisure time during the
summer months is occupied in practising or promoting boat-racing, foot-racing, and other athletic
sports. Their muscular sympathies extend also to
pugilism, for an appeal to " honour the brave "—that
is, to take a ticket for the benefit of Dan Bosher, the
Metropolitan Crusher ; Bill Burker, the Birmingham
Buster ; or some other idle ruffian—generally meets
with a liberal response from the islanders. There is
a public reading-room on the island, but it is scarcely
so well attended as might be expected, when it is
considered that so many of the inhabitants are of " the
intelligent artisan " class ; but this is to a certain extent accounted for by the fact that great numbers of
the men take in the cheap daily newspapers.

There are a great number of boys employed in the
various workshops on the island, and the diversions
of these young gentlemen have a decided tendency to
the boisterous, and lean slightly to the predatory.
They are great in the performance of intricate shuffles
and break-down dances, and are noted for the early
acquirement and energetic singing of the popular
melody of the hour. A number of the bright particular stars among them, who are known as the Peep o'
Day Boys, levy black mail from those who are trying

to sell their goods in the roads near the workshops. "Give us something to leave you alone," they will say to the proprietor of a stall; and if he is wise he does not refuse. It may be asked, why not set the police upon these young scamps? The question is one I do not presume to answer. In the course of my visits to the island I have seen divers street and public-house rows, but I have never seen a policeman.

From time to time (generally once in from five to seven years) a disastrous change comes o'er the aspect of the island and the fortunes of its inhabitants. A long run of brisk trade results at length in the over-stocking of the ship market, or commercial crises or money panics arise, and one or a combination of these causes brings about what is known as "a slap of dull trade" in the shipbuilding business. Orders do not come in to replace the work completed or nearing completion, and employers begin to discharge "hands," and this sometimes goes on till there are not hundreds employed, where thousands were before. Large numbers of men are then to be seen lounging idly about the streets, at hours when in busy times only women and children were visible. At first they are pretty well dressed, and are healthy and comparatively cheer-ful, as they are in hope that things will soon take a turn; but things only take a turn for the worse, and the hopes and means of the men alike fail them. Those who are members of trade unions are in these cases the most favourably circumstanced, but even they are great sufferers. Their "do." (donation) from the union will certainly keep a roof over the heads of themselves and families, and with careful management, and perhaps a little occasional assistance from previous savings, will keep them from absolute starvation; but still, ten shillings per week is not much for the support of a family. It should be borne in mind, too, that there is a good deal of the "I cannot dig, to beg I am ashamed" principle involved in the position of a mechanic out of work. There is a certain understood dignity and exclusiveness of caste pertaining to the artisan class which every individual of it is practically compelled to respect and support. A mechanic when out of employment can scarcely take work as a labourer, even if it is offered to him. If he were to do so, labourers would strongly object to his being brought amongst them. "Here," they would say, "is a fellow with a trade in his fingers, and yet he is coming to take the bread out of the mouths of us poor labourers;" and then the men of his own craft would say, "Here's a pretty character for you; he had his share of work when trade was good, and he has his club money, and now he's degrading himself and the trade by working as a labourer." In this matter the mechanic, when out of work, is in a far worse position than the labourer, for the latter can seek employment in any trade, and if unable to obtain regular work can generally pick up something in the way of odd jobs; the mechanic must, as a rule, work at his trade or not at all. But the out-of-work pay of a trade union, though comparatively small, enables the men entitled to it to tide over the dull time with much less of suffering than is endured by men who are not members of unions.

When the dull time has fairly set in, when ship after ship is launched, while none are laid down, and it becomes evident even to the most hopeful that things will be worse before they are better, the unemployed islanders naturally lose heart and begin to look anxious and careworn. Their little savings, however carefully handled, are soon expended, and small shopkeepers, however long-suffering, cannot go on giving credit for ever. The time inevitably comes when a little ready money *must* be raised; and then spare clothing and articles of furniture are parted with; next, necessary clothing, bedding, and furniture have to go, and want and misery sit down in the once comfortable home. When reduced to this strait, those who have friends able and willing to give them shelter, go to those friends. Many of the Clyde men return to Scotland, and numbers of the Lancashire and Staffordshire operatives tramp down home, where—if, as is generally the case with the iron trade mechanics of those counties, they can turn their hand to general work— they often find employment. But for the islanders who have not these resources, there is nothing left but to "hang on." They manage to live, as they say themselves, "God knows how;" the man, when knocking about in the hope that he may possibly "hear of something," occasionally meets with old mates who are in work, and who give him a shilling or two, or take him home to dinner with them. The wife manages to get a limited supply of bread upon credit; and other wives, whose husbands are among the fortunate few who are in work, make excuses for asking her to tea with them occasionally, and the little ones frequently come in for "pieces" when playing about the doors. And so in one way and another they contrive to exist till the turn of trade comes; for the longest period of dull trade, as well as the longest lane, has its turning. A rumour gets about that this or that firm has got an order; but so thoroughly disheartened are the unemployed that they receive the rumour very doubtfully. In the course of a day or two, however, when the workmen still employed in the firm are seen engaged in laying " ways," the good news is known to be true; and the foremen of the establishment are besieged by applicants for work. In about a week hands begin to be engaged, and this goes on from day to day until the establishment is " full-handed." Then comes the report that the tender of another firm on the island has been accepted for " a big job," and this report likewise turns out to be true. So, one by one, the shops fill again. Once more piecework, overtime, and large wages prevail; clothes are redeemed from the limbo of the pawn shop; homes are refurnished. In short, the Isle of Dogs becomes itself again, and its people are restored to comfort and prosperity; but those of them who have suffered in it never forget " the time when they were so hard-up in 18—," while any of them who had not previously had a taste of hard times will from thenceforward have more of fellow-feeling for the unfortunate.

A noticeable feature in the Isle of Dogs is, that while it is almost entirely inhabited by the working classes, the dwelling-houses upon it are singularly ill-adapted to the requirements of a working man's home. They are large houses of from twenty to thirty-five pounds a year rental; and as the houses, and especially the rents, are too large for a working man, the consequence is that from two to four families, or two families and a number of lodgers, live in each house. Though this may not be regarded as any great inconvenience by Londoners who have become habituated to living in rooms, it is severely felt by those workmen and their families who come from the provinces, and who have been used to living in " self-contained " cottages. The living in upstairs apartments has a decidedly demoralizing influence; as the great labour involved in managing a household without the aid of many conveniences which are only to be found on a ground-floor, and the too close proximity of the sleeping to the household apartments, are productive of uncleanly and slovenly habits. Nor are these the only evils that arise from several families living in one house. The social habits of the various families are often totally different, and this is the cause of much unpleasantness and ill-feeling. Thus, the workman who occupies the lower apartments may be in the habit of retiring to rest at an early hour, while the " single young man " who lodges with the tenant of the upper apartments may be given to coming home during the small hours, howling popular choruses and practising acrobatic feats in his bedroom, previous to finally " turning in," or otherwise disturbing the rest of the more orderly inmates of the house. Or it may be that he of the upper apartments is the one who goes early to bed, while the occupant of the ground-floor, who is a member of a workshop brass band, practises on the cornet-à-piston till midnight.

This system of several families dwelling in the same house also interferes materially with that family and domestic privacy so necessary to home happiness, and developes joint-stock tea partying, gossiping, and other undesirable qualities in women.

ONLY A LODGER.

A few years since, one of the chief topics of the " silly
season" was, whether or not 300*l.* a year was a sufficient income for a man to marry upon. Among
matrimonially-disposed gentlemen of limited income,
marriageable young ladies, and mothers with marriageable daughters, this important question is still a
debated and undecided one, though the present extravagance of living almost inevitably tends to a negative
decision. But whatever doubts there may be as to the
prudence of marrying upon an income of 300*l.* a year,
there can be no doubt that for a clerk or an " intelligent artisan," whose income only reaches 80*l.* or 90*l.*
a year, but who yet likes to be decently dressed,
or to indulge in such luxuries as the purchase
of a favourite book or a summer's holiday, marriage
is an act of folly, if not of crime. And as many
of the young men thus situated have the good
sense to see their position in its proper light, and
others of the same class are bachelors by predilection,
the result is, that in manufacturing and mercantile
districts there are always numbers of young men with
incomes of less than a hundred a year who are unmarried. Now, though a man with an income of
300*l.* a year may not consider himself justified in
marrying, he can at least afford to live in chambers.
Or he can rent apartments in the house of a
family of " highly Christian" or " strictly Evangelical"
principles; or he can take the " sitting and bedroom"

which are "to be let furnished" in the dwelling of a
family of "cheerful and musical disposition." In any
case, he may be well provided for.

The clerk or mechanic with less than a third of 300*l.*
a year, cannot go and do likewise. Neither in chambers
nor furnished apartments will their income permit them
to take up their abode. No! When a young man in
this rank of life leaves the parental roof, he must make
up his mind to enter his next dwelling-place in the
humble position of one whose individuality is from
thenceforward to be merged into that of his landlady—
who will speak of him as *only* her lodger ; while by the
inhabitants of the neighbourhood he will be known,
not by his own name, but as Mrs. So-and-so's lodger.
And though some of the more ambitious of these
young men may, on the principle of calling a spade
an agricultural implement, bring themselves under the
heading of "residence, with partial board," they know
that that high-sounding phrase is a mockery, and that
practically they are only lodgers. Why a single man,
who in the office or workshop is considered "as good
as the best," should, merely because he is a lodger, be
regarded by those among whom it is his lot to live as
an inferior being, who is not able to take care of himself, and towards whom it is not necessary to observe
the customary courtesies of society, I am at a loss to
understand. I have been a dweller in the houses of
lodgerdom for a number of years, and I have pondered
the question deeply ; but I am constrained to confess
that I have not been able to arrive at any satisfactory
conclusion. To a superficial observer, it might appear
that a lodger is thus contemptuously treated because
he does not marry and get a home of his own. But
this is not the case ; for when a lodger gets married,

his landlady invariably declares that he is a fool, and did not know when he was well off.

There is certainly no positive harm in being a lodger, and even if there was, to be a lodger is in many cases —my own, for instance—an unavoidable necessity, and the hardships which are inseparable from a state of lodgerhood are sufficiently hard to bear. That a lodger who " pays his way," and is a source of profit to those with whom he lodges, should be " treated as one of the family" in such disagreeable points of domestic government as being compelled to have cold dinners on washing days, and (metaphorically) having his nose snapped off when, by the smoking of the kitchen chimney, the breaking of some portion of the household crockery, or other domestic mischance, his landlady has been " put out," is bad enough. Such treatment as this is, however, a natural result of being a lodger, and, like many other disagreeable things, is nothing when you are used to it. But when in addition to having to endure evils that are to a certain extent unavoidable, you are treated as though you were a big child, are allowed to have no will of your own, and are always spoken of as only a lodger, it is rather too bad. None but those who have suffered from having it applied to them can fully estimate the utterly humiliating power of the word " only." I have read that

> " All that poets sing or grief hath known
> Of hopes laid waste, knells in that word alone ;"

but for my part, I would be disposed to give the palm for an utter misery-conveying sense to that word *only*. " It is not good for man to be alone," but to speak of a man as being alone does not necessarily imply that he is contemptible, while to speak of him as being *only* anything does. However insignificant a man may be, whether he is a German Prince or "a pauper whom nobody owns," you have merely to prefix *only* to the description of his insignificance, and you intensify it a thousandfold. It is the constant use of this terrible word "only," in conjunction with the term "a lodger," that has been chiefly instrumental in producing the now generally received opinion that a lodger is a person to be despised. Is a man in his wife's "black books," or does he find himself powerless in his own house, he in either case fully expresses his position by shrugging his shoulders and simply observing, "I'm only a lodger." Even beggars know that a lodger is a person of no consideration in a household, for if by chance you open the door in answer to the knock of any of those importunate personages, you have merely to say, "I'm only a lodger," and the most persistent beggar will immediately take him or herself off; though in the street, they would probably have stuck to the same lodger until they had succeeded in extorting black mail from him. So well is this last phase of the powerlessness of a lodger understood that it has become a regular practice with many men who are householders and fathers of families to get rid of mendicants, collectors of missionary funds, and other importunate callers, by boldly asserting that they are only lodgers.

One of the most aggravating circumstances connected with the social position of a lodger, is that landladies, the persons to whom lodgers are the most profitable, should be the first to cause their (the lodgers') humiliation. The alliterative description "fat, fair, and forty," would have conveyed a very accurate idea of the personal appearance of my first landlady, who had been represented to me as "a nice motherly woman," with whom it would be a great advantage for

a young man fresh from home to lodge. She was an
eminent sister of a Primitive Methodist congregation,
of which her husband was one of the local preachers,
and was supposed by herself, and such of the sisters of
the congregation of which she was a member as were
not envious of her fame, to be possessed of at least all
the terrestrial virtues. Having ascertained that this
good woman was willing not only to receive me
as an inmate of her house, but likewise to under-
take the superintendence of my religious training
(of which last generous offer I did not avail myself),
I waited upon her, and was not long in arranging terms.
" Don't you think the terms are reasonable ?" she
asked when she had named them. " Very," I answered ;
and indeed they were, for the house was comfortably
furnished, and the sister a neatly-attired, pleasant-
looking, and comely dame. " Ah, you see," she said,
when I had assented, " we are not taking you to
make money out of you ; we are trying to live in the
fear of the Lord, and are not greedy after the things of
this life ; but as we have no family of our own, we
thought a respectable lodger would be company for us."
I became a dweller in Sister Jones's house on a Monday
morning, and up to the following Sunday morning all
went merry as a marriage-bell, and I began to think
that I was going to escape the ills that I had heard
lodgerdom was heir to. But on the Sunday morning
a circumstance occurred which, though slight in itself,
was sufficient to indicate that sooner or later the fate
of my race would overtake me. After breakfast I
had taken up the " Weekly Screamer," and was in-
tent upon a more than usually scurrilous and illogical
leading article, when the paper was suddenly snatched
from my hands by my landlady, who sternly asked me
if I thought reading newspapers on a Sunday morning

was proper behaviour in the house of a God-fearing couple. And before I could reply to this abruptly-put question she bounced out of the room (taking the paper with her) to get ready for chapel. " I wont stand that," I said to her husband, when I had recovered self-possession enough to speak. " Oh, pray, sir ! pray, sir !" he said, in an alarmed tone, " don't say anything to her. She'll soon come round, and she's one of the sweetest creatures in the world so long as you let her have her own way, but if you rouse her she's a regular devil, and when she once gets in the tantrums it lasts for weeks, and then she leads me an awful life." I thought this rather curious language for a preacher to use, but as while he had been speaking I had become cool enough to consider that what had occurred was not worth leaving comfortable lodgings for, I calmed his fears by telling him that I would take no further notice of the affair. The donning of her chapel-going garments seemed to exercise a soothing influence upon the temper of the sister, for on coming downstairs again her countenance wore its usually serene expression, and she observed in as apologetical a tone as it was possible for a landlady to assume towards so inferior a being as a lodger, that although she did not wish to interfere unwarrantably with any person's freedom of action, she considered it her duty as an unworthy servant of the Lord to remonstrate in a Christian spirit with those whom she found wandering in the path that leadeth to destruction. It occurred to me that, applied in the eminently practical manner in which it had been in my case, this doctrine might occasionally be productive of unchristian results; but I kept my thoughts to myself, and merely replied that the sentiment was doubtless a highly commendable one. And this acquiescence, and a little judicious praise bestowed at dinner-time upon the excellent cooking of the Sunday joint (it was nearly raw, the oven having got cold while the sister was at chapel), fully restored me to my landlady's good graces. For a month afterwards all again went so pleasantly that I once more began to entertain hopes that I should yet escape the humiliations of lodgerhood. But on giving my usual knock one afternoon on going home to tea, I heard a great shuffling of feet and rattling of cups and saucers within doors; and while wondering why my knock should have caused this commotion, I heard my landlady say, "Oh never mind, my dears, don't disturb yourselves, *it's only the lodger ;*" and the next instant she opened the door. On entering I found about half a dozen ladies seated round the tea-table, upon which one of them was just replacing a bottle of spirits which she had been attempting to conceal, saying to my landlady with a sigh as she did so, "Laws, my dear, what a start it give me; though I might have known by the time of day that it was only the lodger." A glance at the now composed countenances of these ladies convinced me that from that time forth they would regard me and speak of me as " only a lodger ;" a person whose good or bad opinion was of no consequence, and before whom the sisters of Zion might openly put a strong " lacing " of brandy in their tea, and disparage their neighbours' characters. For during the quarter of an hour that I remained in the room with them, they discussed the character of a widow whom they were one and all in the habit of gushingly addressing (to her face) as " my dear," and unanimously arrived at the conclusion that "if everybody had their own," she (the widow) would not go to market in a silk dress, and, in the case of the unmarried daughter of one of the local preachers of their congregation,

a verdict was returned to the effect that she set her cap at
every marriageable man that she met, and that she was
no better than she should be. Nor was this openly contemptuous treatment of the sisters the only humiliation
I was destined to receive at their hands. One Sunday
morning, a few weeks after the episode of the tea-party, I
consented to go to chapel with my landlady; and as I was
at that time " young and foolish," and given to coming
out strong in the matter of elaborate Sunday costume,
I flattered myself that I should create a sensation
among the plainly dressed congregation of " The Primi-
tives." Nor was I altogether disappointed. On entering
the chapel I felt that I was the observed of all observers. I had scarcely taken my seat when I had the
satisfaction of hearing a pretty young woman ask in
an eager whisper of an elderly female, whom I afterwards recognised as one of those who had been at my
landlady's tea party—" Who is that nicely-dressed
young man?" Here then was a pleasing recognition
of the impressive character of my attire, and the due
effect of a gold guard and a signet ring. With a
sense of extreme self-satisfaction pervading my mind I
listened intently for the answer. " Who do you
mean?" asked the elderly female. " Him," whispered
the pretty Primitive. " Him?" repeated the elder sister
in a contemptuous tone, " He's only Sister Jones's
lodger." From that moment I was conscious that any
interest which this young sister might have felt in
the " nicely-dressed young man" was dispelled. This
was the unkindest cut of all. That the whole of the
brethren, and the old and plain-looking among the
sisters of Little Zion, should have known that I was
only a lodger and contemned me accordingly, would
have been to me a matter of supreme indifference.
But that the interest which a young and beautiful

sister had seemed disposed to evince for me should have been turned to indifference, if not contempt, by the knowledge that I was only a lodger, was humiliating to the last degree.

But notwithstanding such small miseries as these, the period of my residence with Sister Jones was a comparatively happy one; for though like the rest of her sex the sister had her little weaknesses, she was in all the more important transactions of life a kind-hearted woman, and in the broadest and most essential principles of Christianity, a true Christian. And though I was only her lodger, I shall ever recall the memory of the kind, comely sister with grateful affection; for she nursed me through a violent and malignant fever with all a mother's tenderness. Dear, kind old landlady, she has long since gone "to the land of hallowed rest!" and when, some years after I had ceased to be *her* lodger, I entered Little Zion for the second and last time, it was to hear her funeral sermon preached; and though a fastidious critic would have considered the preacher vulgar and bombastic, I know that one at least of his hearers bowed his head and wept before he had made an end of it.

On leaving Sister Jones's lodgings I went further and fared worse in the matter of landladies. In the town to which I then removed lodgings were few and far between, and choice of landladies extremely limited. The landlady in whose house I was, owing to these circumstances, compelled to take up my quarters, was a decidedly disagreeable person to live with. She was of a most violent temper, and on the second day of my residence with her she informed me, in reply to a remark of mine to the effect that I would like to have my dinner at a regular hour, that she never took any d——d im-

perence from a lodger. And when I had been with
her a fortnight, she was committed to gaol, without the
option of a fine, for seven days, for husband-beating;
the beating in question having consisted in laying her
husband's head open with a saucepan. But this imprisonment had anything but a subduing effect upon
her temper; for on the day that she came out of prison
she again violently assaulted the unfortunate being
who, by a cruel fiction, was supposed to be her lord
and master. She considered, and not altogether without reason, that it was the sight of his bandaged head,
when he appeared in court to beg of the magistrates to let her go free, which had been the chief
cause of her being imprisoned. At the earliest possible
opportunity I quitted the abode of this termagant,
and was fortunately much happier in my next choice
of a landlady. She was a decent woman and a good
cook, and conscientiously did all in her power to
make me comfortable; and, as I showed a proper appreciation of her efforts in that respect, and tried to
give her as little trouble as possible, I soon became a
favourite with her. Still I was only a lodger, and
the favour with which she regarded me had a decided
air of proprietorship about it. She would talk of
" my lodger " in much the same way that she would
of " my best chest of drawers " or " my new carpet."
Her greatest weakness was an extreme admiration of
muscular Christianity; and her favourite idea was that
it was the chief, if not the whole duty of man, to
" lick " any one who should in any way offend a
female. Moreover, although I was one of the most
peaceful of men, and had never " licked " or attempted
to " lick " any one, my landlady, by some process of the
inconsistent female mind, became possessed with the
idea that I was a sort of unprofessional Tom Sayers,

and openly boasted to her female friends that her
lodger could "lick" any man in the street. Sometimes
her propensity to speak of my supposed prowess was
productive of disagreeable consequences to me. One
morning, in the course of an altercation with a milk-
man, whose mixture she had stigmatized as rubbish,
she said to him that if he gave her any of his impudence she would make her lodger give him a good
"licking." The result of this threat was that the milk-
man, accompanied by a considerable body of friends,
met me at night, and made a number of pressing in-
quiries as to whether I wanted to fight—urgently
inviting me to "come on," and so forth. I confess I
declined to do so. On another occasion a drunken
Irishman, who by some chance had wandered into the
respectable part of the town in which my landlady's
house was situated, was making night hideous by
howling out, "Send out your min, and I'll bate them
all, I will!" For some time no one took any notice
of this midnight disturber of the peace, but at last my
landlady threw up her bedroom window, and addressing the pot-valiant Patlander, ordered him to go away.
"It's not ye I want, ye ould Jezebel," roared the
Irishman, furious at being attacked by a woman;
"send out your min, I tell ye; send out your min,
and I'll give them all a bating, I will, I will."
"Send out your min, indeed!" answered my landlady; "I'll send out my *lodger*, and he will bate *you*,
if you talk about bating." How this encounter might
have terminated I cannot say; but fortunately a policeman appeared upon the scene, and the Irishman took
himself off. But a few days after this occurrence
I was horrified by meeting, in the immediate vicinity
of my landlady's house, a gigantic Irishman, in a
state of intoxication, who asked me if I could oblige

him by pointing out the man that lodged with the
ould Scotchwoman at No. 4. I need scarcely say
that under such unpleasant circumstances I denied
all knowledge of that person. " Well, I tell you,
sur," rejoined the Irishman, " there's not a part
about him that his mother ever touched that I wont
bate when I lay hould of him." Having given expression to this comprehensive threat, this son of Erin
left me to prosecute his search after " ould Jezebel's
lodger." I am happy to be able to state, however,
that he never succeeded in " laying hould " of him.
Nor are such positive annoyances and humiliations as
these the only ones to which the unhappy man who
is only a lodger is subjected. His every movement
in the house, which by the great commercial law of
payment he has a right to consider in some degree his
own, is criticised and found fault with not only by his
landlady, but by every gossiping acquaintance of hers.
If the lodger spends his evenings at home, the gossips
openly speak of him as a mollicot, and inflame his
landlady by telling her that *they* would not have a man
mollicoting about *their* house among a lot of women.
While if he goes out in the evening and returns
to his lodgings late enough to have to use his latch-
key, the gossips will assert that " he is not out to those
hours for any good," and will originate and circulate
dark rumours concerning him ; rumours which, while
they mark the unfortunate lodger as an unquestionable
" bad 'un," leave the minds of those who hear them
in doubt as to whether he spends his evenings in
committing burglary or in the more harmless occupation known as " cupboard courtship."

If landladies were an eminently and distinctively
superior race of beings, the fact that it is they who
have been chiefly instrumental in bringing about the

humiliations of lodgerdom would have less of bitterness
in it.   But they are *not* a superior race.   I am painfully competent to speak on this subject, and I emphatically repeat that landladies are anything but a
superior race of beings ; and though the assertion would
doubtless lay me open to a charge of partisanship, I
would not be asserting too much if I were to say
that as a class landladies are in many respects inferior
to those much contemned members of society who are
only lodgers.   I have known many landladies who were
" given to drink," and I once lodged with one who
drank a barrel of porter belonging to me.   She said it
must have been the rats ; but of course I knew better
than that.   I have known others who have borrowed
their lodgers' money, and—without his knowledge—
pawned his clothes, and refused to repay the one
or redeem the other ; and once, through a quarrel
between a landlady of mine and one of her neighbours,
I learned that she (the landlady in question) having
by some means learned that a self-adhesive envelope
could be easily opened by exposing the gummed part
to the steaming spout of a boiling kettle, had for
months been in the habit of opening and reading my
letters, and retailing their contents to the gossips of
the neighbourhood.

'Tis true that in times of sickness and distress the
woman will in the majority of instances rise superior
to the *landlady*, but even when playing the Good
Samaritan a landlady cannot help showing that she
considers a lodger an inferior being, and one who is
incapable of taking care of himself.

I have spoken principally of my own sorrows as a
lodger, but that I have at the same time spoken also
as a representative man, thousands of unhappy lodgers
could bear mournful testimony.   As the ill-used class

to which I belong is not considered competent to have
a voice in the election of the legislative body, it has
no *claim* on the attention of "honourable members,"
and those who compose it (the lodger class) have no
means of "ventilating" *their* grievances in "the
house." But though public business, private bills, and
the grievances of free and independent electors, may
exclude legislative discussion of "the lodger question,"
or the introduction of a bill for the erection of homes
for lodgers, there can be no reason why private enter-
prise should not take up this important subject; and
it is a matter of surprise that in this age of companies some energetic promoter has not started a
"Lodgers' Home Company (Limited)." That such
an undertaking would pay there can be no doubt,
for were it once known among lodgers that there
was a prospect of their becoming inmates of a
home, in which each would have the exclusive use
of his own little room, with the privilege of using, in
common with the other members of the establishment,
a comfortable dining-room, and smoking-room! and
where they would be attended to by cleanly and competent servants, instead of being held in abject sub-
jection by domineering landladies, and waited upon by
miserable slipshod little slavies of tender years and
weak frame—they (the lodgers) would take sufficient
shares to "float" the concern. And once floated, success would be certain; for the prices paid for lodgings
of a very inferior class would be sufficient to pay a good
per-centage on the amount of capital required for successfully carrying out an undertaking of this kind. A
plainly built "home" of three stories, the lower one
comprising dining-room, smoking-room, cooking department, and servants' sleeping apartments; and the
two upper ones consisting of fifty small rooms each;

each apartment being made to combine sitting-room and bedroom, and thus affording accommodation for a hundred lodgers—could, I believe, be built and furnished for eight thousand pounds, and managed for about five hundred pounds per annum. At a rental of five shillings per week per lodger, there would be an eager competition to obtain lodgings in an establishment such as I have attempted briefly to sketch, and an income of thirteen hundred pounds a year would thus be assured to the proprietors of the establishment. Nor would the rents be the only source of profit. In commercial and manufacturing towns—and those are the towns in which homes for lodgers are chiefly required—the majority of lodgers get their meals in eating-houses, so that the functions of an eating-house might be added to a home with advantage to its inmates and profit to its proprietors. And now, as I think a little reflection will show that the establishment of a " home for lodgers" would be a happy blending of philanthropy and profit, I trust that the day is not far distant when the hearts of those who are only lodgers will be gladdened by the sight of a prospectus of " The Lodgers' Home Company (Limited)."

THE END.